FEB / /2020

BRAD,

I'M GLAD THAT YOU ENJOYED THE
BOOK AND THANKS FOR YOUR REVIEW.

Mark

Caught Between Two Devils

Caught Between Two Devils

MARK CREEDON

IGUANA

Publisher: Meghan Behse
Editor: Jane McNulty
Front cover design: Meghan Behse
Interior book design: Heather Bury

Front cover photograph: The cover photograph depicts Jadwyga and Maria
sitting on the barge that took them and Antanas from Kaunas, Lithuania, to
Elbing, Germany. The man standing beside them is a Wehrmacht soldier.

ISBN 978-1-77180-360-1 (paperback)
ISBN 978-1-77180-361-8 (epub)
ISBN 978-1-77180-362-5 (Kindle)

This is an original print edition of *Caught Between Two Devils*.

To the loving memory of Antanas and Jadwyga Paskevicius and Maria Vasiliauskas. This novel is a tribute to their real-life experience and the love and courage that they brought to the world.

Table of Contents

Chapter 1

A Final Decision

As part of Operation Pomeranian, the Red Army had reached the outskirts of Elbing, Germany, by January 23, 1945. The German generals pleaded with Hitler to make a conditional surrender, but he ordered them to keep fighting.

Elbing Work Camp, February 3, 1945

Jadwyga spotted the U.S. markings as the bombers thundered across the cloudless sky. She stood on a small snow-covered hill with her husband Antanas and his sister Maria. The knoll from which they gazed upward was just beyond the spruce-planked warehouse that the Wehrmacht (the unified armed forces of Nazi Germany) had assigned as a foreign workers' mess hall. Jadwyga felt as if the earth might split beneath her from the roar above. She covered her ears.

"They're mostly B-24s with a few of the big B-29s! And they have Mustang fighter escorts!" Antanas shouted to the women over the rumbling of the bombers' engines.

"We aren't the target this morning, but what about tonight?" Maria asked worriedly as the planes disappeared overhead. "We can't stay here much longer. If the Americans don't kill us, the Brits will!"

Jadwyga turned to Maria and cautioned her in a low voice. "Quiet, the guards."

Maria spat into the snow. "The Germans keep telling us that Hitler is winning the war. But the Germans are finished—and it won't be long now before everyone knows the truth."

At thirty, Antanas was the oldest of the three. He was a fine-looking man of average height. Prematurely bald, he had a well-shaped head, a square jaw, and soft brown eyes. His build was slim and muscular. He had been a graduate electrical engineer in Lithuania. Then in April

1944, the Wehrmacht had ordered him to travel to Germany to assume the role of head mechanic of the Elbing Transit System. He was technically part of the Wehrmacht but really he, Jadwyga, and Maria were all prisoners of the Third Reich. They were forced labour imported from Lithuania.

Jadwyga was twenty-four. She had raven hair, fair skin, and the captivating smile and dark blue eyes of a movie star. Maria, at twenty-one, was the youngest but also the feistiest. She had the body of an athlete and her beautiful pale blue eyes revealed a strong and determined spirit.

Antanas waved for Maria and Jadwyga to come closer to him. "Listen. There's another sound that's more terrifying than the bombers. Can you hear it? It's Soviet artillery. It sounds like it's east of Elbing now but how long will it take the Red Army to reach us?"

Maria peered towards the east. "They would love to level this city," she said gravely.

Antanas nodded in response. "Yes, they want to destroy the war munitions stockpiled in Elbing. Besides the Soviets, the British and the Americans are closing in. Elbing will be a pile of rubble soon."

They had all witnessed the kind of damage that the Soviets could inflict when the Red Army seized control of Lithuania and Eastern Poland in the early part of the war. Antanas stared up at the sky and saw two ravens circling the German-controlled compound where he, his wife, and his sister had been forced to live and work for the past ten months. "Living under the heel of the Germans has been bad enough, but we must avoid liberation by Stalin at all costs," he said with an anxious expression.

He glanced around to see if anyone was within earshot. "We'll leave tomorrow night. There'll be no moon by then. I'll need some time to steal a truck," he said decisively.

Jadwyga's face turned white. "How can you steal a truck?" she asked.

"I'll take one from the garage. I've been hiding diesel for a while now," replied Antanas.

"I don't like this plan," said Jadwyga fretfully. "If you get caught stealing diesel from the Wehrmacht, they'll kill you on the spot. Look what they did to Wladek, just for having a crystal radio set." Jadwyga reached out and took Antanas's hand in hers as she clasped Maria's arm protectively.

Antanas gently squeezed Jadwyga's hand, but Maria pulled away. "And you have a better plan?" Maria confronted her sister-in-law. "We can't stay here! The Red Army soldiers will rape every single woman in Elbing and they'll kill every single man."

"But the Wehrmacht forced us to come to this work camp; it wasn't *our* choice," replied Jadwyga.

"There are no excuses where Stalin is concerned," Maria said grimly.

"But Maria, we aren't Germans!" uttered Jadwyga.

"That doesn't matter," Maria responded, shaking her head. "The Russians don't care that Antanas and I are Lithuanians, and they despise Poles like you, Jadwyga. They hate the Poles as much as they hate the Germans."

A whistle blew once and then a second time. The three hurried back to their respective work stations. Jadwyga returned to the sewing and tailoring shop, Maria to the cleaning depot, and Antanas to the garage where the German army unit's trucks were serviced.

Antanas knew he would need help to steal a truck from the garage. He had already selected one of the vehicles for their escape. He was acutely aware that it was a risky move, but he had decided to ask Maria's German boyfriend, Private Peter Baur, to help them. He needed the assistance of someone who knew the Wehrmacht guards' procedures and routines. It was indeed a dangerous move. Private Baur had the power to hand them over to his commanders in return for a reward. However, Antanas reassured himself by focusing on what he knew of Peter's character. *Peter's just a good farm boy. He's no Nazi.*

***

Shortly after work, at about 5:40 p.m., Antanas saw Peter enter the garage. Tall and slim, Peter had brown hair and dark blue eyes. Before the war, he had been a farmer. When he was fourteen, a belt flew off his father's thrashing machine, splitting his skull. He had a nasty scar as a result, but his thick hair covered most of it. Antanas knew that his sister loved Peter, and he also understood why. *He's handsome and intelligent, but more importantly, he's brave and he's kind.*

Antanas beckoned for Peter to join him in a spot in the garage beside some barrels of grease. They often met there to share a cigarette. Antanas set a large tin full of tobacco on top of a forty-litre grease drum and he checked for papers for rolling cigarettes stored in his overalls. He opened a jar of purple cleaning jelly to remove the grease from his hands before wiping them with a clean rag. Antanas needed a few moments to collect his thoughts. He pulled out two papers from his overalls and rolled two perfect cigarettes. He handed one to Peter and stuck the other one between his lips. He lit the cigarettes and they both took a long drag.

Peter believed that this particular spot in the garage was a relatively safe place to meet. For one thing, Captain Johan Ninehaus, who was Antanas's boss, trusted Antanas. He appreciated the fact that Antanas did an excellent job keeping the buses of Elbing in good working order. He also acknowledged that Antanas didn't complain when the garage became increasingly short of the proper parts and tools needed to run the buses. Consequently, Captain Ninehaus gave Antanas a lot of slack, and he looked the other way when he observed Antanas and his mechanics talking to Wehrmacht soldiers, including Peter. Officially Antanas was a member of the Wehrmacht but he was not a soldier. He was a Lithuanian mechanic forced to work for the Wehrmacht. Captain Ninehaus should not have trusted him but he did.

The garage was large enough to work on three buses and two cars at the same time. It was a relatively safe place to seek protection when the Americans or the British dropped bombs on the camp. But the concrete walls and roof amplified sound, so it was not the best place to conduct a covert conversation.

Antanas pointed to the yard outside. "Peter, let's go talk behind the garage." Beyond the back of the garage was a large dumping area about twenty-five metres by thirty-five metres. Here, two broken-down old buses, a green army car missing tires, and the chassis of a black 1925 Mercedes-Benz sedan had been stripped for parts. Ten empty grease barrels were lined up against a chain-link fence. The snow crunched under their feet as the two men stepped outside. They could see their breath and the cold air stung their cheeks.

As they walked towards the desolate area, Peter laughed in a gently mocking way as he asked Antanas, "What's so secret that you have to drag me out to the vehicle graveyard to have a talk?"

Antanas didn't reply. He motioned for Peter to follow him into the closest abandoned bus. Antanas brushed snow from the torn cushion seats, sat down, looked seriously at Peter, and spoke. "Peter, I'm going to tell you something that could risk my life and the lives of Maria and Jadwyga." Continuing to look Peter directly in the eye, Antanas said, "Then I'm going to ask you to do something that could risk *your* life."

"You have my full attention," replied Peter, his eyes alert.

"We're planning to run away from the camp and to try to make it to Bavaria. We need a truck to get there and I need your help to steal one. Will you help us?" Antanas stared intently at his friend.

Peter's face went ashen. He stood up, walked slowly to the end of the bus without speaking, and then returned to his seat. Tears welled up in his eyes for a moment, but then a slight smile crept over his face. He took a long drag on his cigarette. "It will break my heart to see you all leave. But yes, I will help you," he said quietly.

Peter blew on his hands to warm them. His thoughts flew back to the first day he had met Maria at the work camp. They had literally bumped into each other as they rounded the corner of a building from opposite sides. As she dropped some bedsheets, she had sworn: "*Scheisse!*" Peter was fascinated by the way this lovely young Lithuanian woman swore in German with no trace of an accent. She was strikingly beautiful, but what had eventually captured his heart was her loyalty to those she loved and her passionate vision of a better future together. Over the past eight months, Peter and Maria had met secretly with the aid of Antanas and Jadwyga. They had fallen in love and were even discussing marriage. And now she was planning to escape. *Scheisse.*

Antanas poked Peter gently in the ribs. "What are you thinking about?" he asked.

Peter turned and faced Antanas. "Never mind what I'm thinking. Which vehicle are you planning to steal?"

"The 1936 Mercedes-Benz truck that I was working on this morning," replied Antanas.

"And what about diesel?"

"I emptied out a huge cleaning fluid drum, and I've been siphoning fuel and storing it in the drum for weeks now. I have enough to fill up the truck. This will get us started and still leave a small reserve. Once that's used up, I'll have to steal more fuel by siphoning diesel from unguarded trucks along our way."

"How many of you will be escaping?"

Antanas held up his fingers on both hands and smiled. "Ten. That's how many people we can fit into the old Mercedes and still have room for luggage, extra fuel cans, and a few tools."

"But how will you explain your passengers and your cargo to the camp guards and to the road patrols?"

Antanas patted Peter on the shoulder as he responded, "This is where I need *you*. Can you help us?"

Peter took a drag on his cigarette, and then exhaled a little longer than usual.

"Yes, I'll help you," he said finally. "I wondered when you Lugans would actually jump off this sinking ship."

"It's not uncommon for me to work in the evening, and Captain Ninehaus trusts me," Antanas spoke reflectively. "He's even allowed me to drive repaired and serviced cars, trucks, and buses to other sites in town. Still, I'll need your help with the night patrols. It won't be easy to give them a plausible explanation as to why I'm driving a truck out of the camp carrying nine passengers."

"The camp guards are supposed to patrol every hour on the hour until midnight, and then every two hours until the light of dawn," Peter explained. "If you can leave by 10:15 p.m., you probably won't be challenged. The guards will be too busy staying warm in the bunkhouse and drinking beer, if there's any left. They usually don't poke their noses out of the bunkhouse on a cold night until about 10:30 p.m. They still have *some* military discipline left, but now they're fighting for themselves and their comrades—not for Hitler and not for Germany."

"Will they desert?" Antanas asked.

Peter butted out his cigarette in the snow on the seat of the bus and sighed. He sat up straight, removed his soldier's cap, and ran his fingers through his hair. "No, they won't desert. Where would they go? They can't surrender to the Soviets because the Red Army would either kill them or enslave them. They can't wait for the Americans or the British to arrive because the U.S. and British troops won't be coming this far east. If they try to run home and hide, they'll be killed by their own officers—either the SS or the Gestapo."

Antanas stood up and placed his hand on Peter's shoulder. "What options do you have?" he asked sympathetically.

Peter shrugged as he answered, "Let's get back to *your* plans."

"What can we expect from the soldiers in this camp?"

"Things are deteriorating fast. Discipline is reduced and routines are less predictable. This should make it easier for you to escape, but you still need to be extremely cautious. I'll find out which gate I can unlock for you, and I'll try to have a guard there who knows you and who won't question why you're driving a truck full of foreign workers at night."

"What about papers?"

"I'll call in some favours from my friend Walter, who issues transit papers for our regiment. If you have papers and you're stopped, you'll have a reasonable excuse for transporting a group of foreign workers out of Elbing. I'll get him to say that you're a tractor mechanic and that the women are farm workers who are needed to plant seeds in Bavaria this spring."

"Can you join us?"

"No, I can't. That would put you in even greater danger. If a patrol were to stop us and suspect that I was a deserter, they would likely kill me and everyone in the truck, without hesitation. You're all safer without me. I'll meet you here tomorrow night at 9 p.m. sharp."

Chapter 2

Exodus Part 1

The Red Army was pressing forward hard on the Eastern Front. German defenses were still formidable, but German forces were losing ground and their strength was diminishing. The Red Army outnumbered the Wehrmacht by a ratio of five to one in terms of soldiers and six to one in terms of tanks.

Old Town, Elbing, February 3 and 4, 1945

After his conversation with Peter, Antanas returned late to the flat in the Old Town of Elbing that he shared with his wife and his sister. He recalled the risk that he, Jadwyga, and Maria had taken when they moved from the barracks at the work camp into a flat rented out by a woman named Frau Brewer. That had been three long years ago. It was now time to say goodbye to this phase of their lives.

When Jadwyga heard her husband's footsteps on the stairs, she raced to the door. "I thought you'd been arrested by the Wehrmacht—or worse, the Gestapo!" she exclaimed, as the fear drained from her face.

Maria rushed towards her brother. "Did you speak to Peter? Can he do something to help get us out in time?" she asked breathlessly.

"Yes," Antanas responded as he stepped inside the common room they shared. "He's willing to risk his life for us. I'll meet him at 9 p.m. tomorrow night in the yard at the garage. I'll pick up the truck. Then I'll drive to the cleaning depot and meet the two of you in the back courtyard at 9:30 p.m. sharp."

Maria stared down at the floor as she asked her brother in a whisper, "Is Peter coming with us?

"No," said Antanas. "He knows he would endanger everyone by joining us."

Maria burst into tears and fled to her room. Jadwyga and Antanas stood together in silence, feeling completely helpless.

Antanas broke the silence. "We can invite seven of your closest friends to join us—but no more," he told his wife. "I'll let you and Maria make the final choices about which friends to invite. We've discussed who our fellow travellers should be several times already, and you know what I think. We're placing our very lives in their hands. All of them must be absolutely trustworthy."

Jadwyga nodded to signal her understanding. "What about luggage?" she asked.

"Each of us can bring only one suitcase. That's all we can fit into the truck."

"I'm going to go check on Maria. She needs comforting," Jadwyga said as she headed towards Maria's bedroom.

After a while, Maria and Jadwyga exited the bedroom slowly and joined Antanas at the table in the common room. None of them felt hungry, but they each forced down half a bowl of watery borscht.

As they sipped their soup, they debated whether or not to invite their landlady, Frau Brewer, to join them in their escape attempt. After some discussion, they concluded that it would be too dangerous.

"She's been a good landlady, but our relationship with her is strictly business, not personal," Maria said. "We can't be certain that she wouldn't betray us to the authorities."

"War is still being waged and Frau Brewer is German. We cannot take her with us," Antanas said firmly.

With this crucial decision made, Jadwyga stood up and began to pace back and forth. "Let's figure out what to bring with us," she said.

This proved to be a slow and painful task. Jadwyga packed practical things first: a pair of wool slacks, three pairs of socks, a pair of long underwear, two shirts, and her underthings. She would wear her wool coat, her old sweater, a scarf, a hat, and gloves. The only special items she would bring along were a small photo album of her family in Vilnius, a few photos of Antanas, Maria, and herself, some amber jewellery, and her embroidered nightgown. As she packed her few belongings, she thought longingly of her mother and sisters whom she had had to leave behind in Vilnius.

Maria packed all her practical belongings first as well, followed by her photographs of Antanas and their family in Kaunas and a few pieces of amber jewellery. She wept silently as she gently ripped up the only picture taken of Peter and her together. It was dangerous enough to hide this picture in her room, but to have it found on her person if and when a Wehrmacht patrol stopped them in their getaway truck would be fatal for both of them.

Antanas packed his work clothes, his long underwear, some socks, and a sweater. He knew that Jadwyga and Maria would bring along their family photos, so he packed only one photo of his beloved dog. Nero was a large, intelligent, handsome German shepherd. He was Antanas's best friend. Antanas had had no choice but to leave him behind in Kaunas with his parents. Antanas wondered if Nero was still alive. He hoped with all his heart that his parents were still alive.

Antanas planned to pack some tools, but they were stored at the garage. That task would have to wait until tomorrow.

Elbing Work Camp and Old Town, Elbing, February 4, 1945

Antanas usually arrived at the garage at 7:45 a.m. each day. His mechanics left work for the day at 5:30 p.m. He liked every one of the men who worked for him, and he even liked his German boss, Captain Johan Ninehaus. However, he strongly suspected that one of his men, Vytautas Belskas, had made a treacherous deal with Major Braunshiedel, the commander of the work camp. Because of likely betrayal on the part of Vytautas, Antanas could not risk inviting any of his men to join their escape attempt.

Vytautas was short, slim, and handsome. He had a thin nose, pale blue eyes, and curly brown hair. He was an extrovert who could strike up a conversation with anyone. He laughed a lot and often kidded with the other mechanics. He also liked to drink, and he had shown up at work drunk several times. No one knew how or where Vytautas got his schnapps and his wine, but in all likelihood someone in the Wehrmacht was securing it for him. Antanas was convinced that this person was Major Braunshiedel.

Braunshiedel was a zealous Nazi who was feared by everyone. Antanas trusted the rest of his men, but he knew that Vytautas would be able to read their faces if they harboured a secret. If Vytautas were to report to Major Braunshiedel that he sensed something unusual going on behind the scenes at the garage, the Gestapo would be called in to investigate. Antanas wiped away tears as he silently confirmed within himself his decision to exclude his entire crew of mechanics from the escape plan.

At about 6:15 p.m., Antanas arrived home for dinner. Jadwyga had made him a little soup and coffee. He could drink the coffee, but his stomach would not tolerate food. At 7:40 p.m., as Jadwyga handed him his coat, hat, and gloves, she told him reassuringly, "Don't worry. Maria and I will bring your suitcase to the camp. It would be hard for you to explain why you're carrying a suitcase to the garage. I have a scheme to justify the suitcases for all of us. Maria and I will ensure that the guards don't think our suitcases are part of an escape. We've thought of a good excuse. We'll see you at 9:30 p.m. by the cleaning depot."

Jadwyga hugged Antanas with all her strength, and then gave him three small pieces of meat wrapped in paper. "This is for the guard dogs in case they don't recognize you," she said. She kissed her husband tenderly and returned to the kitchen. Maria held open the door for Antanas and he stepped out into the cold, moonless night.

The temperature had fallen another six degrees. It was now minus eighteen degrees Celsius. The cold, crisp air amplified the sound of his footsteps as Antanas walked in the direction of the work camp.

Antanas took in his surroundings and was struck by the impact that the Allied bombing had had on Old Town. In the early phase of the bombing, the British and the Americans targeted only Elbing's factories and warehouses. Beginning in 1944 and continuing into 1945, however, they bombed everything. Antanas reflected on how random the damage seemed. One house would be demolished while the house next door to it remained unscathed.

When Antanas arrived at the gate to the camp, his face broke into a warm smile when he saw that the guard on duty was Hans Muller. Antanas knew this man well. Hans often joined Jadwyga, Maria, and other foreign workers at lunchtime to swap stories and to sing together.

"Hans, are you cold enough yet?" Antanas asked in a joking tone.

"Yeah! It's colder than Major Braunshiedel's heart," Hans replied. They both laughed.

"What brings you back to the camp on such a cold night?" Hans inquired.

Antanas blew on his hands and stomped his feet as he said, "Captain Ninehaus wants me to have a bus ready to roll by 7 a.m. tomorrow and we couldn't finish the repairs on it this afternoon."

"Why are you alone? Why didn't you ask one of your men to help you?" asked Hans.

"No, it's okay; what's left to do is a one-man job," replied Antanas nonchalantly.

Hans tipped his hat to Antanas as he said, "You're too soft on those mechanics of yours. But have fun working tonight in that cold barn you call a garage."

Antanas waved at the guard as he strode past. "I'll do my best," he said.

As he drew near the garage, two Doberman Pinschers approached him slowly with their ears pinned back. Both dogs were larger than the average Doberman, but they had the breed's classic black and brown coat, large black ears, and flashing white fangs. The smaller of the two was named Panzer and the larger was named Tiger. They growled menacingly at first, but when they realized it was Antanas who was entering the garage, they went quiet. He was a favourite with both dogs because he had fed them scraps ever since they had first begun guarding the camp.

"Here, boys, take this meat and be happy," he said as he tossed them the scraps that Jadwyga had packed for them. After eating, the dogs rolled in the snow and then ran off towards the north fence. Antanas used his key to open the door to the garage. It was a large sliding door that one man could manage to open with some effort. As slowly and quietly as possible, he succeeded in shoving the door open.

The escape vehicle that Antanas had chosen was a military transport truck. Even though the crew at his garage worked mostly on buses belonging to the Elbing Transit System, Antanas and his men were sometimes ordered to fix army cars, trucks, and tanks. The truck that Antanas had selected for their risky plan was a beauty—a 1936 Mercedes-Benz heavy-duty transport vehicle that could carry twelve people and a reasonable amount of luggage. Because of the extra fuel can, tools, and ropes he needed to bring along, however, Antanas knew that the truck could only transport ten escapees.

Antanas had stealthily siphoned eight litres of diesel into the truck's fuel tank the previous evening, after his men had finished work for the day. Tonight, he filled the reserve fuel can to the brim and stored it in the back of the truck. That extra can would give them another twenty-five litres of fuel.

With ten passengers and their luggage, plus his tools and the weight of the extra fuel cans, Antanas calculated that the truck would travel between 280 kilometres and 360 kilometres on a full tank of fuel.

How far they progressed would depend on various factors: the maximum speed they could attain given the weight being hauled, the road conditions, the weather, the terrain, and any idling time they needed. The reserve diesel would get them another 88 to 113 kilometres. Antanas realized that this amount of fuel would not get them all the way to Bavaria. He would have no choice but to siphon diesel from unguarded vehicles at night as he and his companions fled. He knew that if he was apprehended stealing fuel, he would be shot point-blank.

Antanas heard a sudden rap on the window of the garage's back door. His heart froze for a moment before he stepped quickly towards the source of the sound. Peter stood at the door. "Thank God, it's you," Antanas said as he let him in.

"Who did you think it was—the Führer making a surprise inspection?" said Peter in an amused tone.

"Help me put this tarp on the truck," Antanas said. There was clearly no time to banter.

The truck had a large cab that could accommodate three people and its body consisted of metal poles and beams that would enclose the rest of the travellers. Once the tarp was fastened over the poles and the beams, the truck would become a kind of covered carriage that would protect the passengers from wind, snow, and rain, but not the cold. Anticipating freezing temperatures, Peter had stolen five large woollen blankets from the barracks and placed them in the back of the truck.

Antanas threw Peter a section of tarp and they worked swiftly together to secure it in place with ropes. When they were finished, Peter leaned in closely towards Antanas and whispered into his ear, "Leave by the south gate tonight. I left it unlocked."

Antanas nodded and then loaded his personal toolbox onto the truck. It contained the equipment he would be most likely to need on the journey. *Complete sets of screwdrivers and wrenches, check. Metal strips for setting spark plug gaps, check. Wire brushes for cleaning spark plugs, check. Small engine parts, check.* Antanas tossed a hacksaw, a jar of grease, some rags, six spark plugs and three litres of oil to the back of the truck. He threw two long pieces of rope into the back of the truck as well, and then used a shorter piece of rope to tie one of two shovels to the driver's side of the vehicle. Peter did the same on the passenger's side. Then Antanas remembered that he would have to bring along a two-metre rubber hose. He would need the hose to siphon diesel fuel.

After he had loaded all the equipment into the truck, Antanas paused and checked his watch. A worried frown creased his brow. *Damn, it's 9:37 p.m. already! I can't be late. We have to make it out of the camp before the patrols have a chance to stop us.* He climbed into the cab of the truck and turned the ignition key. The motor sputtered and then died. *Bastard truck!* Frantically, he tried again. This time the truck's engine turned over and started to make the clacking and popping sounds so typical of diesel engines. Antanas let the engine run for five minutes to warm up. Then he depressed the clutch and put the vehicle into first gear. Peter slid open the garage door and Antanas let out the clutch, pressed the gas pedal, and crept forward slowly. He stopped just outside the garage, rolled down his window, and was about to thank Peter when a lump in his throat prevented him from speaking.

Peter said simply, "God be with you."

Antanas saluted his friend.

Neither man would ever speak to the other again.

8:55 p.m.

By the time Maria and Jadwyga reached the little courtyard by the cleaning depot, it had begun to snow. The depot was a three-story wooden structure with a sloped roof that enabled the snow to slide off it. Big snow banks had accumulated below the roof on either side of the building. Clustered in front of one of the snow banks were the women that Jadwyga had invited to join them in their flight to freedom. Tanya Shushkevich held a small bag of clothes. Marion Fedyck spoke quietly with Tanya, and Veronica Norkas sat on her suitcase as she listened to their conversation.

9:10 p.m.

Maria watched her housekeeping colleagues trudge into the courtyard. First came Birite Balsys and Jurate Matulionis. Maria knew Jurate from high school in Kaunas and Birute was Jurate's cousin. Maria nodded a greeting to the two women. *These two I would trust with my soul.*

Then she spotted Agafya Gorokhov and Sarah Friedman marching into the square. Inviting these two women to join them had sparked considerable debate with Antanas during the past few days.

When Maria and Jadwyga first recommended her friend Sarah, Antanas had thrown up his hands and exclaimed, "But Sarah's a Jew!"

"So?" Jadwyga and Maria replied in unison.

"If Major Braunshiedel discovers we've tried to assist a Jew to escape, he won't just kill us. He'll torture her, and then us, to death as an example to everyone else!"

Jadwyga had raised her arms towards the heavens. "From what Wladek said, it won't be long before the Red Army is here and Major Braunshiedel will have more to worry about than a frightened Jewish girl and a bunch of foreign workers."

"Look what happened to Wladek. Is that what you want for us?"

"No, but dear husband, you're a good man. Remember the Kaunas massacres. The Germans lied to the Lithuanians and claimed that Jews had led the Soviet oppression of their country. The mob believed them and killed thousands of innocent Jews. Afterwards, I promised God that I would do something to right that terrible wrong. This is our chance, Antanas!" Jadwyga clasped her hands in a gesture of prayer. "This girl has lost her family. And, based on what Wladek told us, the Jews of Eastern Europe are being destroyed. Right now, in this camp, we are the eyes, the hands, and the feet of God. We *must* help Sarah."

"I agree, brother; we have to include her," said Maria.

"All right," said Antanas. "But that leaves only one more spot."

Jadwyga remembered distinctly that at this point in the argument Maria had crossed her arms and faced her brother squarely. "Then it has to be Agafya Gorokhov."

"Maria, she's Russian. We would have the same problems that we would have with Pavel."

"No, there are big differences. She's not a POW, she's not a former Red Army soldier, and she's not a man. She wouldn't be viewed as a deserter by the Red Army."

"Antanas, I support Maria," said Jadwyga. "Agafya is a gentle and intelligent soul who will do us no harm."

Antanas threw up his arms. "Okay, you two, but Agafya is the last person we can take with us."

9:40 p.m.

Jadwyga believed that of all the women with whom they had worked, these seven were the ones they could trust with their lives. *We gave the lucky ones only twelve hours' notice. Secrecy and surprise are our only weapons.*

Jadwyga now saw two new women arrive. One of them held a little boy by the hand and carried an infant girl. Jadwyga grabbed Maria by the shoulders and shook her. "Oh, my God! Those are two of the local German women, and one has brought her infant daughter Katrina and her little boy Sebastian."

Maria shook her head worriedly.

Jadwyga knew what these women wanted. They desperately needed to get out of Elbing, just as they all did. Jadwyga was also acutely aware that there was room for only ten people in the truck. She didn't know what to do and her heart started to pound.

Suddenly, Jadwyga recognized the women. She whispered to Maria, "The children belong to the older woman. Her name is Carola. Her husband was killed fighting the Soviets in Poland. I think her friend is called Johanna."

Maria's face grew tense. "There can only be ten of us. Our caravan must consist of the three of us plus seven of our closest friends. That is what we decided last night."

As Jadwyga and Maria conversed, Carola approached them. "I'm pleading with both of you. I know what the Soviet soldiers do to German women. What will happen to my babies if I am raped and killed? And I cannot leave my friend Johanna."

Jadwyga did not know who had told Carola about their escape plan, but now that these two women were here, she needed to take action. She glanced at Maria and then took Carola by the hand. "I'll speak to my husband Antanas. He's a good man."

When it appeared that there would now be fourteen escapees, four of whom were German, Jadwyga and Maria were anxious to leave right away. It was 9:44 p.m. and there was no sign of Antanas. He was already fourteen minutes late. The pain of the cold was nothing compared to the icy fear gripping their hearts.

Then, at 9:47 p.m. they heard the low rumble of the truck and they watched in relief as it drove into the courtyard. When Antanas climbed out of the cab and saw the number of women and children who had gathered, he became angry and alarmed.

"I said there should be ten of us, not fourteen! Two of these women are German. Why didn't you just invite the camp commander as well?"

Jadwyga drew close to Antanas. "This was not our idea. I don't know how they found out. They just showed up. They're here now. Are we to send them home? Even if you don't care about them or their children, think about what they might do if we reject them. Do you want them screaming at the guards to stop the truck?"

"How will we fit all of them in there, plus our luggage?" asked Antanas in exasperation. He paused and frowned. Then an idea struck him and he called out to Maria. "Little sister, climb to the top of the truck and spread your body evenly over the tarp and the metal beams. You're going to help us secure the luggage to the roof."

"Have you gone mad, big brother?"

"No; it's the only way we'll be able to cram fourteen people into this truck."

Maria did as she was instructed and scampered to the top of the truck. *Don't let me rip this tarp. Dear Jesus, let me do this right*, she prayed. Antanas, Jadwyga, and the other women carefully passed the suitcases to Maria using a long rope slipped through the luggage handles. Maria, in turn, spread the suitcases over the ribs of the carriage roof and handed the other end of the rope to Antanas. He fed the rope through the brackets on both sides of the truck. He also fed it through the bracket at the back of the cargo compartment. Then Antanas threw the remainder of the rope to Maria. She crawled over the roof again and pulled the rope through the luggage handles once more. Then she extended it to the front of the carriage. She dropped what was left of the rope to Antanas. He pulled hard on it to give him more length. Finally, he tied it to the bracket at the front of the carriage.

The women and children boarded the back of the vehicle swiftly and silently, while Antanas, Jadwyga, and Maria entered the cab. Antanas started up the engine and drove towards the south gate of the camp. As they approached the exit, Antanas spotted a soldier, grimaced, squeezed the steering wheel hard, and thought: *Who the hell is that? Is our escape going to end here?* Then he realized that the soldier was Peter and his shoulders and arms relaxed.

Peter opened the gate and motioned them to drive through quickly. Once they were out of the camp, Peter closed and locked the gate, saluting as they drove past. Antanas saluted in return. Peter blew a kiss to Maria, who began to sob. Jadwyga put an arm around her. Antanas checked his watch: it was 10:15 p.m.

Antanas's guts tightened another notch as they passed through the heavy manufacturing area of Elbing. The factories in this area had huge walls made of reinforced concrete. Many of these walls, although tough, were broken from the frequent Allied bombings, and more than half the warehouses had been levelled by bombs as well. Smoke still hovered close to the ground from the last raid.

After another thirty minutes of driving, Antanas made a three-point turn and headed back towards Elbing. Having gone about 400 metres, he made a hard right and headed south down a little-used country road. As the truck lurched, a couple of the women yelled. Sebastian, Carola's three-year-old squealed in delight, and his baby sister screamed.

"What was all that about?" Maria asked.

"I just realized that the road we were on is well travelled by local farmers and army trucks. That road has enough traffic to warrant frequent army patrols, but this road going south leads to marshes and swamps. It's a passable road, and it won't have as many Wehrmacht patrols."

"Okay, big brother, that makes sense, but please make the turns a little less dramatic next time."

***

The farther they drove from the camp, the more relaxed everyone felt. However, at the south end of Lake Druzno, the route deteriorated from a two-lane gravel road into a one-lane dirt road. After driving a few kilometres along this road, Antanas began to worry that this might be a dead end. After another kilometre he observed that a major thoroughfare joined the road to the right. He turned and proceeded west along this bigger boulevard.

Travelling along a major roadway made Jadwyga extremely nervous.

Maria handed Jadwyga her rosary. "Pray and you'll be all right."

Jadwyga fingered the rosary constantly, praying quietly: "Jesus, Mary, and Joseph, please, please help us get to Bavaria."

They had been driving for two hours when Jadwyga suddenly spotted a Wehrmacht patrol up ahead. Five soldiers awaited them. The tallest of the soldiers was standing on the edge of the road moving a lantern in a circle with his right hand and pointing to the side of the road with his left.

Antanas eased up on the accelerator and pulled the truck onto the shoulder. The sound of the soldiers' footsteps crunching in the snow made Maria sit up straight. The truck had driven about thirty metres past the patrol, but none of the soldiers had fired upon them. Antanas hoped fervently that the transport documents that Peter had furnished him would pass inspection. Maria reached down and touched a metal pipe concealed beneath her seat. She was prepared to use it.

Jadwyga continued to pray quietly. "Mother Mary, spare me, Maria, and the other women from rape, and Antanas from death."

As a sergeant approached the truck, Jadwyga's stomach cramped, sweat broke out on her forehead, and her arms began to shake. Then she fainted. Maria propped Jadwyga up on her shoulder to make it look as though she was sleeping, and then smiled at the sergeant who was rapping on the glass.

Antanas rolled down his window.

Chapter 3

Jadwyga's Family

The Poles and the Lithuanians had been allies under the banner of the
Confederacy for many centuries, but when Poland drove the Red
Army out of Poland and Lithuania in 1919, they rewarded themselves
by keeping the Lithuanian capital, Vilnius, as a Polish city, renaming
it Vilno. This act created huge tensions between the former allies.

Kaunas, early May 1923

Jadwyga was only three years old and did not understand much of
what her family was talking about. But she knew that her sisters were
angry and afraid. She saw her sister Nika reluctantly hand her father
a note that had been written by Mrs. Valanciunas, the principal of her
school. The note was addressed to her mother and father but it had
been given to Nika to deliver.

"I thought about throwing this note into the ditch, but then I
figured that you need to know how mean they are to Wisia and me at
school," said Nika.

Jadwyga watched her father Piotr and her mother Marija pick up
the letter, stand up, and read it together, silently. Jadwyga could see
that her sisters, Nika especially, were afraid of their parents' reaction.
She watched her father's mouth and her mother's eyes. Her mother
had a round face, brown hair, and soft blue eyes; she looked gentle,
but she could be firm. Nika and Wisia were both surprised when their
mother calmly asked Nika to explain what had happened at school.

"My teacher ordered me to answer the arithmetic question in
Lithuanian and I refused," said Nika.

"Why didn't you answer in Lithuanian?"

"My answer to the arithmetic question was correct, but it was in
Polish. I forgot the Lithuanian word."

"So, what happened?"

"Mrs. Bernatas sent me to the principal's office."

For months, Marija and Piotr had listened to the girls' complaints and they had tried their best to help them fit in at school. Nothing seemed to work. After eight months of watching his daughters suffer, Piotr decided to pay a visit to the principal.

"I'll go to the school tomorrow and speak to your principal. We'll work out a solution and life will be better for you two rascals. Still, you must both promise me that you'll try harder to speak Lithuanian at school."

"Why can't Wisia and I go back to St. Monica's? We could speak Polish there."

"Nika, you know why. We need a house that is big enough for my tailor shop and for us to live in. The extra rent means we had to move you and your sister out of St. Monica's. Your mother and I can't afford both the extra rent and private school tuition."

Jadwyga was shocked when she saw Nika fold her arms and stare hard at her father. "You can talk to Mrs. Valanciunas if you want to, but things won't get better. She's mean," Nika declared.

Marija cleared her throat. "I have to work at the store tomorrow, Piotr, but my thoughts and prayers will be with you and the girls."

***

The next morning was Friday and Piotr had no customers scheduled at his tailor shop. So, after asking a neighbour, Mrs. Klamitis, to look after little Jadwyga, he decided to ride his bike to Wisia and Nika's school.

He waited until he knew the students would be settled into their classes before riding his Polish-built bicycle the one-kilometre route to the school. It was a pleasant ride past their neighbours' homes and a cedar grove halfway to the school. He loved the sweet smell of the cedars. The aroma reminded him that this lovely grove was one of the reasons why they had chosen to live in this neighbourhood.

The local public school was a three-story, red-brick building with many windows. It accommodated 220 local children, seven teachers, a secretary, a janitor, and a principal. It had a pot-bellied stove in every third room and the classroom doors were never closed so that heat could be evenly distributed. This was not a cold day, however; it was early May and the air was warm and fresh. Piotr felt invigorated by his brisk bicycle ride.

When he entered the building, the school secretary greeted him. Piotr explained that he was there to see Mrs. Valanciunas. "I wish to speak to her about the note that she sent home with Nika yesterday."

Mrs. Valanciunas entered the waiting area and offered her hand to Piotr. "*Labas, labas diena, Ponas Sosnowski.*" ("Hello, hello and good day, Mr. Sosnowski.")

Piotr shook the principal's hand and replied, "*Labas, labas diena, Pone Valanciunas.*" ("Hello, hello and good day, Mrs. Valanciunas.")

They made an odd couple. Piotr was tall and stocky. He was balding but had a pleasingly symmetrical, shaved head. Dressed in a three-piece navy suit and sporting a thick, black moustache, he was handsome in a rugged way. Mrs. Valanciunas was petite and blonde with light-green eyes. She was attractive but she never seemed to smile. She wore a conservative brown dress and a necklace of medium-sized, yellow amber stones.

Piotr was struck suddenly by a bad feeling about Mrs. Valanciunas. *Maybe Nika is right about her.* The principal led Piotr into her office. They stood facing each other.

"I have come to respond to your note about Nika. I would like to work with you to help Nika and Wisia enjoy school, make friends, and learn Lithuanian faster," Piotr began in perfect Lithuanian.

"First, Nika must apologize to her teacher, Mrs. Bernatas," Mrs. Valanciunas replied firmly.

Piotr nodded. "Done."

"She must also apologize to me and to her class."

"Done."

"She must always speak Lithuanian when she is in school."

"Done."

Piotr then took a step forward. "Now, can I ask something of you and of Wisia and Nika's teachers?"

Mrs. Valanciunas stepped back and folded her arms. "What do you want from us?"

"Can the teachers be kinder to Wisia and to Nika? Can they encourage the Lithuanian girls and boys to help my daughters to speak Lithuanian more fluently? Can you discourage them from teasing Wisia and Nika for speaking it less than fluently?"

"If they're not willing to speak Lithuanian properly, don't blame the other children. They've been in class for eight months, and if they don't want to speak Lithuanian, why don't you take them back to Poland?"

Piotr's heart began to pound and his breathing escalated, but he told himself to remain calm.

"We're talking about my Wisia and Nika; they're nine and seven years old. They aren't revolutionaries—they just want to learn, make friends, and avoid being bullied."

"They bring it on themselves."

"Tell me, are there any other Polish girls in the school?"

"Of course, there are many, but they speak beautiful Lithuanian."

"Did they speak Lithuanian before they came to this school?"

"Yes, they did, but what has that got to do with Nika and Wisia?"

At this point, Piotr raised his arms skyward. "Don't you think that my children may need extra help because they didn't speak Lithuanian before coming to your school?"

Mrs. Valanciunas took another small step backwards and enunciated slowly, "No, I don't think so. And if Nika continues to refuse to converse in Lithuanian, she'll fail her year."

"Why would you do that to her? So she'll hate school even more?" Piotr asked.

"I think that you and your wife should have prepared Nika and Wisia better for school. Why don't you take Nika back to Poland and show her that things are not perfect there?"

Piotr's jugular was throbbing and his mouth went dry. The few hairs he still had on his neck stood at attention. He chose not to lash out, but he also made a deliberate decision to answer the principal in Polish. "*To jest bardzo dobry. Do widzenia.*" ("That's a very good idea. Goodbye.") Piotr turned his back and left the principal's office, brushing past the secretary on his way out. He left the school through the main door, mounted his bicycle, and raced home.

***

Later that day, Jadwyga saw her mother return from her work at the general store, just in time for supper. Her father stood stirring the cabbage soup, but he was far more steamed than the soup. He told his wife about his unsatisfying conversation with the principal. "Some Lithuanians teach their children to hate the Polish."

Her mother replied, "Most of my comrades at the store are good to me, but my boss, Daiva Petrauskas, treats me unfairly. I'm sure it's because I'm Polish. My dear husband, I've never told you this before because I didn't want to disrupt your business or interfere with the girls' schooling, but maybe now is the time to reveal the whole truth."

Jaywyga's father put down his spoon and stared at her mother.

"Mrs. Petrauskas makes me do the inventory every week. You already know that, but what you don't know is that I'm the only one who must stay after hours to do it. I told her that it takes me until 8 p.m. and I'm afraid to be alone in the store. Mrs. Petrauskas said, 'A good strong Polish woman like you can't be afraid,'" her mother explained with tears in her eyes.

"Do you want your Lithuanian colleagues to stand by you in solidarity?"

"Yes. I would like their company and their help."

"It's too bad Poland didn't do the same for Lithuania. Poland stole Vilnius from us. A strong Polish woman like you, you should do fine on your own."

Piotr threw his mug onto the kitchen floor and it shattered. Wisia, Nika, and Jadwyga all jumped. Their mother froze on the spot.

"I brought you to the outskirts of Kaunas because it seemed like a small, peaceful, beautiful village, but I now know that a few of the locals still harbour a very serious grudge against Poland. Marija, you and the girls are paying the price."

He rose to his feet, put his arm around his wife, and looked down at Wisia, Nika, and Jadwyga.

"I don't believe that most Lithuanians hate the Poles, but a few still do, and they're harming our family. Our absence will be their loss. We'll return to Poland."

Wisia and Nika were thrilled by their father's declaration. They jumped up and down, laughing and screaming in delight. Jadwyga knew only that the family was going somewhere new and it sounded exciting.

Despite the distaste that some Lithuanians felt for Poles, Piotr knew it was illegal for his family to return to Poland at that time. He analyzed their dilemma. *The Lithuanian government does not want Poles to return to Poland. They want us to stay here so they can "Lithuanianize" us. Our family is caught in an impossible situation. But I have a plan. We'll have to sneak across the border.*

Chapter 4

Crossing the Nemunas

Most Lithuanians and Poles co-existed well, but the loss of Vilnius
was a persistent sore in their relationship. Even the naming of the
city was a source of tension. The Lithuanians held on to the name
"Vilnius," while the Poles referred to the city as "Vilno."

Kaunas, late May 1923

The journey from Kaunas to Vilnius became a family legend that
young Jadwyga heard told many times by her mother, father, and
sisters. As Jadwyga remembered it, her father finished all his orders
for making suits, shirts, blazers, and pants and he took on no new
business. He sold most of his rolls of fabric to other tailors and kept
three rolls to take with him. He packed three pairs of scissors, his
sewing machine, a tape measure, and one mannequin. He placed his
best navy three-piece suit in a box. He and Marija sold the family's
winter coats, sweaters, scarves, mittens, and gloves because they were
too bulky to transport. Piotr would make new winter clothes for his
family in Poland.

Jadwyga's mother packed clothes and shoes for herself and the
rest of the family. She knew she would miss Kaunas and the friends
she had made here, especially Antanas and Stephania Paskevicius. But
she also knew that Wisia and Nika would never be happy in Kaunas.

She gathered together three pots of different sizes. Marija was a
skilled cook and she wanted to bring all her cooking implements with
her. Piotr reminded her, however, that they would have to carry
everything across the Nemunas River in boxes, so they decided to sell
all their household items and furniture to neighbours.

Marija lied and told her colleagues at work and her neighbours
that they were moving to Alytus, a Lithuanian city south of Kaunas.

She told the truth only to her good friend Stephania. She knew that her secret would be safe with Stephania and the Paskevicius family.

Marija told the girls they could each bring one special item on their journey. Wisia packed her paintbrushes and some paint. Nika packed her skipping rope. Jadwyga chose the rag doll her father had made for her. Marija pulled out a bottle of vodka.

Before leaving their home, Marija had also suggested to Piotr that they bring along their cow, Anya. "Once we are in Vilno, we can sell her for cash. The money will give us a fresh start."

They crammed all their belongings into large wooden crates that were strong enough and buoyant enough to cross the Nemunas River. To assist them in crossing the river, they hired a man who owned a large wagon and two strong horses. On May 29, 1923 they moved out of their home secretly, piling all their belongings into the wagon. They departed around 2 p.m., which gave them enough daylight to locate a place to enter and cross the river. Most of their things were jammed onto the wagon, but everyone had to carry personal items as well. Little Jadwyga held on to her rag doll.

At first, everything went well. Jonas, the wagon driver, was friendly and helpful. He assisted Piotr in loading the crates and then he tied Anya to the back of the wagon.

He drove the wagon through the forests near the river, where the birch and fir trees hid them from sight. During the first several hours of travelling, Piotr, Marija, Wisia, and Nika took turns either walking on the road or sitting in the wagon with Jadwyga and Jonas.

At around 8:30 p.m., Jonas pulled on the reins and stopped the horses. "This will be a good place to cross. The Nemunas is not so wide here. It will be dark soon, but there will be enough moonlight to guide you across."

The Nemunas River formed part of the border between Lithuania and Poland. The Poles called it the Niemen and the Lithuanians called it the Nemunas. Whatever the river's name, Marija knew there was a problem. She pointed at the water.

"The river here is too deep, cold, and fast for the girls to cross. Even I would drown in such a place."

Piotr gazed at the river. "There may not be any better places to cross."

Jonas unloaded some thick boards on which to place the crates. Then he gave them some bad news. "I don't swim, and the Nemunas is too strong for me to cross at my age. I'm afraid that my part of your journey must end here."

Jonas said goodbye to Marija and the girls and Piotr paid him his fee. "Good luck crossing," Jonas said before leaving.

Just then, a Lithuanian man stepped from the woods. He had been picking mushrooms earlier that evening but had grown tired and fallen asleep. The girls' excited chatter had awakened him. But when he saw how frightened the girls were now, he decided to offer help.

The man approached Marija and Piotr. "My name is Vytas. I'm visiting from Alytus so I don't know the river well here, but I'm strong and I can swim. I would like to help a young family like yours but, before I do, I must know why you're attempting something so dangerous. Why not travel by road across one of the bridges?"

Wisia ran to her mother. "Do we have to swim across the river?"

"Wait, darling, I'm talking to this gentleman. He has offered to help us cross."

Nika pulled on her mother's skirt. "Do we have to swim all the way to the other side?"

"We'll answer your questions soon, but first we must make a plan," Marija responded patiently.

Marija spoke softly to Vytas. "We're Poles living in Kaunas and we feel that we're hated by some of the Lithuanians. They have made my life and the lives of my two older girls too painful to stay on this side of the Nemunas."

"It's illegal for Poles to return to Poland from Lithuania, and yet my daughters can't do well here in Kaunas. We're crossing the Nemunas here because if we use a bridge, we'll be stopped. The guards could arrest us," added Piotr.

"What would happen to our girls if Piotr and I were thrown in prison?" Marija began to cry.

Piotr placed his hand on Vytas's shoulder. "Will you help us, or will you report us to the authorities?"

Vytas looked up and down the shoreline. "I know something about the bad feelings towards Poles in Lithuania. But like most Lithuanians, I see the Poles as our friends and allies. I have daughters of my own in Alytus. I could never turn my back on your girls."

"Thank you," said Piotr, giving Vytas a hearty slap on the back. Marija handed him her bottle of vodka. Vytas accepted the bottle and took a gulp. Piotr and Vytas spent the next hour unloading the wagon and placing the crates onto the boards, which they lashed together.

Piotr attached metal rings to each of the makeshift rafts and then attached a rope to each ring. Marija took on the job of entertaining the girls and keeping them calm and quiet as the men worked. Marija glanced at the river, pulled her St. Christopher necklace away from her throat, kissed it, and then tucked it back inside her shirt.

The Nemunas is a large river, but at the spot where Jonas had dropped them off, it was only forty metres across to the other bank. The depth of the water was hard to judge, but it appeared to be about two metres or so. There were no rapids in this spot, but there was a swift current. The water was also cold—very cold.

Piotr and Vytas finished unloading the wagon and building the rafts made from the crates. Together, they pushed the first raft into the water and loaded some of the boxes onto it. Vytas held the first raft in place. Their plan was to pull the small rafts across the river with the boxes perched on top, but first Piotr needed to lead Anya across the river. Piotr stepped off the riverbank. The water was up to his waist as he tried to pull Anya into deeper water. Anya balked at crossing the river, but then Piotr noticed something interesting. He called out to Marija. "Anya is heading downriver following the bank. Let's see where she goes."

Anya walked fifty metres downriver and around a bend. There the river widened, but the level of the water dropped from the cow's shoulders to her stomach.

"She found shallow water for us, thank God," said Piotr.

The rest of the family followed Anya and Piotr along the riverbank. The banks of the river were steep and Wisia and Nika entered the river with a splash. They screamed, shivered, laughed, and then started to swim. Marija was not laughing, however; she was losing her battle with the current. She could still touch the sandy bottom of the river with her feet, but the current had knocked her off balance several times and she had gulped water twice.

Vytas called to Marija over the roar of the water. "Let me lift you onto my shoulders."

Marija waved him off, yelling, "No!"

Despite her protests, Vytas grabbed her and lifted her onto his shoulders in one movement, carrying her to safety on the other side.

Piotr saw that Jadwyga was not sitting still on the riverbank as she had been told to do. She was walking towards the water. Piotr left Anya a third of the way across the river and rushed back to shore. He picked up Jadwyga, carried her all the way across the river on his shoulders, and placed her safely in her mother's arms. He looked over at Wisia and Nika. They had swum across the river on a diagonal and had made it across.

Piotr returned to Anya and led her the rest of the way across the river before leaving her in the care of his wife and daughters. "Take good care of our cow. I'm going back for the crates," he said before returning to the other shore.

Piotr met up with Vytas on the Lithuanian side of the river and they towed the boxes that they had placed on the wooden rafts. Piotr and Vytas dragged the largest boxes across the sandy shore and pulled them onto the rafts that were floating in the water. The banks were steep, so the rafts made a huge splash when the boxes landed on them. Piotr began to swim as he pulled a raft behind him, while Vytas pulled another as the current threatened to topple him over.

Piotr hauled his load with the current at his back. Water swept over his head and he swallowed a mouthful. He stopped, stood up, and coughed until he could breathe again. Then he resumed his journey to the other side.

Vytas was stronger and he had a somewhat lighter weight to haul. He arrived with his load on the other side before Piotr. He waited for Piotr and helped him to pull his heavy boxes up onto the shore. Piotr then helped Vytas lug the boxes off the other raft.

They jumped up and down on the riverbank to get their blood flowing again. Then each man re-entered the river until the waves reached chest level. They dove into the water and fought their way across. When Piotr pulled the last raft onto the Polish shore, he turned to Vytas. "We've done it. You've saved our lives. May you live a thousand years."

Marija ran to them and handed them the bottle of vodka. "You've saved our girls!"

Vytas smiled and pointed at Anya, who was grazing in the grass near the bank. "You're not giving enough credit to your cow."

"How can I ever repay you?" Marija asked.

Vytas smiled and glanced over at the girls, who had discovered a field of fireflies. They had shed all their wet clothes except for their underwear. They were completely engrossed as they chased the glowing creatures. He looked intently at Marija. "You can live well and be good to one another." Then he took another long swig of vodka. "How are you going to move these boxes?"

Marija smiled. "My sister Julia, her husband, and some friends will meet us somewhere on the road beside the river. When I sent her a message, I couldn't be certain exactly where we would cross. On a map, I restricted the possibilities to the narrowest crossing points within a kilometre of each other. They'll be travelling between those points by wagons, looking for us."

Just then they heard people singing songs in Polish and they could see two wagons, each guided by its own lantern. It was Marija's sister Julia, her husband Marek, and two of their friends. Marija ran to the wagons and Julia jumped down onto the road. The sisters embraced. "Thank God, you're all alive. I brought some dry clothes for all of you."

Julia resembled her sister, but she had hazel eyes and blonde hair. Marek was tall, lean, and muscular. He had light brown hair and grey eyes.

After the family greetings, Marija saw Vytas walk towards the river's edge. She waved and shouted, "Thank you!" She and Piotr watched as he crossed the Nemunas to the Lithuanian bank for the last time. He gestured from the other shore and they waved back. Marija turned and marshalled the girls onto Uncle Marek's wagon.

***

For two months, the two families lived together on Marek and Julia's farm with their young sons Andrew and Stefan, along with Julia's and Marija's Aunt Zofia. The Sosnowskis helped with chores on the farm. In early August, Piotr took a trip to Vilno, where he found a job and a place for his family to live. The following week, the family moved to a flat in the centre of Vilno.

We fled Lithuania because of the anger some Lithuanians felt as a result of Poland's annexation of this city. Piotr thought. *Now we live here.* The irony was not lost on Piotr.

Soon Piotr began to attract customers to his tailoring business, while Marija found a job in a nearby bakery. They lived on the main floor of a spacious two-story home. The house was built of yellow bricks accented by white window frames. The homeowner lived upstairs, and she turned out to be jovial and helpful. She loved all the girls and was happy to babysit when needed.

Jadwyga loved the house and thought it was pretty. Wisia thought it was wonderful because she had her own room. Nika was the only one to complain. "I have to share a bedroom with Jadwyga." After a while, she got used to it.

Chapter 5

Courtship

Anticipating a possible German invasion, Poland made overtures to
Lithuania to renew their alliance.

Kaunas, early February 1938

Fifteen years later, Marija and Piotr returned to Kaunas to visit their
old friends Antanas Sr. and Stephania Paskevicius. They hadn't seen
the couple since living there in 1923, and they wished to get
reacquainted.

The Paskevicius family had been the only family in whom they
entrusted knowledge of their secret escape to Poland. When postal
service resumed between Poland and Lithuania in 1937, they started
corresponding with each other. Marija and Stephania did most of the
writing, but they always included hellos from Piotr and Antanas Sr.

The relationship between Poland and Lithuania was changing.
Fearing a German invasion, Poland forced Lithuania to reopen
diplomatic relations. The Lithuanians still resented the Poles, but they
feared the Germans more. Therefore, travel between the two nations
became possible once again.

Antanas Sr. was a congenial man with brown eyes and a broad
smile. He was not a large man, but he was fit and lively and he had a
warm heart. He held a good job in the Ministry of Agriculture, and
he was proud that his wife did not have to work outside their home.
Stephania was a tall, slim brunette with blue eyes. She was beautiful
and always well dressed; she loved to wear stylish clothing. At times
she was warm and flirtatious, but at other times she could be cold.

Antanas Sr. and Stephania greeted their guests at their front door
and then gave them a tour of their two-story home. The brick house
had three bedrooms, birch shutters, and maple floors. Antanas Jr.'s

bedroom was given to Marija and Piotr during their visit, while Antanas slept in the living room. Jadwyga had accompanied her parents on the trip and she bunked with the Paskevicius daughters, Janina and Maria. Wisia and Nika were unable to get time off from their respective jobs, but they vowed to come along on the next visit.

Marija and Stephania sat down to enjoy a cup of tea and to catch up on how their respective children were doing.

"Wisia is now twenty-four, Nika twenty-two, and our little one, Jadwyga, will be eighteen in July," said Marija.

Stephania brought out an album of photographs to show Jadwyga. "Antanas Jr. is almost twenty-four now, his sister Janina is nineteen, and our baby, Maria, is fifteen."

Although it was unspoken, it was clear to Jadwyga that Antanas and Maria were their mother's favourites. Antanas Sr. loved Janina as much as his two other children, but Janina reminded Stephania of a shameful time from her past. Later, Jadwyga learned that Antanas Sr. had been a drafted soldier in the Russian army for many years. The Czar's thugs had conscripted him in 1914 to serve during World War I. During the time that Antanas Sr. was essentially kidnapped, he and Stephania had only a baby boy, Antanas Jr. The Russian Army disengaged from the war in 1916, but Antanas Sr. was not released until 1919. Upon his return, he found that he had now had a daughter named Janina. At first, he was beset by anger, jealousy, and sadness. Ultimately, however, he forgave Stephania for her extramarital affair and accepted Janina as his own child. Stephania, however, could never forget that Janina was not her husband's flesh and blood.

The visit lasted three days. Just as the Sosnowskis were about to leave, Stephania said teasingly to Marija, "Would you let Princess Jadwyga come and visit with our Maria over the Easter holidays? They get along so well and are such good friends."

Unlike her two sisters, Jadwyga had no emotional block about speaking Lithuanian. Although she was not yet fluent, she knew enough of the language to easily make herself understood by her new friend Maria.

Piotr accepted the invitation without hesitation, but his wife became a little teary-eyed. This would be the first time that she and

Jadwyga had ever been separated. Piotr pointed out that it would be good for their youngest child to experience a bit of independence. Marija relented. "Yes, they are such good friends; it will be good for both of them."

When mid-March arrived, Jadwyga prepared for her journey.

"Do you have enough sweaters? Do you have nice clothes to wear for Good Friday and Easter Sunday? And what about a fancy coat for walking from church to church on Good Saturday?" her mother asked.

Jadwyga became annoyed with her mother's fussing and overattentiveness. "Do you think I'm a small child? Don't you believe that I can think and dress for myself?"

In reality, this was the first overnight trip of Jadwyga's life, and she was more than a little anxious. A million questions ran through her head. *Will Mr. and Mrs. Paskevicius treat me as well as my parents do? Will Maria and I get along for two weeks? What will Maria's brother and sister be like? I'll be in a foreign country; what if the police don't want me to stay there?*

Jadwyga did not wish to worry her parents, especially her mother, so she kept her fears to herself. She enjoyed a relationship with her mother that was as close as could be. Her sisters teased her about being the baby of the family. Wisia asked, "Who is going to feed you if mama isn't there?"

I'll show Wisia and Nika and mama and papa and everyone that I'm an adult now, thought Jadwyga. *I will act like a grown-up and not voice my worries out loud.*

On the day of her departure, Jadwyga's parents accompanied her to the Vilno railway station. As they sat together in the streetcar, Marija struggled to hold back tears. *My baby is almost eighteen years old. Where did the time go?*

When they arrived at the railway station and disembarked, Piotr carried Jadwyga's suitcase as mother and daughter walked arm-in-arm towards the passenger area. It wasn't long before the train chugged into the station. Just before boarding the car, Jadwyga kissed her father and mother goodbye. Mother and daughter cried and a lump formed in Piotr's throat. Moments later, the whistle blew, and it was time for the train to leave.

The journey was uneventful until Lithuanian border guards stopped the train, entered Jadwyga's car, and checked everyone's passport. Jadwyga was terrified of the guards, but she tried to conceal her fear. She presented her passport and flirted nervously with the younger of the two guards. "You look very much the handsome soldier in that uniform," she said.

The soldier was even younger and shyer than Jadwyga. "Thanks," he blurted self-consciously, and then he proceeded down the train to check the remaining passports.

When Jadwyga arrived at the railroad station in Kaunas, Maria and her brother Antanas were excitedly awaiting her on the platform. After the train blew its whistle and jerked to a stop, Jadwyga descended onto the platform from the train. Maria spotted Jadwyga and ran to her. Maria and Jadwyga laughed and chattered about how great their visit was going to be. Antanas picked up Jadwyga's bags and carried them to his car as the girls accompanied him arm-in-arm.

"This is Antanas's 1926 Fiat," Maria explained. "Not many people can afford a car, but he turned an old wreck into this shiny sports car."

Jadwyga smiled appreciatively. "He must be a very good mechanic."

"Yes, he is. I'm very proud of him. He's not only a great mechanic—he's a graduate electrical engineer."

"Oh, my!" Jadwyga was truly impressed.

"He'll be a terrific catch for some woman. Too bad he's too old for you, Jadwyga," Maria said with a mischievous smile. Jadwyga giggled and Antanas blushed.

On the drive to the Paskevicius home, Antanas found himself glancing at Jadwyga in the rearview mirror. *She's stunning*, he thought. *She's charming and lovely. I want to get to know her better.*

When they arrived at the house, Jadwyga saw that the ice was still solid on the Nemunas River, which flowed behind the Paskevicius residence. Maria told her that she, Antanas, and Janina skated on the river during the winter and swam in it during the summer. Stephania confided to Jadwyga one day that Antanas had built his own kayak and was an accomplished paddler. Because Maria still had two days of her high school term to finish, Jadwyga and Stephania had time alone to get to know one another. At first, Stephania's austere manner unnerved Jadwyga, but once Stephania began telling stories about her family, Jadwyga warmed up to her.

***

When Good Friday arrived, Jadwyga and the Paskevicius family started a three-day odyssey of church attendance that was no different from the one she observed at home. Mass on Easter Sunday was followed by a feast consisting of ham, goose, sauerkraut, buns, potatoes, Napoleon cake, and coffee. There was more than enough food and laughter for everyone, and even a glass of wine for Jadwyga. *They are treating me like an adult,* she thought.

After the feast, Jadwyga, Maria, and Antanas began to plan activities for the rest of their time together. Antanas worked as the head mechanic for the Kaunas Transit System, but he had taken his holidays to coincide with Jadwyga's visit.

At the beginning of Jadwyga's stay, the three of them went skating and tobogganing every day and to the movies every other night. Hollywood movies were all the rage, but so were films from Sweden, England, Germany, Czechoslovakia, and Italy. *Golden City,* a tragedy starring the famous German actress, Christine Snahore, was Maria and Jadwyga's favourite. Antanas preferred Errol Flynn in *The Adventures of Robin Hood.* Movie tickets were expensive, and Jadwyga wondered how Antanas could afford to take them to the cinema so often.

One night, Antanas asked Jadwyga to walk down to the river with him. As they were standing by the riverbank, he asked, "Will you go to the spring dance with me?"

Jadwyga was stunned. "Will Maria come as well?"

"No, you have to be eighteen or older to attend this dance."

"I'm not eighteen."

"Yes, but you're almost eighteen, and you look old enough. Please come with me. I bet you're a good dancer."

She was a good dancer, thanks to practising steps with her sisters.

"Okay," Jadwyga found herself saying, before adding, "But I don't have a proper dress for a dance."

"That's not a problem. Mama and Maria will take care of it."

When Jadwyga was preparing for bed that night, she slipped into Maria's room and told her what had happened. "Your brother asked me to the spring dance, but I have no dress fit for such an event. I already said yes, but I have nothing to wear. Maybe I should tell him that I've changed my mind?"

Jadwyga worried that Maria might be angry at this turn of events because the dance would be a date that separated them as a trio. At the very least, she believed that Maria would be surprised, if not shocked by this news, but it was Maria who astounded Jadwyga.

"Don't worry; momma and I will get something for you to wear before Saturday night."

"Did you know that your brother was going to ask me to the dance?"

"To be honest, I wondered if he would. I know him well and I can tell he likes you a lot."

Janina was away from home with friends for the holidays, so they decided to lend Jadwyga one of her dresses. It was the same deep blue colour as Jadwyga's eyes. On the evening of the dance, Maria and Stephania helped Jadwyga to apply eye-liner, mascara, and red lipstick. Jadwyga looked radiantly beautiful.

Antanas wore a double-breasted navy suit and he carried a single red rose, which he pinned to Jadwyga's dress. "Thank you," was all Jadwyga could think to say, but she was truly moved by such a romantic gesture. Antanas blushed when she thanked him.

Jadwyga and Antanas were both good dancers and they commanded the dance floor like Ginger Rogers and Fred Astaire. Antanas became completely caught up in the dancing. When he finally glanced at his watch, his smile disappeared. It was 11:30 p.m. "We have to go now," he told Jadwyga. "I promised mother that I would have you home before midnight."

They rushed to the car, intent on getting home as quickly as possible. When Antanas tried to start the car, however, it made a loud bang; black smoke billowed from the exhaust and then the motor stopped completely. During the holidays, Jadwyga had dubbed the old Fiat "Zabka," which meant "little frog" in Polish, because of its green colour and small size. That night, however, Antanas was not calling his Fiat by any cute names.

"Bastard, why don't you start? Why do I even ask? I know what the problem is. Zabka was overdue for a tune-up before Holy week, but I was so busy at work that I had no time. Then, I was having so much fun with you and Maria that I neglected her."

Antanas popped the hood, got his tools from the trunk, and went to work. He quickly determined that the spark plugs needed cleaning. The carburetor needed an adjustment and the timing chain required a fix as well. But there was no time for these latter two procedures, especially with a flickering streetlight as the only illumination. Antanas cleaned the spark plugs and soon old Zabka was operational again. Antanas set off for home. It was a thirty-minute ride at legal speeds but Antanas did it in twenty. He was a highly skilled driver, but even he could not make it back in time to meet the midnight curfew.

***

Stephania was beside herself when Antanas and Jadwyga had not returned home at midnight. *Where are they? Did they have an accident? Did Antanas make advances towards Jadwyga? What will Marija and Piotr say?* When Antanas Jr. and Jadwyga finally walked through the door, Stephania pounced on her son. "I convinced your father that taking Jadwyga to the dance was a good idea and that you could be trusted. This is how you repay me?"

"We're only ten minutes late," said Antanas. He explained what had happened with the car while Jadwyga remained silent and stared at the floor, tapping her left foot constantly.

Antanas Sr. stood up and faced his wife. "The only thing that our son has done wrong is to forget to do his regular maintenance on old Zabka. Maybe Zabka is jealous of Jadwyga because, up until now, she has been the special one in Antanas's heart."

Stephania laughed despite herself. "There has been enough foolishness tonight already, and now everyone should go to bed."

***

The next day Antanas, Maria, and Jadwyga decided to try a little spring skiing. Skiing came easily to Antanas and he loved it; he had even made his own skis out of maple wood. Maria, too, had long ago mastered skiing. For Jadwyga, however, it was a terrifying sport. Nonetheless, she forced herself to learn to ski because she had so much fun being with both of her friends, no matter what they were doing.

During the second week of their holiday, Antanas sometimes asked Jadwyga to accompany him on evening dates that did not include his sister. They usually went to the movies but, when the weather allowed, they would simply go for romantic walks. Jadwyga found herself very attracted to Antanas, but she still missed Maria on these outings. The two girls had become tremendously close. Jadwyga greatly admired Maria, even though Maria was three years younger than she. Maria's intelligence, maturity, and sense of humour made Jadwyga forget the difference in their ages.

One Friday evening, after they had returned from seeing the British movie *Pygmalion* and after Maria had said good night, Antanas beckoned Jadwyga to join him for a walk along the banks of the Nemunas River. Jadwyga kept repeating movie lines to Antanas but, eventually, she could no longer ignore the fact that Antanas had been quiet for a long time.

"What are you thinking, Antanas?" she asked.

"Jadwyga, will you marry me?"

Jadwyga stumbled backwards, then straightened herself and took hold of Antanas by the arm. "I'm flattered by your offer of marriage," she said. "But I'm not yet eighteen and we really don't know each other very well."

"You can take your time, and I'll wait for you. Just know that I love you for more than your beauty. I know that you are kind to everyone that you meet, you're intelligent, and you enjoy life. You're the woman I want to marry. I hope that I haven't frightened you with my honesty. Don't answer my proposal now—but tell me the moment that you can say yes."

***

That night, Jadwyga couldn't sleep. She tried to drift off, but finally she got up, put on her robe, crept to Maria's room, and knocked on the door.

"Maria, are you awake?"

"I am now."

"Your brother has proposed."

Maria sat up and took hold of Jadwyga's hands.

"I told him it was too soon. I need time to think." Jadwyga blurted.

"That's a good answer. And don't worry; he'll wait." Maria counselled.

"But I leave tomorrow."

"Don't worry; he'll wait."

When Maria and Antanas said goodbye to Jadwyga at the train station the next day, the three of them were visibly sad. It felt like the breakup of the Three Musketeers and possibly the separation of Romeo and Juliet. There were lots of tears and promises to write. Finally, Jadwyga had to board the train.

***

When Jadwyga arrived back home, she began to receive letters. Some of them were from Maria, but many more were from Antanas, who was writing at a pace of four letters a week. He told Jadwyga of his daily activities at the garage and at home, but he also expressed his deep love for her. He made it clear that she was his one and only true love. Jadwyga was at a disadvantage because she had told no one except Maria about his proposal. Jadwyga wrote to Maria: "I like your brother very much and I want to see more of him, but I'm not sure that I'm ready for marriage."

"I know one thing," Maria wrote back. "He has chosen you and you're the one."

Antanas began to visit Jadwyga and her family. It was 100 kilometres from Kaunas to Vilno, but Antanas made the trek to the Sosnowski home most weekends. He usually took the train, but occasionally old Zabka was pressed into service. Over time, Piotr and Marija discovered that they liked Antanas very much.

He would be a good husband for Nika, but I didn't expect Antanas to pick our youngest, mused Marija.

The visits extended from May of 1938 until April of 1939. Finally, Antanas received the answer he had been waiting for. He and Jadwyga were walking hand in hand in downtown Vilno on a balmy spring evening when Jadwyga suddenly stopped. She turned and faced Antanas, took his hands into her own, smiled, and whispered, "Antanas, I love you and I accept your proposal."

Antanas lifted her up and twirled her around joyfully. He set her down gently and they kissed. He still had one concern, however. "What about your parents? Do you think they'll give their blessing to our marriage?"

"Yes, I believe they will," Jadwyga replied. "They like you, Antanas, but you'll still have to ask them both for their permission."

On his next visit to the Sosnowski home, Antanas summoned his courage, got down on his knees, and asked Piotr and Marija together, "Do I have your permission to marry Jadwyga?"

Piotr looked intently at Antanas. "Do you love her?"

Antanas smiled and returned Piotr's gaze. "Yes!"

Marija took Antanas by both hands and stared into his eyes. "Will you keep Jadwyga safe, healthy, and happy?"

Antanas stood up and said firmly, "Yes."

Marija held out her hand. "Antanas, you and Jadwyga have my blessing. Be good to her."

Tears welled up in Piotr's eyes. "I, too, give you permission to marry my little princess."

Chapter 6

The Battle of Vilno

Since September 1, 1939, the Polish Army had been waging war against the Wehrmacht and the Luftwaffe in the west of Poland. At first, the Poles were overwhelmed by the German blitzkrieg, but they learned how to defend themselves against it and they were beginning to hold their own. Then, on September 17, another threat emerged when the Soviet Red Army attacked Poland from the east.

Vilno, September 17, 1939

It was a cool Sunday morning, and Jadwyga and Antanas were awaiting the beginning of mass in an old Catholic church named St. John. It was located in the centre of Vilno. Antanas was admiring the elaborate marble pillars and the paintings that framed the altar. Usually he did not take time to appreciate the grandeur of their church, but Father Jonas Stasys was ten minutes late for the 8 a.m. mass.

When Father Jonas finally approached the marble and wooden podium, the congregation rose to their feet. Father Jonas cleared his throat, paused for several seconds, and then said in a low, clear voice, "Please, sit down."

The congregation obeyed and sat down in the wooden pews.

The pastor delivered devastating news. "Don't panic, but Vilno is under attack from the Soviet Red Army. The Polish Army is doing everything they can to protect us, and Lieutenant Colonel Podwysocki has asked that everyone leave the church and go home in an orderly manner."

Jadwyga could hear people gasping and many of the women began to cry. She noticed that most of the men were glancing towards the exits and almost everyone was shivering from the combination of the cool morning weather and the terrifying news.

"There are two things we'll do this morning," said the young pastor. "We'll go to our homes, but first we'll pray together." He raised his arms and the congregation stood.

"Let us pray. Our Father, who art in heaven, hallowed be thy name…"

At the end of the prayer, Father Jonas made the sign of the cross and uttered the Latin words that always concluded mass. *"Dominus vobiscum."* ("God be with you.")

Jadwyga observed that despite their trembling bodies and tear-filled eyes, the parishioners gave the usual response: *"Et cum spiritu tuo."* ("And with your spirit.") Antanas and Jadwyga genuflected beside their pew and walked quickly towards the side exit.

Everyone left the church without panicking and walked briskly back to their respective homes. As Jadwyga and Antanas drew close to the Vilnia River, huge clouds of black smoke from the artillery barrage engulfed them. Antanas handed Jadwyga his handkerchief and said, "Take this, breathe through it, and protect your eyes." He pulled his jacket up to shield his own eyes with his left hand as he took Jadwyga's hand with his right.

Without warning, bursts of artillery and heavy machine gun fire broke out at close range. Jadwyga and Antanas threw themselves to the ground. As soon as there was a lull in the firefight, they ran up a street that led away from the river. Once they were far enough away from immediate danger, Jadwyga lifted her face to the sky and cried out, "Mother of God, what's happening to us? What's happening to Poland?"

As they hurried up the cobbled street where the Sosnowski family lived, they could hear the artillery barrage and machine gun fire resume. Nearing the back door of the Sosnowski residence, Antanas took Jadwyga by the arm. "Hurry, Jadwyga, let's get you inside."

Jadwyga ran up the stairs from the back door and entered the kitchen. "Mother, father, Nika—the Soviets are attacking Vilno!"

Piotr stepped towards Jadwyga. "We guessed that it was the Red Army, but the radio station is shut down and we've not heard any news," he said.

Marija said, "We went to our neighbours the Kaprowskis' house to phone the police, but the telephone wires are down. Jadwyga, your eyes are so red and watery."

"Smoke irritated my eyes when we were near the Vilnia River. There is terrible fighting going on there."

Marija looked out the window and down their street. She could see smoke rising. "Mother of God, what can we do?"

"We can pray and keep safe," replied Antanas. He felt trapped between his loyalty to the Sosnowski family and to his own family. He knew that the Sosnowskis were in a better position to defend themselves from misfortune. Piotr had developed more local political and parish connections compared to Antanas's family. What frightened Antanas most was that his sister Maria was only sixteen.

He began to pace.

Marija said, "Antanas, is there something that you want to say?"

"I know that this is a terrible time to leave you, but I need to get back to Kaunas. I must protect my parents and my sister Maria."

"How will you get home?" Piotr inquired.

"With this kind of fighting going on, the trains won't be running, so I'll walk."

"That's 100 kilometres."

"What choice do I have? I must leave now. But I'll return as soon as I can."

Tears streamed down Jadwyga's face. "Be safe, my darling. Come back to me as soon as you can."

"Don't worry, Jadwyga."

Jadwyga went into the kitchen and when she returned, she handed Antanas a loaf of rye bread. "Here, take this and we'll pray for you every day."

Antanas placed his hand gently on Jadwyga's shoulder. She clasped his hand and drew it close to her heart. They kissed, and Antanas began his long walk home.

Vilno, September 19, 1939

It was Tuesday and there had been no word from Antanas since Sunday morning. Just after dark, a soldier knocked quietly on the back door of the Sosnowski residence. He was dirty, his uniform was ripped, and blood was oozing from his left arm.

Marija was afraid, but in the dim light over the back door she could see that the young man was a Polish soldier. Marija held her breath and opened the door just a crack. "Who are you and what do you want?"

"I'm Sergeant Wladek Szudy. My mother said to come to you if I ever needed help in Vilno. I have your address in my wallet and I found you."

"You are the son of Ewa Warszawara and Colonel Lech Szudy?

"Yes, I am."

Marija removed the latch and opened the door wide. "Come, everyone, meet Sergeant Wladek Szudy, the son of my best friend."

Piotr noticed the blood on Sergeant Szudy's uniform. He rolled back the young soldier's sleeve to reveal a deep gash on his forearm. "You're bleeding badly, young man."

"A Red Army soldier swam across the Vilnia. He surprised me as he pulled himself from the river, but when I saw him, I shot him in the leg. He stumbled, but recovered his balance for a moment and he bayonetted my left arm when he fell."

"What did you do then?"

"I shot him again and hit him in the chest. The force of the gunshot pushed him backwards into the river."

"Come into the kitchen and I'll wash your arm."

Sergeant Szudy followed Piotr to the kitchen and stood in front of the sink. Piotr cleaned the young soldier's wounded arm with soap. A heavy stream of blood circled the bottom of the sink and mixed with the running water as it flowed down the drain. Sergeant Szudy's facial muscles tightened.

"Was that the first man you killed?" Piotr asked.

"No, sir. I have killed many German soldiers. This man was my first Russian."

Marija walked into the kitchen carrying a white cloth for Wladek's wound. "Why did you knock so quietly on our door? No one heard you but me."

"The streets are full of Red Army soldiers looking to kill what is left of the Polish Brigades. I didn't want to attract attention."

The rest of the family was standing in the kitchen when Nika appeared. She stared at Wladek. "You're filthy," she said.

"Do you think fighting for Poland is a clean job?"

Nika ignored his reply and asked her mother, "Who is this man?"

"This is Sergeant Wladek Szudy. He's the oldest son of my best friend, Ewa Warszawa. We were inseparable until her family moved to Warsaw when we were both seventeen. Wladek's father is Colonel Lech Szudy of the Polish Army."

"Oh," said Nika. "I'm sorry for being rude." She offered the solider her hand.

Sergeant Szudy kissed her hand. "I understand. It's late and many Red Army soldiers are patrolling the streets. You're all afraid and my presence puts you in danger."

"Nonsense," said Piotr as he wrapped Sergeant Szudy's arm with the white cloth. "You're risking your life to defend us, and to defend Poland. Come, sit at the kitchen table."

As he moved from the sink to the table, Jadwyga noted Sergeant Szudy's commanding presence. She estimated that he was in his early twenties. He stood just under two metres in height and he had blue eyes and sandy hair. Despite his cuts and bruises, he still maintained a proud military demeanour.

Piotr frowned. "What's happening in the battle?"

"It's a bad time for Poland. Colonel Okulicz-Kozaryn was the leader of the Polish forces here in Vilno until Sunday. He informed us that Hitler and Stalin have joined forces against Poland."

"Were you expecting this?"

"Not at all. When we first saw the Russian tanks, some of our soldiers went out to welcome them. They thought they had come to fight with us against the Nazis."

"What happened to them?"

Sergeant Szudy paused before answering. "Those soldiers were mowed down by the Red Army tanks' machine guns."

"What about Poland's allies?"

Sergeant Szudy clenched both fists. "May the devil burn those idiots! The British and the French have scolded Hitler for his theft of neighbouring lands, but they have failed to fight. I apologize to you ladies for my cursing."

"Wladek, you think we've never cursed? If ever there was a time to be angry, this is it," Marija responded.

"Why didn't they come to Poland's aid?" Piotr persisted.

"Joseph Goebbels and his propaganda machine have duped the British and the French. They've used falsified newsreels to create two big lies."

"What lies?"

"The first lie is that the Wehrmacht and the blitzkrieg are invincible. It's important for you all to know that after losing tens of thousands of comrades, the Polish Army regrouped, and we were starting to push the Germans back until Stalin unleashed the Red Army on our eastern frontier."

"What's the second lie?"

"That the Polish soldiers and the air force, although brave, are ill-equipped, poorly trained, and hopelessly outnumbered."

"Is that a lie?"

Sergeant Szudy grimaced as he sat down on a kitchen chair. "The truth is that we have a modern army and air force and we can fight as well as anyone. We've held off the Germans for almost three weeks, but I don't know how much longer we can fight on two fronts."

Marija stepped up to the table. "It's late, Wladek; you're wounded and you need sleep. Piotr, you can talk to him tomorrow. For now, we all need to sleep."

"I'm the intruder, so I can sleep on the floor in the living room."

"No, you will sleep in Jadwyga's bed and she can bunk with Nika."

"No, I can't make so much trouble for Jadwyga and Nika."

Jadwyga noticed how Sergeant Szudy was shivering and she threw up her hands. "This is war, Sergeant Szudy. You're a soldier fighting for Poland. You're our friend and you're wounded. You'll sleep in my bed and I'll sleep with my sister."

"All right, I will bow to your request, but upon one condition."

"What is that?" inquired Jadwyga.

"That you all call me Wladek. I am your friend and your guest, so please don't be so formal with me."

"Okay. Good night to everyone," said Marija. "Sleep well."

Vilno, September 20, 1939

Wladek slept until late afternoon the next day. He was making up for all the sleep that he had missed in the previous sixty hours.

When Jadwyga saw him descending the stairs, she smiled. "Wladek, you've shaved and there's colour in your cheeks."

"Thank you, Jadwyga, for your kind words. And thank you, Piotr, for the use of your razor."

Piotr beckoned Wladek to join him at the kitchen table.

"What do you think will happen next?" asked Piotr.

Marija tugged on Piotr's arm. "Leave him alone. He's just a young sergeant; he just takes orders."

Wladek straightened in his chair. "That's not completely true. I was the driver for Colonel Kozaryn, and when the fighting began in Vilno, the protocols were tossed out and I attended some pretty important meetings. Everyone either trusted me or they forgot that I was there."

Piotr apologized. "I won't exhaust you with questions. Please tell me if there are things that you can't answer because they are confidential."

"I'll tell you what I can," said Wladek.

Wladek proceeded to explain that the Polish Army in Vilno had only 14,000 soldiers against a Soviet invading force of over 35,000. The Polish High Command had moved most of their army out of Vilno to fight the Germans when the German army invaded on September 1. The number 14,000 was deceptive, however, as most of those troops were volunteers with no guns and no training. In an act of good conscience, Colonel Kozaryn sent the volunteers home. That left the Poles with only 6,500 professional soldiers.

Jadwyga's mind kept drifting from the conversation. She was wondering what all these battles would mean for Antanas. Would the

Soviets invade Lithuania too? Would Antanas be required to serve in the Lithuanian army? Had this happened already? She was brought back to the moment by her father's voice.

"What kind of armaments did you have?"

"Our tanks left when most of the infantry moved out to fight the Germans. We were left with lots of small arms, twenty-two pieces of artillery, and forty heavy machine guns."

"What did the Soviets have?"

"They had hundreds of T-26 tanks and a few heavy BT-7 tanks. They had plenty of 76 mm artillery as well. It wasn't a fair fight."

Piotr combed his hands through his thin hair. "What did your colonel do next?"

"After assessing the relative troop strengths, Colonel Kozaryn decided not to defend Vilno at all but rather to use most of the professional soldiers to escort citizens of Vilno towards the Polish-Lithuanian border."

"Why, then, were you still here fighting?"

"Most of the Polish troops left with Colonel Kozaryn, but Lieutenant Colonel Podwysocki decided to stay. He chose to defend Vilno with what was left of our Polish brigades."

"Why didn't you leave with Colonel Kozaryn? You were his driver."

"Lieutenant Colonel Podwysocki asked me to stay. Colonel Kozaryn gave me the choice to go with him or to defend Vilno. I chose to stay."

Tears welled up in everyone's eyes. Piotr spoke for the family when he quietly uttered, "*Dziekuje.*" ("Thank you.")

Wladek peered out the window towards the Vilnia River. "We were vastly outnumbered and outgunned, but we were lucky at first. The Russians underestimated the depth and the power of the Vilnia River. They tried to cross it before dawn on Sunday, but many Red Army tanks slid to the bottom of the river. Their crews were trapped inside and drowned," Wladek recalled. "We repelled the first assault."

But then Wladek's expression darkened. "Still, it was just a matter of time before the Red Army regrouped and prepared for a second attack. By 10 a.m. the Red Army engineers had started building temporary bridges."

Jadwyga began to weep and to shake. "That was just a little while after Antanas left for Kaunas. Sweet Jesus, please protect him."

"We're all praying for him," Nika said, putting an arm around her sister.

"Go on," Piotr said to Wladek after a few moments of silence.

"We used our artillery and heavy machine guns to stop them from spanning the river, but they countered with their tanks and artillery fire. We killed some of their engineers and soldiers, but despite our best efforts they managed to build the bridges. Their tanks and infantry crossed the Vilnia on Monday morning. By noon on Tuesday, it was all over for Vilno."

"What are you going to do now? How can we help?" Piotr asked.

"You've already helped by tending to my wound, giving me a safe bed, feeding me, and listening to me. I'll leave you tonight."

"Wladek, stay with us," Marija implored. "You can burn your uniform and wear some of Piotr's clothes. We'll tell the Red Army soldiers that you're our son and that you are a Polish citizen and not a soldier."

"No, the Red Army is already searching homes for surviving soldiers. They won't believe any of us if we deny who I am. My wound will be damning proof of my identity. If I stay, I would be putting all of you at risk. If they caught me out of uniform, they would label me a spy and kill all of you."

"We'll take that risk," Piotr said gently.

"No. I'm a sergeant in the Polish Army and I must get back to our fighting forces in Western Poland."

"You have no weapon," said Jadwyga.

"That's not true. I've hidden my rifle away from your property."

Wladek talked a while longer with Piotr and Marija and then asked Piotr if he could borrow his Bible. He read it for a couple of hours. When Marija saw his head nod from drowsiness, she spoke softly to him. "Wladek, you're exhausted from fighting and you need that wound to heal. Go back to bed and we'll wake you at 10 p.m."

***

Jadwyga entered Wladek's room at the appointed time. She woke him gently and invited her cousin to join them for dinner. Marija had prepared a meal of cabbage rolls and roasted potatoes. They ate in silence, knowing it would be their last meal together.

Wladek broke the stillness. "Thank you for this meal and for harbouring me. Because of you, I'm ready to go."

Jadwyga frowned. "What will you do when you leave?"

"I'm travelling under cover of darkness, so I hope to meet up with my comrades before I meet the Red Army."

Marija left the kitchen and returned with a satchel for Wladek.

"This bag has two straps that Piotr sewed onto it. You can carry it on your back."

"It contains socks, underwear, and a blanket. It has some dried salami and a small wheel of cheese, a flask of water, and two apples."

"You've thought of everything, but you're sacrificing your own family's supply of food to feed me."

"Don't worry about us. We're not rich, but we're not poor, either. Not yet," said Nika.

"You're a wonderful family," said Wladek. "My mother was right. I hope to see you all again, in better times."

Wladek disappeared into the night on September 20. Jadwyga and her family wondered fearfully what would happen to their cousin.

The Sosnowski Home, October 6, 1939

Piotr gathered Marija, Nika, and Jadwyga into the kitchen. He had just come from the home of their neighbours the Kaprowskis. There, they had listened to the radio for news about the war. What they heard had shocked them.

"Marija, Nika, Jadwyga, I have very bad news. The Red Army is now broadcasting throughout all of Lithuania and Eastern Poland. They are boasting that the Polish Army has surrendered."

Marija brought her hand to her mouth and Jadwyga and Nika held onto each other.

"There is a pact between Hitler and Stalin. Eastern Poland has fallen under the heel of the Red Army. Warsaw and Western Poland have become the property of Germany," Piotr continued as Marija wept.

"The Red Army has given our city Vilno to Lithuania. I can only hope that the Lithuanians are not fooled by those devils." Piotr sighed and then fell silent.

Vilno, October 28, 1939

As Jadwyga paced back and forth in the kitchen, she gazed frequently out the window. She saw trees stripped of their leaves and rain clouds in the sky, but there was no one in the street. It was too early for all the birds to have flown south, yet no birds sang. Vilnius was cold and silent. Jadwyga had been quiet and brooding most of the week. Her mind was tormented by the fear that Antanas had been sent to a Russian work camp.

"There's been no word from Antanas for almost six weeks. He should be here. Where is he? Why has he not sent word?"

"This is war," Nika answered. "Communications are shattered. Just pray that Antanas is alive."

Suddenly, there was pounding at the back door. Marija descended the stairs. She peered out the small window hoping it would be Sergeant Szudy, but she quickly recognized the uniform and the stripes on the sleeve of a Red Army corporal. He was unshaven and a lit cigarette dangled from his mouth. His skin was sallow and his eyes were red. His uniform appeared to be two sizes too large.

Marija was terrified, but she answered his knock and opened the door. *Please, Jesus, may he not be here to take my husband away to a Russian slave camp.*

Piotr joined Marija at the door. They both trembled until the mysterious corporal spoke.

"Don't be afraid. I have a letter from Antanas Paskevicius for Jadwyga Sosnowski."

Piotr took the letter from the soldier's hands and called out for Jadwyga.

Jadwyga appeared at the top of the stairs. She quivered at the sight of the grizzly Red Army soldier, but then summoned her courage. "What do you want, father?"

"This man has a letter for you. It's from your Antanas."

Her father handed her the letter and she hastily opened it.

Antanas's Letter

October 7, 1939

Dear Jadwyga,

How are you and your parents? I am okay and I will come to Vilno as soon as I can.

Love,
Antanas

Jadwyga jumped up and down in excitement. "He's alive! Our prayers are answered!"

Nika and Jadwyga locked arms and danced a little polka until they could no longer catch their breath. Piotr wondered why this Russian soldier was helping two lovers who were from enemy countries, but he did not say a word.

Marija offered the Russian corporal a drink of water, and he drank thirstily. She then gave him a bottle of wine, which he placed under his cloak as he bowed and backed away onto the dusty road.

Neither Jadwyga nor Antanas ever discovered the identity of this Russian soldier. They never found out how he got the letter from Antanas, but they were both eternally grateful to him for his act of kindness.

Chapter 7

Living with the Russian Bear

The soldiers of the Red Army, including most of the officers, were poorly educated; many were illiterate. They were the sons and, in some cases, the daughters of poor farmers or labourers from Russia and other parts of the Soviet Union. Most of these women and men had little military training. Nonetheless, they were cocky and proud of their conquests. Having been humiliated by the Polish Army in the Soviet–Polish War of 1919, the Red Army perceived that it was time for revenge.

Vilnius, October 31, 1939

At about 11 p.m., Jadwyga heard her parents on the back stairs. They were laughing so hard they could barely make it up the flight of steps. "Piotr, please stop making me laugh. You're going to get us both killed. Get up these stairs and into the house now." Marija exclaimed.

Jadwyga opened the door and her parents tumbled into the landing. Jadwyga shut the outside door, and Piotr and Marija ascended the next flight of stairs and entered the kitchen. Jadwyga asked if they wanted tea, and her parents replied with a resounding "Yes."

Nika came into the kitchen to ask what was causing such a commotion.

Piotr stopped laughing. "Tonight, the Poles and the Lithuanians of Vilnius achieved a minor but sweet victory."

"Tell us about it." Jadwyga was eager to learn the details.

"As you know, your mother and I attend the opera from time to time. For years, I've made the suits for Jurgis Kalnietis, the Lithuanian conductor of the opera house. He's one of my best customers. To show his gratitude for the well-fitting suits I've made for him, Maestro

Kalnietis makes sure that Marija and I can attend at least one opera performance a year. He always gives us the best balcony seats in the theatre. Tonight, we saw a performance of *Figaro*—"

"Yes, Papa, we know all that, but what victory was won?" interrupted Nika.

"Well, many Polish and Lithuanian victories start out badly. This was no exception," said Marija.

"Yes, your mother is correct. The opera began at 8 p.m., but the Russian Comandarm, Pavel Korsakov, his mistress Tanya Markov, and his bodyguards arrived at 8:15 p.m. The eight guards presented themselves at our balcony and the captain said, 'You six, make room for Comandarm Korsakov and his party.' We were the only ones who were not asked to leave.

"Marek Rafalski, past president of the St. Casimir Credit Union, asked the captain what he meant. 'How can we make room? The seats are all filled.'

"The captain pointed at Mr. Rafalski and the sergeant standing closest to him thrust his rifle butt into the old man's stomach. The poor man doubled over and I thought the blue vein on his temple was going to burst. The other five people sitting in the disputed seats jumped up quickly, helped their injured colleague to his feet, and fled.

"We had witnessed the guards' viciousness at close range. But Comandarm Korsakov and his mistress sat down right beside us as though nothing had happened. At this point, Marija was shaking."

Marija took a swig of her tea and joined Piotr in describing their harrowing situation. "The Comandarm kissed my hand and Piotr did the same for Miss Markov. The Comandarm and Piotr shook hands. Four bodyguards sat to the left of Miss Markov and the remaining four instructed the patrons in the row behind the Comandarm to vacate their seats so the guards could sit behind him. So, we were surrounded by Russian bodyguards."

"Why were the bodyguards so brutal?" Jadwyga inquired.

"They would never have been so bold if they had not been ordered to do this in advance," Piotr responded.

"But who would give them such an order?" Nika asked.

"Comandarm Korsakov is the most brutal of the Russians. The Polish underground has labelled him as the one to watch," Piotr explained. "The reaction of the audience to the cruelty of the Russian guards was as you would expect. Everyone just went silent. They were in total shock.

"But then, something changed. The audience began to laugh. At first it was just a few titters, then quiet chuckles spread throughout the entire hall. Of course, there had been no laughter at first, when the soldiers were forcing the patrons to vacate their seats. But the hilarity started when the Comandarm and his companion became the focus. Even without the violence, this couple would have been the centre of attention. He's a tall chunky man who is probably forty but he looks older. He has a square face with a narrow nose, broad shoulders, a barrel chest, a triple chin, a thick neck, and brown eyes. He has blond, thinning hair, cut short in the military style. His mistress, Tanya Markov, is about eighteen, tall, and beautiful. She has long blonde hair and green eyes that attract everyone's attention. She has a perfect complexion and a shapely figure."

Jadwyga was puzzled. "Clearly, the Comandarm was trying to impress the people at the opera, but I don't understand why the audience laughed."

Marija spoke up. "You're at a disadvantage because you could not see what the rest of us could see. I'll describe everything for you, but first I'll tell you about the danger your father and I were facing."

"Now you really have my interest," said Jadwyga.

Marija continued. "The laughter caused the Comandarm to go red in the face and he started clenching his fists. I thought that he was going to scream or maybe even shoot someone, but then he seemed to calm himself. He leaned towards me and asked me in Russian, 'Why are they laughing at us?'"

"What was your answer?"

Marija put down her tea cup. "I can speak Russian fluently, but this was the most difficult question that I've ever been asked in any language. I knew exactly why the people were laughing, but I was terrified to tell him. It seems that, in his efforts to impress everyone, he had instructed Miss Markov to make herself look as beautiful and sophisticated as possible. She had chosen an outfit that matched her green eyes. Unfortunately for her, it was a nightgown."

Jadwyga smiled. "Please, tell us how you answered the Comandarm."

"I paused for about three seconds, which seemed like three eternities, but then I had a moment of grace. I knew what to do. I understood that the Comandarm would appreciate an honest answer. I whispered in his ear, 'Your guest appears to be unfamiliar with Polish opera garments and has mistaken a nightgown for an evening gown. A nightgown is meant to be worn to bed and is normally seen only by one's lover or one's children.'"

Nika opened her eyes wide. "What did he say?"

"Korsakov's face went red; he took a long breath and he kept his voice low as he told me, 'Thank you for your honesty and your courage.'

"Then he kissed my hand and told his guards, 'We'll return to my home now.' He glowered at Miss Markov, pulled her to her feet, and ordered her to follow him. She tried to do so, but stepped on the nightgown and fell against his chest. He raised his right arm, glared at her, but then lowered his arm. She began to cry."

At this point, Marija and Piotr broke into gales of laughter as they recalled how the Poles and the Lithuanians had had the last laugh at the opera house. It brought them great satisfaction to think of the exquisite embarrassment that Comandarm Korsakov had obviously experienced.

"What do you think will happen to Korsakov's mistress?" Jadwyga asked.

Piotr raised his eyebrows. "I would rather not think about that now. We're having so much fun at the Comandarm's expense."

"Do you think he'll beat her?"

"Of course, he'll beat her. He might even kill her; it will depend on how angry he is when he gets home."

"She looked afraid when she left the balcony," Marija said.

"She has good reason to be afraid. The Comandarm is not only a cruel man—he's a proud man. Her ignorance made him look like a fool," Piotr surmised.

Marija's eyes flashed. "It wasn't her fault; she's a peasant girl. How is she supposed to know what to wear to the opera?"

Piotr reached out for Marija's hands. "Russian comandarms don't accept excuses. Ever."

Vilnius, November 1, 1939

The next day was All Souls Day. The Sosnowskis had attended early mass at St. John and Maria was preparing porridge. Wisia, Nika, and Piotr were hungry and looked forward to their late breakfast. They were not expecting anyone, but just before they began to eat, there was a knock at the front door.

Nika opened the door and shrieked, "Antanas!"

Everyone came running from the kitchen to greet him. They all eagerly asked him how he was and what he had been up to since they had last seen him.

"I've been working at the same garage, as the head mechanic for the Kaunas Transit System. The Soviets are my bosses now, but we do the same work for half the money. It's better than being shot."

Jadwyga entered the room and ran into his arms. "I'm so happy that you're safe. Why didn't you come to see me sooner?"

Antanas frowned. "It was no longer safe to travel back and forth between Kaunas and Vilno because the trains were stopped. If I'd been caught walking between the two cities, the Red Army soldiers would have accused me of being a resistance fighter. They would've shot and killed me. The trains are running again now, though, so I'll visit you and your family as often as I can."

Jadwyga stepped into the dining room and Antanas followed. As she sat down at the dining room table, she fluffed up her hair and struck a Hollywood glamour pose. "You'd better start visiting often or I'll start dating one of the Russian soldiers."

Antanas took a seat beside her. "Good luck dating a Russian, unless you like men who drink litres of vodka, sing Russian songs, order you to feed them, and then fall asleep." Antanas plopped his head on the table and Jadwyga laughed.

"You make Russian offers sound tempting, but maybe I'll give you a second chance." They smiled at each other, and then they kissed.

Chapter 8

A Bus to Kiev, a Turkey to Kaunas

In 1940, the Soviets gave up any pretense of granting Lithuania autonomy and the NKVD (Soviet secret police) began keeping lists of potential fighters resisting Soviet occupation. On June 14, 1941, the Soviets carried out their first mass deportations of Lithuanians to Soviet work camps. These raids and mass transfers of people had a double impact. They were intended to terrify the population and to prevent resistance. They also provided free labour for the Soviet Union.

Kaunas, June 1941

Despite the Soviet oppression of Lithuania, work at the Kaunas Transit System was going relatively well for Antanas. His Russian boss, Captain Jurij Petrokov, soon realized that he had an intelligent, creative mechanic and supervisor in Antanas. On one occasion, Captain Petrokov's bosses ordered one of the Kaunas buses to be driven to Ukraine. Captain Petrokov chose Antanas to deliver the bus to Kiev, commanding him to return by June 21.

When Antanas arrived in Kiev, he parked the bus, a big old Fiat model, in the Kiev Transit System garage. He was impressed by the huge barn of a building and he was surprised that it was located in the downtown area. He also realized that the building had seen better days. It was originally erected in 1920, but they had used cheap construction materials and parts of the building were already starting to crumble.

Antanas spoke to the manager, who was his counterpart, Jan Barszczyk. Antanas did not speak Ukrainian and Jan did not speak Lithuanian, but both were fluent in Polish.

After Antanas provided instructions about how the bus functioned, he and Jan began to talk about their respective families. Jan was very proud of the fact that he had a lovely wife and four young children. Antanas showed Jan a picture of Jadwyga.

"When are you getting married to that beautiful woman?" Jan asked.

"We're engaged, but the war is making it difficult to make wedding plans. There's a ban on weddings," Antanas said.

"Don't wait too long or you could lose her. Getting married was the best thing I ever did. Even Uncle Joe [Joseph Stalin] hasn't wrecked our lives yet. Say, Antanas, where are you staying in Kiev?"

Antanas shrugged. "I don't know. I was going to ask you to recommend a hotel."

"Why don't you come and stay at my home? The three boys can all sleep in one bed and that will give you a mattress and a small room for tonight. Marion and the kids would be happy to meet a new friend."

"I don't want to cause you or your family any hardship."

Jan grabbed Antanas by the arm in a friendly way. "Nonsense! I'll be insulted if you don't come home with me."

"My boss gave me money for a hotel and a restaurant meal, so let me use it to buy enough food for a feast for your family."

"It's a deal. I'll get in touch with Marion on the office phone. We don't have a phone at our home, but the grocery store nearby has one. They'll get a message to Marion."

It was a warm evening and they walked the cobbled streets in their shirtsleeves. When they reached Jan and Marion's home, Antanas found that they occupied a small but well-maintained house on an old street. The street's cobblestones dated back to the days of Catherine the Great and there were lovely birch trees in many of the front yards. The house had three small bedrooms on the second floor and another bedroom on the main floor. The eight-year-old grumbled when he was told he had to give up his room for the night. But when he saw all the food that Antanas and his father had brought home, he was much more forgiving.

Marion opened her arms to Antanas. "Welcome to our home. Look at all the wonderful food you've brought: kielbasa, ham, cabbage, potatoes, apples, and wine. You can always come and stay with us whenever you come to Kiev."

While Marion, their oldest son, and their daughter helped to prepare dinner, Antanas and Jan moved to the small back yard. There, they shared a bottle of Riesling and two shots of potato vodka. After the vodka and their third glass of wine, Jan leaned forward and whispered to Antanas, "You know what the bus you brought here is for?"

Antanas moved closer and answered in a whisper, "No, I didn't ask."

"It will be used to transport troops. Comandarm Sasha Kupchenko is assembling as many buses and trucks as he can within 400 kilometres. He's the local Russian big shot and he's convinced that the Germans are going to attack. He's doing all this secretly because his boss, Stalin, disagrees with him."

Antanas glanced out the window at the neighbours' fences. "Jan, are you sure you should be telling me this?"

"The wine makes it easier to talk, but I'm a good judge of character. I trust you. You are no communist." He slapped Antanas on the shoulder. "You're just some poor Lithuanian who can't even get married because of Adolf and Joe."

Jan motioned Antanas to lean closer to him. "The brother of one of my mechanics works for the NKVD. He's a terrible drunk and if he likes you and you buy him a few shots of vodka, he not only tells you what he knows, but also what he thinks he knows."

"What has he shared with you?"

"He says that the top brass in the NKVD are convinced that Hitler is about to launch a surprise attack against the Soviets."

"But Kiev doesn't look like a city preparing to go to war, and when I left Vilnius there were no special fortifications being made by our Soviet masters."

"That's because Stalin will not hear of it. He's not yet ready to go to war against as powerful a foe as Germany, and he can't believe that the war could come to him. He's such a fathead that he would rather throw his spies into jail for treason than to listen to what they're telling him."

"Why would Hitler attack?"

"Because Hitler believes that he can defeat the Red Army quickly, and maybe he can."

As Marion came into the dining room, she wagged her finger at Jan. "Keep your voice down or the Black Ravens will come to take us away."

Antanas knew who the Black Ravens were. They were the black box vans and their four-man crews who carried out most of the arrests and deportations in Lithuania as well as in Ukraine.

Marion beckoned the two men to join the children for supper.

The meal that Marion and her two oldest children had prepared was delicious, and she added some rye bread to the feast. After another glass of wine, Antanas stood up and made a toast. "Thank you, Marion, for this wonderful meal."

Marion beamed with pride.

She then urged all the children to help her with the dishes in the kitchen, leaving Antanas and Jan alone in the dining room. Jan stumbled a bit as he approached the liquor cabinet. He crouched down and pulled out a bottle of homemade potato vodka.

"No, I can't drink anymore," said Antanas.

Jan collapsed onto the closest chair. "Let's talk some more about Uncle Joe. In 1929 that fool Stalin formed collective farms in Ukraine. Ukraine was the breadbasket of Europe. After his big scheme was enforced, production levels of rye and wheat dropped like a stone."

"What happened to the Ukrainians?"

"Because Uncle Joe needed the cash, he commandeered almost all the wheat and rye. He kept some grain for the Russians and sold the rest to Western European countries. He left almost nothing for the Ukrainians who grew it. They starved. They died by the millions."

"What happened to you and your family?"

"My parents and my five brothers and sisters died of starvation." Jan paused. His eyes watered but he continued. "I saved myself by getting hired as a mechanic and a carpenter on one of the collective farms. They didn't have much money to pay me, but they fed me a little and I survived. That's where I met Marion. The rest of her family had starved to death as well."

"I can see why you hate Stalin. At least, there was a silver lining. You met Marion."

"Once we found each other, it was not long before we fell in love. I persuaded Marion to leave the collective farm and to try our luck in

Kiev. We were fortunate. I found a job as a mechanic's assistant here at Kiev Transit System."

Suddenly, Jan's head fell forward, and it hit the table where he was sitting. It did him no serious harm and he fell asleep sitting in his chair. Antanas took Jan's alcohol-induced sleep as an opportunity to ascend the stairs and climb into bed himself.

***

The next morning was Saturday. Antanas and Jan woke up with splitting headaches. Marion reprimanded Jan at breakfast. "You have poisoned our guest with alcohol. The least you can do is to walk him to the railroad station."

Marion whispered into Antanas's ear. "Jan doesn't usually drink. He just needed to talk about all that we have lost."

Antanas smiled. "Thank you Marion for your warm hospitality and may you, Jan, and your children have good health for all of your lives."

Jan and Antanas headed down the cobblestone street towards the train station. Antanas remembered that his boss had given him a little bonus for taking this trip to Kiev. He had sewn the money into the bottom of his travelling bag. He pulled out his pocketknife, ripped open the stitches, and pulled out the cash.

"What are you doing?" Jan asked.

"I'm retrieving lost Soviet currency. I noticed that they sold live turkeys at the butcher shop that we visited yesterday."

"Yes, they sell good turkeys there. It's on the way to the station."

Soon they arrived at the small butcher shop. It was clean, with lots of sawdust on the floor. The butcher, Jurij, was very tall and had a muscular build. He had brown eyes and a toothy smile. As soon as he saw Jan enter the store, he called out to him.

"How did you enjoy the kielbasa and the ham?"

"It was great, but my head and my stomach hurt today."

"It wasn't my meat; it must have been that horrible vodka you made."

"There's nothing wrong with my vodka; I just drank too much of it. My friend Antanas here is returning to Lithuania today. He wants to take a live turkey with him."

Jurij was not nearly as fluent in Polish compared to Jan, but Antanas explained what he needed. After a little bartering, Antanas bought a medium-sized turkey.

"I'm planning to take this bird with me on the train to Kaunas. I'm not joking. Do you have any suggestions?"

The butcher laughed, but he gave Antanas some old newspaper for the turkey to sit on and some grain for the bird to eat. "Save your remaining rubles to bribe the conductor or they will throw you and the turkey off the train."

Jan walked Antanas to the station and wished him well. "Whatever you do, don't let your fiancée slip away. Seize the day and get married."

Antanas boarded the train with the turkey clutched under his arm. He slept for most of the journey home. The conductor woke him up in Kaunas. "Comrade, it's time for you and your bird friend to leave us now. Thanks for your generous tip, and may your travelling companion turn out to be very tasty."

When Antanas swung open the door of his parents' home, it was about 9 p.m. His parents and his sister Maria greeted him in turn with great affection. Then he saw Jadwyga emerge from a hiding spot. They embraced each other. The turkey squawked and jumped to the floor. Jadwyga screamed and Maria, Antanas Sr., and Stephania broke into laughter.

"Everyone stop laughing and help me catch this bird," he called out as he chased the turkey around the room.

Stephania and Maria joined in the chase while Antanas returned his attention to his fiancée. "Jadwyga, what a nice surprise! How did you get here?"

"I took the train from Vilno. My father gave me the money so I could surprise you."

"Well, I am surprised! I am very pleasantly surprised."

"You were shocked to see me—but not as much as your turkey shocked me."

Maria and Stephania took the bird out back, killed it, and plucked its feathers. It became the next day's main course.

Chapter 9

Operation Barbarossa

On June 22, 1941, two armies of equal strength met in mortal combat across vast territories of Eastern Europe. The Wehrmacht and the Luftwaffe brought 3,316,000 men and thousands of tanks, planes, and artillery to the battlefield. They faced a Red Army of formidable might, but the Germans employed the element of surprise and the Soviet High Command was in disarray due to a Stalin-led purge of its ranks. The Red Army, however, had a strong intangible factor in their favour: they were fighting on home soil.

Kaunas, June 22, 1941

After enjoying their turkey feast, Antanas, Jadwyga, and Maria went for a stroll. It was a beautiful summer evening. When they reached downtown, Maria stopped, looked up and down the streets, and then peered off into the horizon. "It's eerie," she said. "There are no Red Army soldiers, anywhere."

Then Maria heard rumbling noises in the distance. Within fifteen minutes, she could smell the nauseating odour of diesel fuel. "Look, there are German tanks and trucks as far as the eye can see."

Indeed, hundreds of medium-sized and heavy-medium-sized Panzer tanks were rumbling by. Antanas was awed by their deadly beauty and speed. He noticed that some of the tanks were travelling faster than the trucks in the convoy. He was impressed that a few of the larger Panzers were doing more than forty-five kilometres per hour. *Jan was right about the German attack. I pity the Red Army soldiers*, thought Antanas.

Behind the tanks, the trucks lumbered along as they hauled artillery, troops, and many assorted military vehicles. Meanwhile, Focke-Wulf and Messerschmitt fighters and Junkers dive bombers flew low overhead. The sound was earsplitting. Maria and Jadwyga covered their ears as Antanas stared hard at these birds of prey.

Kaunas Transit System Garage, June 23, 1941

The next morning, Antanas reported to his garage and joined some of his men.

At 7:30 a.m., Jurgis Abraiyis was already smoking his third cigarette. He grabbed Antanas by the arm and asked him, "What do you think they'll do with us?"

"I'm not sure, but I think we're about to find out."

Just at that moment, a tall German officer accompanied by ten armed Wehrmacht soldiers marched to the first hoist in the garage. A rough-looking sergeant yelled, "*Achtung!*" Everyone went silent and stood stiffly at attention.

Captain Uwe Baun stepped forward. He wore sunglasses and a long trench coat over his uniform. His officer's cap was pulled down low enough to cover his forehead.

The captain cleared his throat and then spoke in a distinct and steady voice. He addressed the men in German. "The Führer has asked me to be merciful to you. He could have ordered me to kill all of you for working with the Soviets. Your previous boss Captain Jurij Petrokov is now our prisoner. Don't mistake mercy for weakness. You must work hard for the Führer or you will feel the German boot."

At this point, he kicked over an empty barrel. It rattled across the floor and landed in a pit that was used to drain oil from the buses. If he wanted to get their attention, he had succeeded.

Antanas did not flinch. He remembered Captain Jurij Petrokov from his first day at the garage in October 1939. Jurij had spoken in Russian and had put on a similar show full of sound and fury, but he had turned out to be a good man. Antanas wondered if Captain Jurij Petrokov would survive under the heel of his Wehrmacht captors. He would miss Jurij. He looked at Captain Baun and wondered, *What kind of man is he?*

When the barrel stopped rattling in the pit, Captain Baun spoke again. "If you work hard and don't cause trouble, you'll keep your jobs and your lives. Now, get to work."

Over time, Antanas found Captain Baun to be efficient, hard-working, loyal, and merciful. Like Captain Petrokov, Captain Baun recognized what an excellent mechanic and supervisor Antanas was, and he therefore kept him on as the head mechanic.

Chapter 10

Wedding Plans

Operation Barbarossa eventually covered a 900-kilometre front from Finland to the Black Sea. At first, things went well for the Wehrmacht and the Luftwaffe, and badly for the Red Army. German tanks were gaining eighty-three kilometres per day and by late October they were just a little more than 100 kilometres from Moscow. Leningrad and Stalingrad were under siege. The Wehrmacht had captured more than 800,000 square kilometres of Soviet territory. Millions of Soviet soldiers and civilians were killed. Millions more were wounded, and 3 million Red Army soldiers and officers were captured. Then the Red Army regrouped, and middle-ranked officers were promoted to senior command. Factories were relocated east of the Urals and reinforcements were brought in from the eastern regions to fight for Mother Russia.

Kaunas, October 5, 1941

Returning home from the University of Kaunas, Maria flung open the front door and screamed at her mother: "Those German pigs shut down the universities and the churches! They've made going to school and attending mass crimes! The Soviets and the Germans are all devils. I hope they destroy each other!" With these words, she threw her textbooks on the kitchen floor.

Stephania walked slowly towards her daughter. "Don't ever say those things to anyone but your family."

"What the Germans are doing is stupid."

Stephania put her arms around her daughter. Maria began to cry, and Stephania gently stroked her back. "Maria, our German masters don't care about our lives."

Maria knelt and picked up her books. Stephania bent down to help her and they both fell silent.

Vilnius, November 12, 1941

The German High Command shut down the universities and the churches to limit opportunities for citizens to meet and plan rebellions. The Paskevicius and Sosnowski families agreed that it would be better to wait until the Germans reopened the churches before making any wedding plans. Antanas disagreed. He was determined to have the wedding proceed, and soon. The following Sunday, Antanas met with Jadwyga and her parents in the Sosnowski home to discuss an idea.

Antanas sat beside Piotr and tapped his fingers on the tabletop. When Marija and Jadwyga entered the kitchen and sat down, he stood up and pointed to the east.

"The Germans have their hands full fighting the Soviets. They need almost every soldier on the Russian front. They can't patrol all the churches twenty-four hours a day."

Piotr said, "What's your plan?"

"We'll have two weddings. The Sosnowski family will attend the wedding in Vilnius and the Paskevicius family will attend the one in Kaunas."

Piotr shrugged. "How will this help? You'll give the Germans two chances to catch you."

"By splitting up the families, we can keep the numbers very small and we can use chapels instead of the major churches. The Gestapo is only watching the big churches."

"Fine, but how can we find a priest willing to take the risk of marrying you?"

"Piotr, many of the priests in Vilnius are your tailoring customers. Can't you get one of them to preside over a secret ceremony?"

"I can ask around, but why are you in such a rush? To ignore the Wehrmacht's ban is foolhardy. The fighting might be over by June and the church ban will be lifted."

Antanas struck his left hand against his forehead. "I first proposed to your daughter in March of 1938. In time your daughter said yes, but then the Red Army invaded in September of 1939. They applied their own temporary ban on weddings. When they lifted the ban, we applied for permission to marry, but Soviet bureaucracy slowed everything down. Then the Germans kicked the Soviet bureaucrats out in June of this year. In October, they banned all weddings. Now it's November 12, 1941, and soon it will be 1942. Enough is enough."

"Couldn't you wait another six months?"

Antanas stood behind Jadwyga, placed his hands on her shoulders, and looked directly at Piotr and Marija. "The Germans and the Soviets both want to own the world. They are like two titans trying to kill each other. They seem to be of equal strength. It could take a long time for one to destroy the other. Little people like Jadwyga and me, we must go on living. We shouldn't have to wait to see who'll win."

Jadwyga stood up and grasped Antanas's hands. "Darling, I want to marry you with all of my heart, but we'd be risking our lives and the lives of our families."

Antanas pulled her close to him. "Do you trust me to protect you?"

"Yes."

"Then trust me on this and help me make it work."

Jadwyga nodded slowly. "Yes, I trust you, but we need help. Mama, Papa, will you find us a priest and a safe place for us to wed?"

Marija took Piotr's hand and smiled. Together they faced Antanas and Jadwyga. "Yes," they said.

The next morning, Piotr walked to the Basilian monastery in Vilnius. He did paid work for the Basilians, but he also did some free tailoring for the priests and the monks of that order. He had been educated by Basilians and he felt a bond with them.

He had decided to visit his friend, Father Kazlauskas. Piotr always loved walking through the courtyard of the monastery, as the birch leaves gave off a sweet perfume. There was a mat of fall leaves on the cobblestones beneath his feet. As Piotr opened the outer door and entered the wood-panelled hallway, Father Kazlauskas caught sight of him. "My old friend Piotr, how are you?"

"Do the walls have ears?"

"I really don't think so, but the Gestapo certainly don't like us Basilians."

Piotr leaned close to Father Kazlauskas and whispered in his ear. "Will you marry my daughter and her fiancé?"

Father Kazlauskas stroked his chin. "When?"

"Early January."

Father Kazlauskas looked skyward. "I like your plan to have your daughter marry under the noses of the Germans."

Piotr smiled broadly. "I must confess, this idea comes from my future son-in-law, Antanas Paskevicius."

Father Kazlauskas shook Piotr's hand. "I offer my services as a priest. I will make the monastery chapel available to Jadwyga and Antanas."

"Thank you, thank you, Father Kaz. You don't know how happy you've made me."

"Go with God, Piotr, and say hello to Marija, Jadwyga, and all of your family."

As he stepped into the courtyard of the monastery, Piotr admired the beauty of the eighteenth-century building. The red-tiled roof contrasted with the dark-brown bricks. The building featured a spectacular courtyard with tall old maple trees and younger birch trees. Together, these trees provided a splendid canopy. Even if it snowed, he thought, the branches would protect the bride.

Piotr dropped by to see Father Kazlauskas again on December 20, two weeks before the wedding. "Father Kaz, how is my favourite Basilian? I've brought you the two cassocks that I finished mending."

"I'm well. How are you and your wedding plans? Last time we met, I forgot to ask an important question. How many people will be coming to this wedding?"

"There'll be my wife Marija, the bride, her two sisters, the groom Antanas Paskevicius, and myself. To keep the numbers small, Wisia's husband and Nika's boyfriend will have to stay home. That makes seven people, including you."

"What about the groom's family?"

Piotr wrinkled his brow. "It would be far too dangerous for them to travel to Vilnius from Kaunas for the wedding here. There'll be a civil wedding later, in Kaunas."

"By the way, we're talking about January 5, yes?"

"That's right, Father Kaz. We'll arrive one or two at a time, between 7:20 p.m. and 7:55 p.m., and the ceremony will take place at 8 p.m."

Father Kazlauskas smiled and pointed to the courtyard outside. "Because this is a monastery, there are priests and monks living here, and some lay people are employed here. In addition, there are always tradespeople delivering things or fixing things at the monastery."

"So, what you're telling me, Father Kaz, is that the German agents are used to seeing people coming and going from these premises?"

"Exactly."

Chapter 11

The Church Wedding

The Wehrmacht and the Luftwaffe were stalled at Moscow, Stalingrad, and Leningrad. The winter of 1941–1942 was killing almost as many Germans as the Red Army was. Hitler, the German High Command, the SS, and the Gestapo were becoming increasingly frustrated.

Vilnius, January 5, 1942

Marija reached the monastery around 7:20 p.m. She glanced up and down the street but saw no one, let alone a Gestapo agent. As she passed the leafless maple and birch trees, her breath was clearly visible on this crisp winter evening. She opened the heavy wooden door of the monastery. Once inside, she stomped the snow from her boots and proceeded down the long wood-panelled hallway to the chapel, where she detected the mixed perfumes of old cedar wood and incense.

Father Kazlauskas strode up the hallway and greeted Marija with open arms. "Marija, welcome to St. Basil's chapel."

"Father Kazlauskas, thank you for hosting Jadwyga's wedding. You are taking a great risk."

"Marija, I've known your family for years and I am pleased to fool the Gestapo."

"Father, I wish I was as brave as you. I'm terrified that the Germans will find out about this wedding and drag us away to their headquarters. How paranoid can they be to ban church weddings?"

Father Kazlauskas beckoned Maria to follow him into the chapel, where he peered through the clear pane of a stained glass window. He saw dark clouds approaching from the west.

Marija took a turn gazing through the pane. "Do the Nazis actually think that every time we Poles and Lithuanians go to mass, we're plotting against them?"

"Yes, they're that paranoid." The priest took another furtive glance out the chapel window. "I heard on the radio that there's a brutal snowstorm on its way. I have faith that this storm will somehow save us."

"How, Father?"

"The Gestapo are thorough, but they're human. They'll stay in their lairs on this stormy night."

Just then, the old chapel doors creaked loudly before opening wide. Marija jumped and covered her mouth with her hand. Wisia and Nika bounded into the chapel.

"You two! You almost sent me to an early grave."

"Mama, we saw a German patrol—an old corporal and two young privates."

"Did they spot you?"

"No, we hid behind one of the big maples."

"Did they see you come into the chapel?"

"No, we waited until they marched out of sight. Besides, they looked like they were more worried about freezing than hunting for saboteurs."

Father Kazlauskas faced Wisia and Nika. "I'm glad that you're both safe. Now, you're going to be the altar servers. Wisia, you'll bring the hosts for communion. Nika, I'm giving you the water and the wine. Here are the Latin prayer books so you can respond to my prayers. Any questions?"

The sisters responded in unison. "No, Father."

✳✳✳

As Piotr and Jadwyga crossed St. Basil's courtyard, Jadwyga could not help but marvel at how the moonlight bathed the snow in a silvery light. "Look at those towers and the gateway we just entered. It makes me think of castles and a magical time long, long ago. The beauty of this place takes my breath away. Thank you, Papa, for choosing this chapel for my wedding."

"It's the perfect setting for my beautiful daughter." Before they entered the monastery, a cold wind swept over them. As Jadwyga looked up, she saw two monstrous clouds covering the moon.

Piotr unfastened the outer door and they entered the foyer. They shook the snow off their boots, walked down the hall, opened the chapel door, and saw the tall figure of Father Kazlauskas, surrounded by the rest of the wedding party except for Antanas.

Father Kazlauskas strode up to them. "Jadwyga, welcome to St. Basil's chapel."

"Thank you, Father."

Father Kazlauskas turned to Piotr. "Where's the groom? I thought it was fashionable for the bride to be a little late, but not the groom."

"Father, I heard on the radio that there's a blizzard coming from the west. I fear that Antanas may be driving in it. He's coming from Kaunas."

Father Kazlauskas shook his head. "That's a hundred kilometres."

Piotr frowned. "When Jadwyga and I arrived just now, we could see signs of a storm approaching and the wind is biting."

Father Kazlauskas shrugged. "Well, there's no point standing around worrying about the storm and the Gestapo. I'll get some glasses and some bread, and there's some wine hidden in the cellar."

Marija gasped. "Father, can we eat and drink so soon before we receive communion?"

Father Kazlauskas gently took hold of Marija's shoulders. "I know that we're all supposed to fast before communion, but I am sure that the good Lord will see this as an exception. Jesus himself made wine for the marriage feast of Cana."

"Yes, Father, but it's our tradition to fast before communion."

"Marija, these are unusual times. We normally have mass first and then eat and drink; tonight, we will do the opposite. If we must wait for Antanas, we should be able to sit down to enjoy a glass of wine, some bread, and good company."

Piotr smiled. "The wine will help us all."

***

Eighty kilometres to the west, Antanas had encountered serious weather problems. He and his faithful green Fiat, Zabka, were struggling to stay on the icy road. A steady northwest wind was causing frequent whiteouts. Antanas was an expert driver, but when he tried to pump the breaks to slow down for a curve, he skidded, spinning like a top. Miraculously, he corrected his course and managed to face east again, but the wind continued to threaten to force him off the road. Another huge gust picked up the car and pointed it towards a car in the opposing lane. Antanas reacted just a little too strenuously, and Zabka went into another spin. This time, the Fiat flew off the road and into the ditch. The other car kept driving and Antanas shook his fist and cursed the driver. It was 7 p.m., but in this weather, it would take another ninety minutes to get to the church. And before he could resume his journey, he had to get Zabka out of the ditch.

Antanas surveyed the damage to Zabka and to himself. The good news was that the snow in the ditch had cushioned their crash, and he and Zabka were all right. The bad news was that they were stuck in a snow-filled ditch. Time seemed to crawl.

Almost an hour after Antanas went off the road, not a single car had passed. He was freezing and he knew that the Sosnowski family was in danger of being discovered by either the SS or the Gestapo. *Maybe Jadwyga was right. Maybe we should have waited to wed.*

Then, in the distance, he saw headlights. It was a bus heading towards Kaunas. Antanas stood in the middle of the road and began to jump up and down, waving his arms.

Antanas was a graduate electrical engineer, and while attending university he had also taught students how to drive. As it turned out, the bus driver, Tomas Revas, was one of Antanas's former students. Seeing Antanas in the middle of the road and the green Fiat in the ditch, he pulled over. One important lesson that Antanas had taught Tomas was to keep a chain in any bus he was driving in case he needed help pulling himself, or another vehicle, out of a ditch. Tomas had paid attention and he had a six-metre chain on hand.

When Antanas saw the driver step out of the bus and run towards him with the chain in his arms, he recognized the tall husky man with the beautiful smile. "Tomas, Tomas Revas, thank God!" he shouted over the howling winds.

"You've saved my life. I'm trying to get to Vilnius for my wedding and I'm stuck in the ditch. I'm already late."

Tomas smiled. "You've taught me well, professor. I have a bus, a chain, and thirty people to help me pull you out of the ditch."

"Thank you, Tomas, thank you," Antanas replied in a tone of great relief.

Tomas and Antanas trudged through the blinding snow and climbed into the bus. Tomas brushed the snow from his coat and asked the passengers for their attention. He told them about the plight in which Antanas found himself, and he implored them, "Can you help a good man who's trying to get to his wedding in a blizzard?"

"Yes." came the resounding reply from all thirty passengers.

"Stay here," Tomas instructed the passengers, "until we have attached the chain."

As soon as they stepped outside again, Antanas rushed to Tomas's side. "Why did you tell them that I'm going to my wedding?"

Tomas moved closer to Antanas so that he could make himself heard over the moaning wind. "What do you mean?"

Antanas cupped his hand over Tomas's ear. "In Vilnius, all church services are banned."

"Relax, professor, I swear there are no spies on this bus. These are all God-fearing Catholics from the Church of St. Gertrude. They're travelling together to visit their relatives in Vilnius over the Christmas holidays."

"You don't think a Catholic can be a spy?"

"Not this bunch. I know them well. Besides, the Gestapo aren't going to peek their heads out in this wild storm."

Antanas thumped Tomas on the back and laughed. "Who a spy is depends on one's point of view, but you may be right about the storm."

"Antanas, do you have papers for driving to Vilnius?"

"Yes, I do. My boss at the Kaunas Transit System is also my friend. He got me papers to travel between Kaunas and Vilnius on a regular basis."

"Why?"

"So that I could visit my fiancée, Jadwyga."

"Does he know that you're getting married tonight?"

"No, it's better that he doesn't."

"Very well." Tomas then yelled over the wind as he handed Antanas the chain: "Okay, let's get you out of the ditch."

Antanas wrapped and tied the chain around a chunk of Zabka's chassis and Tomas did the same to the bus. Then Tomas climbed aboard the bus and asked the passengers to disembark. They put on their coats, their hats, and their mitts and filed out of the bus into the cutting wind. Each of them grabbed a piece of the chain and began to pull on it. They complained to one another about the bitter cold and the piercing wind, but then one of the passengers began to sing the "The Song of the Volga Boatmen." The others laughed at first, but then they joined in to sing a chorus of this traditional song of hard labour. In surprisingly good harmony, they sang, "Yo, heave ho. Yo, heave ho. Once more, once again, still once more."

Tomas returned to the driver's seat and started the ignition. He backed up slowly and prayed. *Don't let me drive this bus off the road.*

Antanas joined the chain gang and pulled with all his might. He joined in the singing as well. "Yo, heave ho. Yo, heave ho. Once more, once again, still once more."

Thanks to the combined strength of the bus and the chain gang, Zabka was slowly hauled up the side of the ditch to the cheers of all the passengers. Piles of snow fell off Zabka as she ascended the deep trench. Antanas could not help but feel grateful for her beauty and her resilience. *Zabka looks like a majestic whale breaching the snow and the ice,* he thought. Antanas raced to the bus and thanked Tomas. Then he quickly thanked every passenger.

Antanas opened Zabka's driver-side door, climbed into his ever-faithful car, said a little prayer, and turned the key. The car engine groaned, and then sputtered out without starting. The crowd hushed and thirty people standing in the cold wind all prayed that Zabka would start. Antanas stayed calm. He thought about Jadwyga and how much he loved her. He exhaled slowly, turned the key again … but still no luck. He feared that he might have flooded the engine. He placed his foot on the fuel pedal and pushed it to the floor. He turned the key at the same time and suddenly the car did more than shudder; it let out a roar—and so did the bus passengers. Antanas pointed Zabka towards Vilnius and honked his horn.

Tomas honked back. The passengers waved goodbye to Antanas before shaking off the snow and the cold and boarding the bus.

***

By 9:30 p.m., Father Kaz was opening a second bottle of wine. It would have been a third bottle, but the monastery had only a few left over from before the war.

Jadwyga paced up and down the aisle. *Where can he be?* Although she loved Antanas with all her heart, it upset her that her fiancé had been so insistent on getting married during the Nazi ban on weddings. She knew that Antanas was twenty-seven years old and she was only twenty-one. She knew that he had proposed almost four years earlier and that he didn't want to wait any longer. But she was still angry with him for not listening to her pleas. She walked to the end of the hallway, opened the main door to the monastery, and watched the storm raging outside. Her thoughts were conflicted. *I love this stubborn Lithuanian and I'll never find a kinder, more loving man in this entire world.*

Piotr came up beside his youngest daughter. He shut the door. "Don't worry," he said.

Jadwyga wrung her hands. "Antanas is so very late for our wedding! He's never late. Who knows if the Gestapo will invade the chapel before he even arrives? Maybe he's been arrested on the way here from Kaunas. Maybe he's crashed the car in the storm. Why did he insist that we not wait for the Nazi ban to be lifted?"

Piotr gestured towards the outside door. "Most likely Antanas is caught in the storm. He needs to drive slowly. It's better that he arrives late than get hurt in a crash."

Jadwyga made the sign of the cross and prayed aloud. "Please, God, don't let him be killed by the storm or by the Germans."

"The bad weather will keep the Gestapo safe in their offices; they're basically a cowardly and lazy bunch," Piotr tried to reassure his daughter.

***

As Antanas proceeded eastward, the wind still buffeted the car, but not as badly. He was deeply grateful for his good fortune in getting pulled out of the ditch. It was now 9:30 p.m., however, and he wondered if his bride and her family were still waiting for him.

I'm already an hour and a half late and I still have a lot of road, snow, and ice ahead of me.

***

Jadwyga was growing more and more agitated. She paced up and down the hallway just outside the chapel. Marija drew near her daughter. "How are you doing?"

Jadwyga grimaced. "Maybe we should leave and go home. We can get married another day."

Marija held Jadwyga's hands. "Let's wait until 11 p.m. If he's not here by then, we'll all go home."

Father Kazlauskas overheard Jadwyga and Marija talking in the hallway and he decided to ask for some divine intervention. He asked everyone to join him in the chapel. He strode to the front of the altar, turned to face the wedding party, opened his arms, and declared, "Let's all pray the rosary together for Antanas, for ourselves, and for the success of this marriage." He raised his arms in prayer. "Our Father, who art in heaven…."

When they had all finished saying the rosary together, they sat in the dark. Some continued to pray, some sat thinking. Everyone was freezing. Nika had fallen into a light sleep. Suddenly, at 10:30 p.m., they saw lights from a car flash across the chapel windows. They heard an engine come to a stop and they listened to the sound of footsteps crunching in the snow. They heard the outside door open, and they felt cold air swirling down the foyer. Wisia squeezed Nika's hand.

The chapel door flew open and there stood Antanas. The wedding party was tremendously relieved to see his snow-covered face. Piotr, Maria, Nika, and Wisia all embraced Antanas and kissed him on both frozen cheeks. Piotr lit candles and light flickered in the chapel.

Father Kazlauskas greeted Antanas and brought him a big glass of wine.

Antanas thanked him, drank from the glass, and asked, "Where is my bride?"

When Jadwyga saw Antanas enter the chapel, she was flooded with strong conflicting emotions. She ran to the sacristy and locked the door. She could feel her head pounding so hard that she thought she might faint. Her feelings were similar to those of a mother whose small child has wandered off for hours, lost in the forest, and then suddenly reappears. Like the mother of the errant child, Jadwyga was relieved that Antanas was alive and unharmed, but once she knew he was safe, her anger bubbled to the surface.

After Piotr told him Jadwyga's location, Antanas hurried to the sacristy and pleaded with her through the closed door. "Darling, what's wrong?" He could hear Jadwyga crying on the other side.

Antanas returned to the chapel and asked Piotr for help. "Please speak to your daughter."

"I'll do what I can, but she's very angry and very afraid."

Piotr walked slowly up to the old wooden door of the sacristy. He placed his face close to the door and whispered, "Jadwyga, come back to the chapel. We need to get you married before the army comes to stop you."

Jadwyga just kept crying.

Finally, Nika stormed up to the sacristy. She pounded on the door. "Open up, Jadwyga, right now!"

Jadwyga hesitated, sniffled, and then opened the door a crack.

Nika pushed the door wide open and marched into the room. "Jadwyga, I've spoken with Antanas and his explanations for being late are more than reasonable."

Jadwyga frowned. "Why didn't he leave work earlier and get ahead of the storm?"

Nika looked Jadwyga directly in the eyes and asked her in a firm voice, "Do you want to get married or not?"

"Yes, of course, I do, but I want a calm and beautiful wedding where everyone isn't afraid."

"Do you love Antanas?"

"Of course. I love him with all my heart!"

"Then why are you stalling?"

Jadwyga snapped back, "He didn't get here until 10:30 p.m.! He was two and a half hours late!"

Nika grabbed Jadwyga by both arms and shouted, "Quit being a princess! His car slid into a ditch and he had to wait for hours to get pulled out. For God's sake, he drove through a blizzard to get here. He risked his life to marry you."

When Jadwyga took in Nika's words, the throbbing in her head subsided and her heart rate settled back to normal.

Nika took her sister's hand and led her from the sacristy to the chapel and down the aisle to the altar. "Okay, Princess Jadwyga, now you must marry your Lithuanian Grand Duke." They both laughed.

Father Kazlauskas gathered everyone in front of the altar. Nika and Wisia stood behind the priest as the altar servers, and Antanas and Jadwyga took their places in front of him. Piotr and Marija stood immediately behind Antanas and Jadwyga. Marija placed her hand gently on her daughter's shoulder. Father Kazlauskas skipped the rest of the mass and conducted one of the fastest weddings in history. When they got to the part of the ceremony in which Antanas and Jadwyga were to say, "I do," they did so enthusiastically. The newlyweds kissed, and everyone cheered and cried. Then they all dispersed and headed back home through the storm.

Jadwyga and Antanas spent the night together in the Sosnowski home, in Jadwyga's own bedroom. Their wedding night was quietly passionate and filled with love.

By the next day, the storm had passed and they were blessed with sunshine and blue skies. When the newlyweds descended the stairs the next morning, Nika, Wisia, Marija, and Piotr greeted them with laughter and applause. They were served a breakfast of bacon and eggs, oatmeal, and rye bread. Marija's sister Julia had smuggled in the eggs and bacon from their farm.

After breakfast, Jadwyga said, "Thank you, mother for such a wonderful breakfast. Please thank Aunt Julia, too, for hiding the food from the Germans."

They all joked about Antanas's misadventures in the snowstorm and they roared with laughter over the happy ending. Piotr poured everyone a glass of brandy. "May you live a hundred years; may you live in health. May you give us lots of grandchildren."

"I'll give you grandchildren, but not until this war is over," said Jadwyga. "Papa, thank you for making all the wedding arrangements with Father Kaz."

Piotr hugged his daughter tightly. "Take care of yourself, and may you and Antanas be as happy as your mother and I have been."

Jadwyga ascended the stairs and went into her room. She packed her clothes and a few pieces of amber jewellery. She squeezed a small album of family photos into her suitcase. Then she gently placed an embroidered nightgown on top of the other garments in her suitcase. This was a wedding gift from her mother.

Jadwyga's mind was filled with worrying thoughts. This was the first time she was leaving her home, with the exception of vacations. *When will I see my sisters again? When will I be able to talk with my father again? When can I share my soul with my mother?*

She began to cry.

Antanas opened the door, saw Jadwyga's tears, and held her in his arms. "I know that you'll miss everyone. When things settle down with the Germans, I'll get Captain Baun to prepare travelling papers for both of us. Then we can visit your family."

Jadwyga blanched. "Won't you be in trouble for not telling Captain Baun that you got married, despite the ban?"

Antanas drew his wife closer. "Uwe is my boss, but he's also my friend. He'll understand."

Jadwyga looked at her husband and smiled. "Okay, let's go."

Wisia and Nika helped their sister carry her bags downstairs and lift them into the trunk of the car. Tears sprang into everyone's eyes and none of the sisters could speak.

As her daughters stood sorrowfully together, Marija walked up to her youngest child. "Please write, take care of yourself, and love Antanas."

Jadwyga climbed aboard Zabka, and her mother and father waved goodbye. Antanas put the car into first gear and started down the snow-covered road. As he shifted into second gear, Jadwyga turned to look out the back window. Her mother was still waving.

Jadwyga never saw her mother again.

Chapter 12

The Beginning of the Marriage

The German attacking force remained stalled at both Leningrad and
Stalingrad. The United States had entered the war in December
1941. By early 1942, the American troops were training in earnest,
and much of the huge United States manufacturing sector switched
from commercial to military products. In 1943, General Rommel
and the Wehrmacht were pushed out of North Africa. By 1944,
much of Italy had been liberated by the British, the Canadians, the
Free Polish, and the Americans.

Kaunas, January 1942–March 1944

Antanas and Jadwyga were now married in the eyes of the church and
in the eyes of the Sosnowski family. However, the marriage ceremony
for the Paskevicius family and for the state took place at the Kaunas
City Hall on Saturday, January 10, 1942. After the ceremony, the
wedding party returned to the family home. Antanas's dog, Nero,
greeted Jadwyga at the door by jumping up and licking her face. A
large German shepherd, when Nero stood on his hind legs he was as
tall as Jadwyga. At first he scared her, but in time they became fast
friends. Jadwyga soon learned that her husband loved Nero almost as
much as the human members of his family.

Nero was loyal to Antanas and to the rest of the family, but he
was aggressive towards strangers, especially police officers and postal
workers. The dog had a low, menacing growl and his exposed fangs
frightened people who passed by the house. To pacify the neighbours,
Antanas kept Nero on a thick chain while he was at work, but he
released him every day upon his return. Nero rewarded him with
boundless affection. In warm weather, Antanas and Nero swam
together in the Nemunas River, right behind the Paskevicius home.

Nero, Antanas, and Jadwyga took walks together every evening. Jadwyga told Antanas about her day helping his mother with housework and listening to her stories about Antanas when he was young. Antanas would blush and change the subject, telling her about the buses he had repaired that day and the men who worked for him. Jadwyga would smile and say, "Don't change the subject. You were cute as a little boy and into mischief as a youth."

One late day in March, Antanas suggested that they walk with Nero into town. Jadwyga threw on her winter coat but quickly changed into her spring jacket when she felt the warmth of the early spring sun on her face. After a couple of blocks, Antanas stopped.

"Jadwyga, watch what Nero does now." Antanas called out, "Nero, sit up." Nero obeyed. "Nero, play dead."

Jadwyga was convinced that Nero wasn't breathing.

"Nero, bark." Nero's deep-throated bark startled her.

"Jadwyga, now do a special trick with Nero. Place a candy on his nose and make him sit there quietly for a full minute."

Jadwyga complied.

Nero remained quiet but alert.

"Now, say candy."

Jadwyga did as she was asked.

Nero tossed his head back and the candy flew into the air; then he snatched it and swallowed it in one gulp.

It was clear to the family how much Antanas and Nero loved each other, and it was just as obvious that Nero and Jadwyga were growing to love each other as well.

Although Jadwyga bonded quickly with Nero, she was a little nervous around her new mother-in-law, Stephania. But when she learned how Stephania had defended the newlyweds, Jadwyga stopped fretting. Although tensions between Lithuanians and Poles had lessened, plenty of prejudices persisted. Some of Stephania's neighbours and friends asked her why Antanas had married a Polish girl rather than a Lithuanian. Stephania's response was curt and to the point: "Antanas chose Jadwyga because he loves her."

Jadwyga missed her mother and father's loving support, but she was learning to love and trust Stephania and Antanas Sr. She wanted children and so did Antanas, but they both felt that they should wait until the war was over.

"It's not fair to bring a child into a country that is torn apart by war," Antanas said.

Jadwyga nodded in agreement. "When do you think the Germans and the Soviets will stop fighting?"

"When one side is destroyed. We must be patient," replied Antanas.

Chapter 13

Farewell to Kaunas

By the winter of 1944, troops at the Russian front had killed millions of German fighters. German citizens were recruited en masse to replace their fallen comrades in the Wehrmacht, the Luftwaffe, and the Wolf Packs of the German navy. These citizens, in turn, were replaced by workers from the occupied countries.

Between June 1941 and the spring of 1944, the Lithuanian resistance increased substantially. Partisans fought in the forests, in the marshes, and in the cities. German mistrust of Lithuanians grew proportionately. Their rage was greatest towards the partisans of the Kaunas Jewish Ghetto and the Rudninkai Forest, but it was directed towards all Lithuanian resistance fighters.

On April 2, 1944, Antanas's boss, Captain Uwe Baun, ordered Antanas to pack up and be ready to leave for Elbing in Germany in two days.

"Antanas, you're going to be the head mechanic of the public transit system in Elbing, Germany. You can bring your wife. Choose three of your mechanics, but leave me Vladas. Next to you, he's the best mechanic in Kaunas. I'll need him to take over your job."

"Where did this idea come from?" Antanas asked, greatly surprised.

Captain Baun stood up from his chair and walked towards Antanas. "This idea comes from the Wehrmacht High Command and God only knows who tells *them* what to do."

Antanas shrugged. "If I must go to Elbing, then I choose Jurgis Abraitis to be my second-in-command. I also request the services of Julius Capas and Vytautas Belskas."

Captain Baun made a pretend bow. "You may have them all. Please tell them to be ready to leave with you."

Antanas chose wisely in selecting Jurgis and Julius; they were mechanics of exceptional talent and men of good character. While Vytautas was the most gifted mechanic of all, his loyalty was later proven to be suspect.

Captain Baun's original perception of Antanas as a highly intelligent, competent mechanic and supervisor was reinforced every day. When his Wehrmacht superiors asked him to recommend someone for the position in Elbing, he did not hesitate to put Antanas's name forward. Over the past two- and three-quarter years, Uwe and Antanas had come to like and trust each other, and they often shared a coffee during breaks. Uwe was not a Nazi, but every officer's job was political to some extent. It was important for him to be at least partially aware of what the Nazi party was planning for Germany and its conquered countries. He knew that Lithuania and especially Poland were in for a very difficult time.

Antanas's brow furrowed. "I still don't understand why the Wehrmacht needs Lithuanians and Poles to work in Germany."

Captain Baun sat down at his desk and stared at the garage hoists in the distance. "Antanas, close the door."

Antanas complied.

"You didn't hear this from me, but the Wehrmacht is losing badly on the Russian front. Since Operation Barbarossa, the Wehrmacht stalled and then retreated. Germans and Soviets are dying by the millions."

Antanas stepped forward, placed his hands on the desk, and asked, "How does this affect Jadwyga and me?"

"The longer this war goes on and the more German soldiers die, the more Germans must leave their civilian jobs and join the Wehrmacht, the Luftwaffe, or the Navy. This has left many vacancies in factories, stores, garages, labs, warehouses, farms, and hospitals. The former head mechanic in the Elbing Transit System has been sent to Minsk. He'll lead a team of mechanics servicing tanks and military trucks."

"My family is here and Jadwyga's family is in Vilnius. What if I declined their offer to move to Elbing?"

"This isn't an offer; this is an order. If you refuse this order, you will be shot as an example to others who have been given similar commands. And there is something else."

Captain Baun paused before he spoke again. "I can't give you specifics, but as the enemy on the Eastern Front slaughters more Germans, civilian life in Poland and Lithuania will worsen. The Nazis, the SS, and the Gestapo will become more paranoid and more vicious. Someone as smart and capable as you are could be viewed as a partisan suspect, and this could lead to interrogation, torture, and perhaps death for you and your family."

"The Nazis and the SS no longer feel invincible?"

"It's ironic, but it will be safer for you and your wife to be in Germany. As your friend, I recommend that you go to Elbing and as your boss, I order you to go," said the Captain firmly.

"Can my youngest sister join Jadwyga and me on this transfer?"

Uwe paused. "I'll consider your request and get back to you tomorrow."

The next day Captain Baun approached Antanas. "Your sister may join you and your wife, but you must all hurry. There is one more thing I need to tell you, Antanas. The Nazis distrust the Lithuanians, but they have a special hatred for the Poles. You must prepare your wife and your sister to say that Jadwyga is Lithuanian, not Polish. If they think she's Polish, things will be much harder for her and for you."

"What does that mean?"

"They'll make her wear an armband with the letter 'P' on it. Hitler forced the Jews to wear the letter 'J' and then he made the Poles wear the letter 'P.' The Poles working in Germany are paid less and fed less and they are not allowed to walk freely in German cities. If a Pole has intercourse with a German, it's a misdemeanour for the German but a death penalty for the Pole. It's imperative that your wife learn to speak German."

"She studied German in high school and she is excellent with languages."

Captain Baun smiled. "That's good. Tell her to use German as much as possible, and the only other language she should use is

Lithuanian. She will need to do this even when she's alone with you. The guards watch all the foreign workers carefully, and if she makes any mistakes or offers any resistance, they will use her actions as an excuse to ship her off to a concentration camp."

Antanas's eyes widened. "What's a concentration camp?"

Captain Baun looked at the floor. "They are like work camps because the people sent there must work, but the conditions are much, much worse. Believe me."

Chapter 14

The Voyage to Elbing

The use of long-range bombers, sonar, and convoys by the
Canadians, British, and Americans reversed the Battle of the
Atlantic. Now the German submarines were no longer the hunters;
they became the hunted. This reversal allowed vast numbers of
American troops to be transported to Britain. By 1944, most of these
troops had undergone training. They were well equipped with
planes, artillery, and tanks. It was only a matter of time before the
promised Western Front became real. The noose was tightening
around the Wehrmacht's neck.

Kaunas, April 3, 1944

When Antanas tried to explain to his mother what he and Jadwyga
had been ordered to do, Stephania wept.

Antanas Sr. reacted more reflectively. "I agree with Captain Baun.
The Germans are frustrated and scared now, and if they lose even
more ground to the Red Army, they will become vicious."

Stephania looked bewildered. "I don't understand."

"The Poles and the Lithuanians will be targets for the frustrations
of the Wehrmacht, and particularly the SS. We'll become their
whipping boys and girls."

"The Soviets have pushed the Germans out of Russia; maybe they'll
do the same in Ukraine, Belarus, Lithuania, and Poland. Then our
children would be safe, wouldn't they?" Stephania asked hopefully.

Antanas Sr. lit his pipe. "They *might* be safe, but our experience
with the Soviets would suggest the opposite. When they ruled Kaunas
and Vilnius in the early part of the war, they deported tens of
thousands of Lithuanians and Poles to the work camps in the Soviet
Union."

Stephania frowned. "You're right. I tried to forget that time. People were arrested for being a priest, a banker, a lawyer, an engineer, or even a farmer who owned land. Anyone who wasn't poor became a suspect."

Antanas Sr. grimaced. "What will happen if the Soviets regain Lithuania and Poland? Would they see Antanas's job as a civilian position or as part of the military? His boss is a captain in the Wehrmacht. Officially Antanas is a member of the Wehrmacht."

"But he's not a soldier. He's not a volunteer," Stephania objected.

"It won't matter to the Soviets," Antanas Sr. replied.

"Maybe it will be safer for Antanas, Jadwyga, and Maria to go do slave labour in Germany," Stephania sighed.

***

On April 4, 1944, Antanas, Jadwyga, and Maria bade farewell to their family. The goodbyes were long and emotional, but the most difficult one occurred between Antanas and Nero. Antanas scratched Nero behind his ear. Normally this relaxed the dog and he would lick Antanas's hand, but this time Nero remained motionless. Antanas pulled out a candy, put it on Nero's nose, waited, and then said "candy." Nero did not move, and the candy fell to the lawn. Antanas picked it up for him and placed it near his mouth, but Nero just whined softly and turned his muzzle away. Antanas stroked Nero's back gently. Then, tears welling in his eyes, he walked away.

Lugging the possessions that the Wehrmacht had allowed them to bring, they climbed into a taxi. It took about ten minutes to reach the docks on the Nemunas River. It seemed to Jadwyga that the trip took much longer than that, and yet at the same time it appeared to occur in a flash.

The barge they boarded was about fifteen metres long by six metres wide. It was flat except for its curved bow. Other than a few tarps, it did not feature much equipment. A one-metre-high fence surrounded its perimeters. The purpose of the fence was to prevent waves from swamping the deck and its human cargo. Fifteen people were gathered on the barge: Jadwyga, Maria, Antanas, the mechanics

Jurgis, Julius, and Vytautas chosen by Antanas, and eight others destined to work in Elbing. There was also one German soldier, Private Werner. Antanas watched their young guard closely. He gave few orders and kept mostly to himself. The guard stood at attention whenever another Wehrmacht soldier approached, but as Antanas studied the machine gun slung over the young soldier's shoulder, he thought that this man looked look like he could never bring himself to use it.

It took only about twenty minutes to load the few items that the Wehrmacht had permitted the passengers to bring with them. Then they began their voyage northwest up the Nemunas River. The river would take them to the Baltic Sea, and from there they would sail southwest towards Elbing in Germany. Their barge was pulled by a large ship that was carrying wounded German troops back home. The Nemunas had been dredged the previous fall by German engineers to allow such ships to traverse from Kaunas to the Baltic Sea.

This large ship had powerful diesel engines that did not have to strain to pull the barge upriver. Jadwyga and Maria objected to the constant smell of diesel fuel. Jadwyga looked all around the barge and wondered where they would sleep that night and what would protect them from the rain. Maria simply sat on her luggage with her head in her hands.

They tried to enjoy the unseasonably warm spring weather as they were gently towed upstream.

"What are you doing?" Maria asked, as she glanced over at Jadwyga.

"I'm waving at those people on the shoreline. They must be local villagers. They've come to the shore of the river to wash their clothes. I'll picture these lovely Lithuanians in my mind for all time."

Maria gazed beyond the banks to the green meadows and rolling hills in the distance. Tears sprang to her eyes.

Jadwyga wondered what her parents and her sisters were doing. She had written to them the day before, but she knew that it would be two weeks before her letter would arrive, if it ever did.

Later that evening, Private Werner ordered them all to pitch a large tarp over the metal poles on the deck to create a tent-like structure. Afterwards, the passengers covered up with a blanket as they lay down on the wooden deck. It was quiet and peaceful. The deck was hard, but they soon fell asleep.

On the second night, a storm blew up and the waves on the river grew high. Water began to cascade over the barrier and to soak their blankets. Some time after midnight, Jadwyga woke Antanas, but he urged her to go back to sleep. "I think the barge can withstand the storm. We'll be okay." Jadwyga closed her eyes.

Around 3 a.m., there was one snapping sound and then another. The barge began to bounce. The ropes holding the barge to the troop carrier detached under the strain of the pounding waves. They were now adrift, buffeted by the mighty waves. Antanas feared that the barge would capsize if they did nothing. Nothing is precisely what the young German soldier was doing. He simply stood erect, holding onto the rail.

"I can't swim. We're going to drown," the soldier whispered to himself, but loudly enough for Antanas to hear.

"Not if you do what I say, Private," Antanas told him.

Private Werner nodded his head.

Antanas stepped up onto a box and pointed at the four burliest of the passengers. "You four men grab the large oars on the barge and get them into the oarlocks. Paddle to the starboard bank."

"Why?" One of the men challenged him.

"Because there's shallow water there and protection from the waves."

"Do as he says!" Jadwyga yelled, competing with the sound of the waves. "My husband knows what he's doing. If you want to live, do as he says."

Jurgis came to stand beside Jadwyga and he screamed at the men who were frozen in fear. "His plan is a good one. Get moving!"

The men obeyed.

Antanas turned his attention to Private Werner. "Fire your machine gun into the air three times. This will let the captain of the troop carrier know that there's a problem. If they shine a searchlight on you, point starboard to let them know that we're trying to veer in that direction."

Private Werner was so terrified that he either didn't notice or he didn't care that he was taking orders from a Lithuanian.

"Yes, sir!" he shouted, and then he fired a burst of bullets into the air.

The noise was deafening to those on the barge, but Antanas feared that the sound of the waves would drown out the clatter of the gunfire before it reached the ship. Luckily, the sentry on the troop carrier heard the shots. He had been unaware that the barge had been cut loose, but now he realized what had happened. The sentry awakened the captain and the rest of the crew. Soon everyone had leapt into action.

Antanas and the other men did their best to row the barge towards the soldiers and the sailors who were approaching them in life rafts. The crashing waves slowed them to a crawl, but once they met up with the men from the ship, they were able to join forces. The barge passengers, sailors, and soldiers spent the next forty minutes adjusting the length of the ropes until they got the tension and the distance from the troop carrier correct. By this time, all the passengers were soaked and chilled, but they were happy to be alive. They continued their journey upriver, but no one slept for the rest of the night.

Early the next morning, Maria led Jadwyga and Antanas to the bow of the barge. She pointed at the sea gulls that were swimming and diving as they hunted for fish. "Look at those birds. We must be entering the Baltic Sea."

Jadwyga stared up at the cloudless sky and then down at the turquoise water. "Too bad the ropes couldn't break again, and we could drift to Sweden; then we'd be free."

Maria laughed. "Keep daydreaming, Jadwyga; they now have us tied to the ship with three solid ropes."

Antanas scowled. "Dream a little longer, but soon we'll all have to wake up when we land in Elbing."

Everyone managed to sleep that night and the next. The following morning, they were awakened by the wretched screeching of another flock of sea gulls. They were approaching the Strait of Baltiysk, which connected Elbing to the Baltic Sea.

Elbing, April 7, 1944

Antanas spotted two sailors rowing the commander of the troop carrier, Captain Menthe, to their barge in a rowboat. Private Werner helped the captain to board, saluted him, and stood at attention. Captain Menthe told the private to stand at ease. "This strait is too shallow to accommodate medium-sized vessels such as our troop carrier, but it's fine for a barge such as yours. The troop carrier will leave you now and keep sailing west on the Baltic. Our destination is still secret, but your end-point is Elbing and you're almost there. It's just a few more kilometres."

"How are we going to make it the rest of the way?" Private Werner asked.

"Your passengers will row. I'll leave you two extra oarlocks, two extra oars, and Corporal Goering. He'll take charge."

Having made that announcement, Captain Menthe had his sailors row him back to the troop carrier. Private Werner, Corporal Goering, and Antanas began to attach the extra oarlocks to the barge. When they finished, Corporal Goering ordered six of the passengers to row. "In an hour, you will be able to rest and six more of your comrades will take your place."

Three hours later, they arrived at the Elbing docks. The passengers disembarked from their floating home. At first, their legs felt wobbly, but after a while they regained their balance. They all doublechecked that their belongings were still stored in their luggage before the Wehrmacht trucks pulled up beside the docks.

When the Wehrmacht trucks drove them away, they passed huge warehouses and even larger munitions factories. These factories were the pride of the Third Reich. Elbing was a major German manufacturing town. Unfortunately for the Third Reich, some of these buildings had already been destroyed by British and American bombing.

They passed an enormous camp, but they didn't stop there as their first objective was to deliver a soldier to his family. En route, they drove through Elbing's Old Town, which Jadwyga found much more interesting compared to the factories.

"Look at those beautiful old houses," Jadwyga shouted over the sound of the truck's engine. "Most of them are four stories high."

"But look at how many of them have been damaged or destroyed," Maria replied. "This used to be a prosperous town, but times have changed."

Jadwyga called out to Maria. "The bumps and the dust and the diesel smell are making me sick. I think I'm going to throw up."

"Don't even think about it," Corporal Goering commanded her.

Private Werner gave Jadwyga a candy. "Take this peppermint; it will settle your stomach."

The candy did not make her feel much better, but she did not vomit and that was all that mattered.

Once they dropped the soldier off at his family's home, they retraced their route and headed for the work camp. When they arrived at their destination, several German officers and thirty Wehrmacht soldiers met the new arrivals. For a small work detail from Lithuania to receive such a welcome was unusual. The supreme commander of the work camp was Major Dieter Braunshiedel, and he wished to meet Antanas. Although Antanas had received an excellent recommendation from Captain Uwe Baun, the major was keen to inspect this man personally. The major was a thin man in his late fifties whose career in the Wehrmacht had stagnated and was of no consequence to anyone but himself. He wore a monocle for effect.

The major never actually spoke directly to Antanas but rather he observed him closely. He commented to Captain Ninehaus, "He unloads his luggage efficiently and effectively. He moves like an athlete or a soldier. Who are these women that he's helping?"

Captain Ninehaus had read their files. "I believe the one with the brown hair is his sister, Maria, and the one with the black hair is his wife, Jadwyga." Antanas's former boss Captain Baun had been careful to falsify the file and had listed Jadwyga as Lithuanian.

"It's good that his wife and sister are with him. He'll be less likely to become a saboteur or a flight risk. His sister looks Lithuanian, but I'm not sure about his wife. Is she Lithuanian or Polish?"

"Major Braunshiedel, the file indicates that she is Lithuanian."

"I'll find out for myself."

Major Braunshiedel spoke to Jadwyga first. "Who are you?"

Jadwyga answered in German. "I'm Frau Paskevicius."

"What are you?"

"Major, what do you mean?"

"Are you Lithuanian, Russian, Belarusian, Polish, or Ukrainian? I can't keep track of all these foreigners."

"I'm Lithuanian." Jadwyga could feel her face flushing and her left hand beginning to tremble ever so slightly. With a supreme effort, she imagined herself swimming in the Nemunas River behind the Paskevicius home. This helped her relax and her hand ceased to quiver.

"With a Polish name like Jadwyga, are you sure you're Lithuanian? I'll be asking the guards and the other slaves about you."

Jadwyga felt both anger and fear ignite within her, but she gritted her teeth and responded simply, "Yes, Major."

The major interviewed all the barge passengers one by one. Finally, he interrogated Corporal Goering and Private Werner. His questions were always the same. "Is this woman Lithuanian or Polish? Did she speak Polish or Lithuanian on the barge? Did she ever speak Polish?"

Everyone backed Jadwyga's story because Jadwyga had followed Antanas's warning, knowing that speaking Polish or admitting to being Polish could mean being sent to a concentration camp. Only Private Werner had ever heard her speak Polish. He did not speak Polish or Lithuanian, but he could hear the difference in the languages. Polish is a Slavic language, but Lithuanian is not. He had heard Jadwyga call to Antanas for help in Polish when the barge had come loose from the troop carrier. However, because he was aware that Antanas's actions on the barge had shielded him from court martial and prison, he said nothing.

Private Werner stood beside Antanas. He knew that he owed his life to this man.

The major called out, "Private Werner, come here, now."

The private gulped and marched towards his commanding officer.

Major Braunshiedel asked Private Werner, "Did this woman ever speak Polish on the voyage from Kaunas to Elbing?"

"No, Major."

"Never?"

"Never."

No one refuted Jadwyga's claim to be Lithuanian. The major could have made inquiries through the Wehrmacht and the Gestapo in Kaunas if he wanted to be absolutely certain, but the matter was not sufficiently urgent to him. He was just using Jadwyga to demonstrate to all the barge passengers that he was the supreme boss and that it was in all their best interests to cooperate with him.

Antanas was assigned to the garage manager, Captain Johan Ninehaus, a man in his early twenties, muscular and good-humoured. Ninehaus had light brown hair and dark blue eyes; he was a good example of what Hitler proclaimed to be the Aryan race. But this man was not a Nazi. Hitler's brown shirts had killed his parents because they were Social Democrats and they had been protesting Hitler's dissolution of the German parliament in 1933. Only fifteen at the time, Ninehaus had gone into shock, depression, and then rage.

After Major Braunshiedel, Captain Ninehaus, and the other officers had finished inspecting the barge passengers, everyone ran to the barracks to claim the best places to sleep. The barracks was a huge spruce-planked building with a faded green roof. The interior was a shock to Jadwyga and Maria. Their first impression was the stench. It was a nauseating mixture of sweat and smoke. There were hundreds of wooden bunk beds and a wood-burning stove positioned every thirty metres. There were no windows and precious few light bulbs. Men and women were housed in the same barracks and it was extremely noisy. The dust and mould in the air made everyone cough, and Jadwyga and Maria could not stop sneezing.

"Grab those three bunks," Maria ordered. "That way we can sleep near each other."

"These beds are nothing but hard boards with worn woollen blankets," Jadwyga muttered.

"There's no privacy. This place stinks," Maria ranted.

Jadwyga's thoughts drifted to her parents' home in Vilnius and she felt a stab of pain in her heart. *Mama could always find the silver lining in any situation. But she's not here.*

Antanas saw that Jadwyga was in deep thought and he put his arms around her. "At least we're alive and we're together. Tomorrow, I'll see what I can do to make things better."

Chapter 15

Life in the Camp

The Nazis operating the work camps knew that they needed foreign workers to replace German workers, but they were ambivalent about this procedure. They knew how much they depended on these slaves, but at the same time they considered them to be vile and inferior.

Elbing Work Camp, April 8, 1944

The morning after their arrival, Antanas reported to Captain Johan Ninehaus. He entered the captain's office at 7:45 a.m., but it was empty. The office was a small, plain room with a desk, a typewriter, and a telephone. The walls were hung with pictures of the captain's family and colleagues. Antanas noticed a photo that included Captain Ninehaus and his former boss, Captain Uwe Baun. They were in a group photo that was labelled "Basic Training, 1937."

As Antanas was examining this photo, his new boss entered the room. "I've heard good things about you, Antanas Paskevicius. Captain Baun is a friend of mine. He recommended you highly."

Antanas stood up straight, looked directly at Captain Ninehaus, saluted, and smiled. "Captain Baun is an officer and a gentleman. He gets things done and is good to his men."

"Yes, I got to know him very well in basic training. He's a good leader and a good friend."

Antanas suddenly blurted out, "Can my sister and my wife be exempted from labour? I could do a double shift and the Elbing Transit System would be better off for it. Neither my wife nor my sister has skills that the Wehrmacht or the town of Elbing couldn't find among the other foreign workers. Could they be allowed to benefit from my extra work?"

Major Dieter Braunshiedel was searching for a form in the next office, and he overheard every word through the thin walls. As soon as he heard Antanas's request for special privileges for his wife and sister, he bolted into Captain Ninehaus's office. He confronted Antanas. "Everyone in this camp must work, especially the foreigners. Let me make it even more clear: every person who wants to eat will work and work hard." With that, Major Braunshiedel stormed out of the office and slammed the door.

Captain Ninehaus looked at Antanas and grinned. "I guess you have your answer."

Major Braunshiedel strode down the hall and returned to his own office. He sat down in his desk chair, but soon stood up and began to pace. He could hear Captain Ninehaus talking with Antanas. He threw his pen across the room, marched down the hall, and reappeared in the captain's office.

"Get out!" he screamed at Antanas.

Antanas stood up from his chair slowly. He exited and walked down the hall to the stairs.

The major snarled at Captain Ninehaus, "Don't be soft with these foreign scum." He saluted his subordinate and returned to his office.

Captain Ninehaus shut his door, sat in his chair, and leaned forward. He placed his head in his hands. Then he looked up and stared at his basic training picture on the wall. *What kind of monsters are we?*

April 9, 1944

Maria and Jadwyga were assigned jobs. Jadwyga was singled out by Corporal Carl Schmidt.

"What use are you to this camp and to the Fatherland? Why should we waste food on you?" he asked her.

Jadwyga faced him. "I can sew and mend, Herr Corporal."

"Good, you may prove to be useful."

The corporal was a tall, blond man in his early twenties. He had piercing blue eyes and a square jaw. His lean body and quick movements reminded Jadwyga of a panther. She wondered why he wasn't riding a tank to glory for the Führer.

That is exactly what he had been doing as a tank commander in successful campaigns in Poland and in France. However, he had an affair with one of Joseph Goebbels's mistresses that almost cost him his life. Jadwyga later learned from friendly guards that Goebbels had discovered the affair. He had considered killing Captain Schmidt, but then decided that demoting him from captain to corporal and removing him from a combat role to supervising foreign women making uniforms would be even more painful for him.

Corporal Schmidt needed to produce results in terms of uniform production and repair. Based on the recommendation of his subordinate, Private Jaszeinka Munsinger, he concluded that Jadwyga would strengthen his team. There were five tailors—four men and one woman—who sewed woollen uniforms and three seamstresses who repaired shirts and replaced buttons on the officers' and soldiers' shirts. In addition, there were three boot- and shoemakers and a floor boss. Again, based on his subordinate's recommendation, Corporal Schmidt made Jadwyga one of the regular seamstresses.

April 10, 1944

Maria was first assigned to clean dishes in the cafeteria under the lascivious eye of Captain Harold Edelhoffer. However, Corporal Joe Schneider asked Major Braunshiedel to transfer her to his unit, and the major agreed.

Corporal Schneider's staff cleaned the foreign workers' barracks and the officers' houses. The corporal was a man too old to fight but too young to be exempt from the Wehrmacht. He was sixty, with grey hair and warm brown eyes. He was ten kilograms overweight and he had a jovial and kind air about him. A veteran of World War I, he had earned a good record. Because of his war service and in deference to his age, the Wehrmacht had given him a safe position. He still wanted to do a good job, however, and for that he needed a strong team of cleaners. When he was in the cafeteria, he was struck by how hardworking Maria was, so he decided to have her on his team.

"What did you do in Lithuania?" Corporal Schneider asked Maria when they met for the first time in his office.

"I was a student. I was about to begin an undergraduate program in mathematics and sciences at the University of Kaunas when the Wehrmacht shut down all the universities. After completing undergraduate courses, I planned to apply to medical school."

"Very impressive, but that plan must go on hold until Germany has won the war. Working here in this unit, you'll be busy killing germs and preventing disease. You, along with seven other women, will be assigned to cleaning the barracks and the officers' quarters."

"Can't I work in the camp hospital or in the Elbing hospital? I could start as a nurse's assistant and, in time, perhaps I could train as a nurse?"

Corporal Schneider laughed so hard that tears streamed down his corpulent face. Then he saw Maria's expression. She was silent but her eyes had narrowed, and her cheeks were beginning to twitch. When Corporal Schneider saw how hurt Maria was, he stopped laughing.

"The work that you'll be doing is hard physical labour. It also involves chemicals such as DDT that some of the women are afraid of, but the army scientists tell us it's safe."

Maria was afraid of the chemicals too, and she hated this job, but not as much as she detested working in the kitchen and having to tolerate her lecherous former boss, Captain Harold Edelhoffer.

***

After her first shift, Maria returned to the barracks and flopped down on her bunk.

When Jadwyga returned from her work to the barracks, Maria sat up on the edge of her bed and burst into tears.

"That idiot Corporal Schneider thinks my request is funny. But why can't I train as a nurse here at the camp hospital? I'm smart. I'm good at sciences. I learn fast. I work hard. I would be a perfect nurse for these Germans."

Jadwyga shook her head. "You're not the perfect nurse for them and keep your voice down. You're Lithuanian. You're the one who told me how successful the Lithuanian partisans have been at killing Germans."

"So, what does that have to do with me training as a nurse?"

"They don't trust Lithuanians to treat Germans medically. They're afraid that if you have a German officer as a patient, you might use the drugs at your disposal to kill him."

"I might, and who could blame me?" said Maria.

Chapter 16

The Work and the Workers

The fact that the Luftwaffe had lost the Battle of Britain was minimized in the German press. The seesaw tank battles between Rommel and Montgomery in North Africa and Allied victories in Italy were never shared in the papers; only German victories were publicized. Soviet victories in Russia, Ukraine, and Belarus were not reported. Instead, German newspapers repeatedly forecast the imminent collapse of the Soviet Union.

Elbing Work Camp, April 8–14, 1944

Maria was scrubbing the floor of the barracks. She deeply resented this physically demanding job. However, it was better than working in the kitchen. There, the noise and the dangers never gave her time to think.

As Maria washed down one of the men's latrines, she gagged from the smell. She yearned to know how the war was unfolding. She knew that the slaves of the Third Reich and even German civilians heard or read news based only on Joseph Goebbels's propaganda machine. According to the Nazi press, the Germans were winning the war handily on all fronts. She kicked open the side door of the barracks to gulp some fresh air. She thought: *I don't believe it. If they're doing so well, why are we here in Elbing?*

As Maria tossed lime down a hole used as a toilet, she kept thinking about the war effort. She knew that events on the Russian front were going badly for the Germans. She had heard rumours in Kaunas, and these rumours were confirmed by the other slaves here in the work camp. Somehow, they needed to establish contact with the German citizens of Elbing. It was fortunate that Antanas, Jadwyga, and Maria all spoke German. Talking to German citizens would not be as informative as listening to the BBC, but they heard about husbands, brothers, sons, and nephews who had been killed, wounded, or imprisoned, or who had frozen to death on the Russian front.

Maria realized that even the German citizens didn't know much, either. She wondered how she could find out more about who was winning the war. She decided that she must speak to Jadwyga and Antanas that very night. *I need hope that these arrogant Germans will be crushed*, she thought.

She desperately wanted to figure out how and when they could escape from this horrible place.

***

The presence of Corporal Schmidt made fear a constant companion throughout Jadwyga's working day, but the work itself was distracting and it made the hours move fast. Jadwyga's job was to sew and iron shirts and to stitch buttons on the uniforms. It was mostly men who sewed the heavy woollen uniforms, but one woman had been promoted to this job as well.

Private Jaszeinka Munsinger was the head tailor in the sewing and tailoring shop and he reported directly to Corporal Schmidt. He had noticed Jadwyga when she first landed in Kaunas. He loved her smile.

The private approached Jadwyga and asked her if she sewed. When Jadwyga had replied yes, he recommended her to Corporal Schmidt and soon she found herself in his work unit.

Jadwyga's days were less physically demanding than Maria's, but they were noisier and more chaotic. Twelve workers occupied a large room with nine sewing machines, plenty of needles and thread, and tools for shoe and boot manufacture and repair. The sewing and tailoring shop was situated in a long, one-story wooden structure with a steep roof to keep off the snow. There was spruce panelling on the walls. Jadwyga was intrigued by the fragrance of the spruce. She reflected on how the smells of the room affected her. On her first day, it smelled like a spruce forest and reminded her of Kaunas and

Vilnius, but on cool days the smoke from the pot-bellied stove dominated the room. When the hot days arrived, it smelled like twelve extremely sweaty people.

During her first week on the job, Jadwyga engaged all the other workers in conversations. Others she got to know within a few days of their arrival. Most of these chats took place in their work setting when Corporal Schmidt was absent, but some of her conversations occurred in the workers' mess hall and on the short walks between buildings. Gradually, Jadwyga pieced together the painful life stories of all her co-workers.

Private Munsinger was terrified of his boss Corporal Schmidt, but he nonetheless did what he could to protect Jadwyga from him. He also gave her some interesting projects and was more than happy to assist her with special assignments. Jadwyga appreciated his help, but realized it came with a price. The private was a short, fat, ugly German. He was a pest, but he was not dangerous like his boss. He spent thirty minutes or more each day lingering at her work station. Jadwyga knew her co-workers noticed how much time he spent with her. They started calling her "Princess," a name she had not heard since her sisters had used it to tease her long ago.

The work was tedious and hard, but Jadwyga succeeded in getting along with everyone. A Lithuanian woman became her first work friend. She was pleased that her new friend, Veronica, sat across from her. Veronica was a tall, attractive brunette, about fifty years old. She had never married and had no children. She was a devout Catholic and Jadwyga enjoyed saying quiet prayers with her while they sewed shirts. Jadwyga knew that Corporal Schmidt would disapprove of their prayers, but Private Munsinger didn't care. Besides, she knew the sound of the sewing machines muffled their voices.

Natasha Putin came from Western Russia, near the Ukrainian border. She had been a mistress of a Russian colonel, but when he was killed and his regiment was captured in Operation Barbarossa, she convinced the German troops that she could be useful to them as a seamstress. In the end, she wound up at Elbing. In some ways, she was like the other women, but she used a very different survival strategy with her German captors: she slept with them.

Jadwyga did not condone Natasha's behaviour, but she liked her nevertheless. Natasha was a beautiful redhead of about thirty, with grey-blue eyes that men found extremely appealing. She always had a German soldier for a boyfriend, and this allowed her to enjoy frequent and remarkably long breaks. This annoyed Jadwyga's protector, Private Munsinger, but he lacked the courage to report Natasha to his boss. He knew that if he did so, whatever soldier-boyfriend she had at the time would pay him a most unpleasant visit. Ultimately, he pretended not to notice.

The other women certainly noticed, though, and they joked about Natasha constantly. "I wonder why Natasha took so long at break? She must have a fever because when her soldier friend brought her back, her face was all flushed and she had beads of sweat on her forehead. Ha! Ha!"

To Natasha's face, the women were always friendly because they were a little afraid of her boyfriends. But Natasha was also a lot of fun. She was always ready to share a joke or a funny story. She was also generous with the chocolates and cigarettes that the soldiers gave her.

Marion Fedyck was a strong peasant girl from Ukraine. She was the best tailor in the camp, but she was prone to bouts of depression. Jadwyga felt very protective of Marion, and Marion, in turn, grew to like and trust Jadwyga. Over time, Jadwyga came to understand the source of Marion's depression.

"When the Germans first pushed the Russians out of Ukraine, the peasants, like my family, welcomed them as saviours from Stalin. However, the SS officers proved to be even more cruel than the Russians. They rounded up all the men and women in our village and, if they were suspected of being communists or even friends of communists, they were tortured to confess their guilt and forced to give names of fellow communists. Some gave names. Many didn't. Those who didn't were shot."

Jadwyga reached out and took Marion's hand. "What happened to your family, Marion?"

"My entire family was killed, except for me. I was only sixteen and I was forced to become the mistress of a German tank commander. I was angry, then sad, and then numb. For a soldier, the tank commader was kind and understanding, but he was transferred to Belarus. Soon after moving there, he was killed in a tank battle near Minsk. His commanding officer heard about me somehow and shipped me to Elbing, to work as a seamstress. I love to sew, but some days I can't even get out of bed."

Jadwyga touched her arm sympathetically. "Why don't they beat you when you are unable to work?"

"Corporal Schmidt could have had me beaten but two things held him back. The tank commander who made me his mistress was Colonel Erik Doan. He had been Corporal Schmidt's mentor in the Tank Corps, years ago. Corporal Schmidt owed something to his former commanding officer. More importantly, I'm valuable to him when I do come to work. My depression reduces my working days, but most of the time, I do work. Sewing is the only thing that I like to do here. When I come to the shop, I do great work. I was the only woman assigned to sew the winter uniforms and I was promoted from general sewer to tailor. Corporal Schmidt recognized that I was better than all the men."

Jadwyga leaned back and laughed. "Marion, you and I will become great friends."

Tanya Shushkevich was from a farm near Minsk, the capital of Belarus. When Jadwyga first met her, Tanya had just turned eighteen. She was tall and slender and had the same combination of jet-black hair and blue eyes as Jadwyga. Jadwyga shared her story with Tanya and then asked her how she had come to Elbing. Her response shocked Jadwyga.

"Shortly after the fall of Belarus, the SS troops began to apprehend Jewish citizens. My best friend was Irina Lukashenka. She was Jewish. With my parents' permission, I hid Irina in our home. After a few weeks, a neighbour reported her suspicions to the Gestapo. The Gestapo agent and some SS troops raided our home. It wasn't long before they found Irina and she confessed to being a Jew. My parents were arrested and put on a truck and taken away. The Gestapo agent told the gathering crowd of neighbours that because my parents were guilty of harbouring a Jew, they would be sent to a concentration camp in Poland. Five SS soldiers grabbed Irina and dragged her to the field behind our farmhouse. They raped her countless times. Finally, they tore her flesh apart with their machine guns. The Gestapo agent held me and made me watch. All the time that Irina was screaming, I was only fifteen metres away from her. When she died, the agent released me."

Tanya began to shake and to cry. Jadwyga held her as she murmured, "Irina, Irina, Irina."

As Tanya slowly composed herself, she added, "The SS men didn't know what to do with me, but when a neighbour told one of them that I was good at sewing, they sent me here."

Jadwyga met her first American when he was introduced to their work unit during her fourth week at the camp. His name was George Dyer. Jadwyga asked him to tell her his story.

"I'm a shoemaker and an American citizen of German descent. I was visiting Germany when war broke out on September 1, 1939. The German government knew I was an American, but once Britain and France declared war on Germany, the Germans drafted me. I demanded to speak to a representative from the American embassy, but my abductors screamed at me that I was German, not American. My kidnappers flattered me. They reassured me that I was tall, blond, and handsome, and therefore I was the perfect model of a good German soldier."

"So, what did you do?" Jadwyga asked.

"Unfortunately for the German propaganda machine, I refused to fight for the Wehrmacht and, as a Quaker, I declared myself a pacifist. The authorities examined my case and considered executing me, but when they found out I had been a shoemaker in Milwaukee, they came up with a better plan. They sent me to a work camp near Munich and then transferred me to Elbing."

Just at that moment, Corporal Schmidt stomped by in a fury. He took notice of neither Jadwyga nor George. Jadwyga leaned forward and whispered in George's ear, "I'm glad the Germans didn't shoot you."

"I'm glad, too, but I'm not the only German sent here to work in the camp. There's Alfred Menthe."

Jadwyga already knew Alfred as a colleague. Jadwyga had met him on her second day in the sewing and tailoring shop. He approached Jadwyga at break time and asked her how she had come to Elbing.

Jadwyga recounted her story and then asked him, "So, as a German, how did you wind up here?"

"How did you know that I'm German?"

"You have no accent; your German is flawless. Your articulation is wonderful. You could be an actor."

"Your powers of observation are excellent. You seem like a person who listens well, so I'll tell you the short version of how I arrived here. I was accused of being a communist by Hitler's brown shirts because my father was a member of the socialist party. I firmly denied being a communist. However, the Gestapo beat me over the next forty-eight hours. They broke four ribs, fractured my left shoulder, and crushed both cheekbones. They knocked out two teeth as well. I figured they'd kill me. They threatened to kill my parents and my sister if I didn't confess. So, I signed the confession."

"Why didn't they execute you?"

"My denials didn't spare my life, but my voice did. I was a singer in the Munich Opera Company before the war, and critics described me as a fine baritone with a promising career. Some career. Now I work as a tailor in a slave camp."

Jadwyga leaned forward in her seat. "I don't understand. How did your voice save you?"

"When one of the senior Gestapo officers came to inspect how the interrogations were going, he recognized me from the Munich Opera Company. He asked if I would prefer to sing or to die. I said, sing. When they found out that I once had a job as a tailor, they sent me here to Elbing. They made me one of the tailors, but they have me sing for the soldiers, politicians, and bureaucrats at all special functions. I feel like their pet monkey."

"Sing for yourself and your family and forget your captors," Jadwyga replied.

Alfred took her hand and kissed it.

Alfred's father was either dead or in a concentration camp but his mother moved to Elbing to be close to her son. Because of his special status as a singer, Alfred could visit her every other weekend. He always returned from his visits with potato pancakes, which he generously shared with others in his work unit.

Jadwyga met Pavel Karmalov in the sewing and tailoring shop on her third day. He was easy to spot as he was extremely tall and thin. She learned that he was both lucky and unlucky. He had been a tailor in Moscow. Drafted by the Red Army, he was sent to serve as a tailor on the front lines.

The Red Army did not have enough uniforms for the young recruits who were replacing the Red Army soldiers killed during Operation Barbarossa. A unit of soldiers stripped uniforms from the corpses of Soviet combatants and handed them in to the tailor shops. There, the blood-stained uniforms were quickly repaired and issued to the replacement soldiers. Before Operation Barbarossa was over, Pavel was captured along with three million other Soviet soldiers and airmen.

Jadwyga shook her head. "What happened to you?"

"The Germans were not kind to French and British prisoners, but they were brutal to us Russians. They barely fed us and we had no shelter, just barb-wired fences. We slept on the ground and when it rained, we were soaked. Despite the deplorable conditions and our weakened health, they forced us to work. Many of my comrades were dead by November, and with the cold winter weather coming, we knew that most of those still alive would perish."

Jadwyga touched Pavel's arm. "What saved you?"

"I'm not proud to say it, but I begged for my life."

"Did that work?"

"No, but eventually I overheard a guard saying that the Wehrmacht needed tailors. I told one of the guards that I could be useful to the Wehrmacht as a tailor. The next day he gave me an old ripped uniform and some needle and thread. An SS officer came by and told me to sew like my life depended on it, because it did. He laughed and left me with the tattered uniform."

"Were you able to impress them?"

"Yes. I worked for two hours on the ripped coat they had given me. Then I used the thread that remained to transform the rag that had been left in the pocket. I turned it into a soldier's handkerchief. The decent guard took the uniform and the handkerchief from me. The next morning, he told me to board the truck on the other side of the camp. He escorted me to a broken-down but still-functioning troop carrier. There were about twenty men already on the truck. I jumped aboard. I yelled thanks to my guard and the truck pulled away."

Jadwyga sighed. "Where did you go?"

"We travelled all day and then stopped in a field and slept there for the night. They gave us old frayed blankets. The meadow was softer than the ground we were used to in our POW camp, so we all had a good night's sleep. We travelled slowly and made lots of stops. I had no idea what part of Germany we were in and my fellow POWs got on or off at various camps. Finally, we arrived here, at this camp."

Jadwyga leaned forward. "What's it been like for you in the Elbing camp?"

"It's been much better here. If I had stayed at the POW camp, I would've died. It was early November and it was already cold. They gave us only one old blanket each and we were sleeping outdoors. If December 1941 didn't kill me, then January 1942 would have. Here in Elbing the barracks are noisy and filthy and there are lots of bugs, but we sleep inside. It's heated a little and they feed us. After two and a half years, I'm still alive. This is paradise."

Jadwyga laughed out loud. "You're funny, Pavel, but you're right."

During Jadwyga's first week in the sewing and tailoring shop, Antanas noticed that his wife looked tired and anxious. "Are you unwell?"

"My body is fine, but I'm sad from hearing the terrible histories of my colleagues. They're my comrades and I want them to be my friends. By listening to their stories it helps them to trust me, but the pain of their stories weighs heavily on my heart."

"Slow down, my darling. There's no urgency. The Germans aren't going anywhere soon. You have time to befriend your co-workers. Don't rush. Time is one thing that we have in abundance."

Chapter 17

Family Reunion

The Polish army fought valiantly against the Wehrmacht and the Luftwaffe in Poland in 1939 and again in France in 1940. Polish pilots who escaped from France distinguished themselves in the Battle of Britain. However, most of the Polish army eventually became prisoners of either the Red Army or the Wehrmacht.

Elbing Work Camp, April 15, 1944

During Jadwyga's second week in the camp, Private Jaszeinka introduced her to Wladek Szudy. He referred to Wladek as a Polish shoemaker from Krakow. Jadwyga's heart was in her mouth. She was terrified because she knew that if Wladek referred to her as his cousin or even if he spoke Polish to her, then her ruse would be discovered. Jadwyga's mind raced as she prayed, *Please, God, help Wladek to act as if he doesn't know me.*

Wladek understood immediately what was going on when he met Jadwyga. He did not hug her and he spoke only in German. He went to his work station after a few words of introduction and Jadwyga returned to her sewing machine. She did not look up from her work for the rest of the day.

At breakfast the next morning, Wladek crept up behind Jadwyga and whispered, "During lunch, meet me at the outdoor table closest to the chestnut tree. We can talk there."

Jadwyga did as Wladek suggested and they began a conversation that was spread out in small segments over five days. The talks were broken up by work, meals, and sleep, but they took advantage of as many opportunities to speak at short intervals as they could.

Jadwyga usually met Wladek at an outdoor table for breakfast, lunch, or dinner and she was normally accompanied by Antanas and

Maria. "We can only eat together for one meal per day without attracting suspicion, so we'll rotate the meal when we get together," Wladek told her. Eventually, the four of them shared their respective ordeals.

"How long have you been here?" Jadwyga asked him.

"I've been in Elbing since July 1940. Almost four years."

Antanas overheard Wladek's answer as he and Maria approached him. "We arrived last week. Why didn't I see you then?"

"Last week, Major Braunshiedel assigned me to live and work at some uniform manufacturing outposts in the factory district of Elbing. Mostly, I was just maintaining and fixing sewing machines."

"What were you doing before you were sent here?"

"I left Jadwyga's parents' home under cover of darkness on September 20, 1939. I recovered my rifle from its hiding place in a nearby garage and then walked at night and slept by day on my trek to Western Poland. I begged for food or stole it from farmers for ten days until I met up with some remnants of the Polish army east of Warsaw."

Jadwyga shook her head. "It must have been a terrible time."

"Yes, it was, but it was not as horrifying as what I saw in the eyes of my fellow soldiers. They looked exhausted, scared, and hopeless."

Jadwyga tried to hold Wladek's hand but he pulled it away. "The guards could be watching."

Jadwyga nodded. "Sorry."

"We Poles were standing up fairly well against the blitzkrieg. You would never know it from the German propaganda, but we had lots of tanks and modern artillery. We didn't have as many planes as the Germans, but we had great pilots. Still, we couldn't fight for long on two fronts."

Jadwyga leaned forward but kept her hands at her side. "What did you do next?"

"Some of us got out of Poland with as much military equipment as we could and joined the French Army as an independent Polish division. The Panzer divisions routed the Belgian, French, and British armies and we Poles were defeated again."

Maria stared intently at Wladek. "What happened to you?"

"Some of the Polish soldiers and many of our pilots escaped with the British and some of the French at Dunkirk. I wasn't so lucky. I was captured by the Wehrmacht and thrown into a German POW camp near Paris."

"How did you manage to survive?"

"The Germans were arrogant and rough, but it could've been worse." Wladek shook his head slowly. "I'm lucky that I was only a sergeant and that I was captured in France and not in Eastern Poland. The rumours I've heard are that thousands of Polish officers were either executed by the Soviets at Katyn in May of 1940 or sent to work camps to die. The Germans fighting in France didn't care much about a lowly sergeant like me."

"I'm glad you're alive, Wladek," said Jadwyga softly. "How did you get to Elbing?"

Wladek waited for two of the camp guards to pass by their table and then he explained that in Krakow, before the war, he used to run a business making and repairing shoes. He also maintained and repaired sewing machines for the tailors in town.

"Many of the tailors in Krakow and almost all the Jewish tailors used my services because I was the best. I hate to think of what has happened to my former Jewish customers."

Wladek glanced around, saw no one approaching, and continued to talk.

"One day, some SS officers came to our POW camp and one of them asked, 'Can anyone mend and make shoes?' Then he shouted, 'Can anyone fix sewing machines?' I yelled out, 'Yes and yes.' and the next day I was on a train bound for Elbing."

Antanas leaned a little closer on the bench. "And what was that like?"

"The Wehrmacht took possession of an old French passenger train and ripped out all the seats. In its passenger service days, each car would hold about forty people, but minus the benches, they jammed over a hundred of us in at once. It was a hot, late July morning so the smell was putrid. There was one large metal can per car that acted as a toilet. If you could squeeze your way through the packed crowd, you could relieve yourself. There was no place to lie down or even to sit. The German guards had not been feeding us much prior to our train ride so it was not a surprise that some of the men were already sick. Some vomited; some fainted. We were packed together so tightly that even if a man passed out, he couldn't fall to the floor. But we knew that the Germans needed us to work for them, so they would likely treat us better than they had in the POW camps."

Wladek paused and stared with curiosity at Jadwyga, Antanas, and Maria. "I've been doing most of the talking. Now let me ask you some questions."

"Okay," responded Antanas. "Jadwyga is our best storyteller, so let her explain our situation. Time is running short, though. Lunch time is almost over."

Wladek glanced around to check the yard once more for guards. Then he directed his remarks specifically to Jadwyga. "Before you return to work, I must tell you something very important. We've been speaking in German and your German is good. Is your Lithuanian good enough for you to pass as a Lithuanian?"

Antanas and Maria both jumped in to confirm that Jadwyga's Lithuanian was very good.

Jadwyga added, "I've been speaking Lithuanian since 1938. I learn languages easily."

Wladek bent closer to Jadwyga and whispered, "Your first name is Jadwyga. Some Lithuanians choose that name for their daughters, but it's a Polish name. As you know, our German masters don't like the Lithuanians, but they have a special hatred for the Poles. They hate the Jews and the Gypsies the most, but we Poles are a close third."

"I understand."

Wladek suddenly ceased talking as emotion halted his speech. Finally, he said, "My friend, my cousin, speak German first, speak Lithuanian when no Germans are around, and *never* speak Polish, even when we talk alone."

Jadwyga nodded. "I understand."

Wladek gazed solemnly at Antanas and Maria. "Do you both understand that you can never allow Jadwyga to speak Polish, even among yourselves?"

"We do."

"Perhaps you do, but if they suspect that Jadwyga is Polish and that she hid her nationality from them, be assured they'll send her to a concentration camp where they'll work her to death."

Chapter 18

From the Barracks to Old Town

In the winter and spring of 1944, Lithuanian and Lithuanian–Jewish partisans intensified their bombings of railways, telecommunications, and Wehrmacht ammunition dumps. German oppression and murder of Jews in Vilnius and Kaunas intensified. More and more Lithuanians and Poles were sent to work camps.

Elbing Work Camp and Old Town, Elbing, May 2, 1944

Jadwyga held her nose. "It stinks in the barracks and the bathroom is just plain nauseating. I feel like throwing up every time I pay a visit to that filthy hole in the ground."

Maria arched her back in discomfort. "The bedding is hard and the bed bugs are vicious. Sleeping is almost impossible. We aren't the only ones who hate this place. All the workers hate it here."

When Antanas entered the western door of the barracks, he thought he could hear Maria and Jadwyga speaking to each other from the other side of the building. As he drew closer, he could hear what they were saying and he became alarmed. He ran across the building, and as he approached his wife and sister, he motioned with both hands as he whispered, "Be quiet!"

Maria stood squarely in front of Antanas. "Big brother, it isn't just the Germans that cause trouble. Some of the foreigners are no better. That Gypsy woman, Magda, she's the worst. She parades around here nude in front of everyone," Maria said in a sneering tone. "She flaunts her body and flirts shamelessly with the men."

Jadwyga chimed in. "No one complains about her, because everyone knows that she's one of Major Braunshiedel's mistresses."

"No one envies her. She is still forced to do physical labour. She works with the crew that paints the buildings. She reeks of paint and turpentine."

Jadwyga nodded. "What's even worse is that she's at the beck and call of the major. Sometimes he's nice to her and she returns to the barracks tipsy. But other times, she returns bruised and she just goes to bed and cries."

Antanas could no longer remain silent. "Please Maria, please Jadwyga—think about where you are and what you're saying."

Maria held her left hand above her eyes in a searching gesture as she pretended to squint into the distance. "Relax, big brother, Magda and the major are far away."

"You don't think he has spies among the foreign labourers? He trades favours for information. Do you two want to be on his special list? Do you want to be sent to a concentration camp?"

Maria just shrugged.

May 4, 1944

Captain Ninehaus was a fair boss, and Antanas had strong, talented men working for him. They were from all over Europe, forced labourers just like he was. Life was okay for Antanas at work, but he was under tremendous pressure back in the barracks. Every evening he could see the stress endured by his bride and his sister.

As Antanas trudged back to the barracks from the garage after work, his thoughts tormented him. *I don't know how long my wife and sister can tolerate living in the barracks. I must devise a plan to get us out.*

May 5, 1944

When Antanas arrived back at the barracks, he asked Maria and Jadwyga to join him in the yard outside. "I've received cigarettes from my boss as a reward for my work, but also from some of the bus drivers and even from the officers who bring us their trucks and military cars. Captain Ninehaus told me that since I became the head mechanic, the number of buses breaking down has been reduced by

20 percent. When Major Braunshiedel heard about this, he gave me a carton of cigarettes."

"Why would the major be so generous?" Jadwyga asked.

"He's not a kind man, but he's a shrewd one. He knows that a happy head mechanic runs a better team, and a good team produces better work. If the quality and quantity of work improve, he can take credit for it with his bosses. Captain Ninehaus is aware of the same game, but he's also a decent man. He gives me as many cigarettes as possible. I use half the cigarettes as rewards for my mechanics and I save the rest."

"That's great, big brother, but what can we do with all these cigarettes?"

"Without permission today, I took the afternoon off and walked into the Old Town of Elbing. I found a house with a sign advertising two rooms for rent. I knocked on the door and a woman named Frau Erika Brewer answered."

Jadwyga grabbed Antanas excitedly by the arm. "What happened?"

"I asked her to let me look at the rooms. She invited me into her home and pointed up to the next level. I climbed the wooden stairs and examined the rooms. They were small but clean, and the house smelled only faintly of smoke. There's a shared bathroom down the hall."

Maria whispered in Antanas's ear. "Is there a kitchen on the same floor?"

"No, the only kitchen is on the main floor."

"Can we use the kitchen?"

"Yes, but we'd still eat our meals here at the camp. We can't afford to both buy food and pay rent."

Maria asked, "Is there a room on the second floor where we can meet just to talk?"

Antanas smiled. "Yes, there's a small common room."

Jadwyga took Antanas by the hand. "How much does she want from us?"

"Let me finish the story. I told Frau Brewer that I was interested in renting two rooms on the second floor."

Antanas sat down on the edge of his bunk. "It was an interesting conversation. Frau Brewer confided some personal things to me. She told me her daughter is studying to be a mathematics professor at the University of Frankfurt. It seems that she comes back home to live and work in the summers. She also has another daughter who is still in high school and a younger boy. They live on the main floor with her."

Jadwyga was eager to hear the rest of the story. "Was Frau Brewer receptive to your offer to rent her flat?"

"She seemed a bit reluctant at first. Then she shared something very sad and personal. Her husband, a pilot, was killed during the Battle of Britain. I offered my condolences and she softened a little. I explained that we didn't have money, but that we could pay in cigarettes. She agreed and asked for sixty cigarettes per month. I offered twenty-five. We negotiated for a while and settled on forty."

Antanas stood up and faced Maria and Jadwyga. "That's my story. Shall I bring the cigarettes to Frau Brewer and close the deal?"

"Yes, my husband!" Jadwyga exclaimed. "Please close the deal. And thank you."

"Yes, big brother, you've done well," said Maria.

***

Antanas visited Frau Brewer the next evening carrying 120 cigarettes in a cleaned-out can from the garage.

"Do you agree that this pays for the first three months' rent?" Antanas asked her.

"Yes, I do," Frau Brewer replied.

***

On Friday, Antanas told Captain Ninehaus about the arrangement he'd made with Frau Brewer. Captain Ninehaus didn't flinch, but he did wonder aloud how Antanas could afford to pay for the rooms. When Antanas told him how many cigarettes he had saved, the captain seemed impressed. Antanas decided to push him for more favours.

"Can you speak to the officer in charge of the barracks so that he doesn't send out a search party for us three whenever we're absent?"

"Yes," replied Captain Ninehaus. "I'll also inform the guards that I've approved your new location."

Antanas frowned. "You're taking a chance with Major Braunshiedel."

Captain Ninehaus smiled slightly. "Leave him to me. I'll keep silent unless someone complains. If you're always punctual and perform well at work, I could still defend you even if you're discovered."

On Sunday, Maria, Jadwyga, and Antanas moved into their new home with what little luggage they had. By about 11 a.m. they were settled comfortably in the small living room on the second floor. Jadwyga gazed at her husband with gratitude. "This arrangement took courage and cunning. For three foreign labourers to be living off the base of the work camp without permission from the major could be viewed as a serious offense. You took a huge risk."

Antanas nodded. "What we've done could still result in severe penalties. The three of us are taking a big chance, but I think it can work. We must be on time for meals and early for work. And we must work hard. The guards will be let in on the secret by my boss, but they could complain to the major, so we must make friends with them immediately."

Jadwyga sat on the edge of her chair. "How do we do that?"

Antanas grinned. "The two of you can flirt with them and listen to their complaints, and I'll give them ten cigarettes each. I still have some saved."

Suddenly, Antanas's expression changed.

"We must all be extremely careful. We can keep our living arrangements secret from the officers for a while, but not forever. My boss already knows, and your bosses will eventually figure it out. But if they're pleased with our work and they don't see us as troublemakers, they'll probably leave us alone."

Chapter 19

Discovery

In late April 1944, Rudolph Vbra and Alfred Wetzler escaped from Auschwitz and gave the first detailed account of the systematic Nazi extermination of Jews. Their account was eventually smuggled to the British. In May 1944, the Red Army liberated the Ukrainian city of Sevastopol during the Crimean offensive.

May 5–12, 1944

Corporal Schmidt had been observing Jadwyga for some time. He had an eye for beautiful women, and he made up his mind that she would bring sunshine into his dark world.

The corporal knew that Jadwyga had a husband who was the head mechanic for the Elbing Transit System. He was more than aware that Captain Ninehaus was Antanas's commanding officer and that he liked Antanas and depended on him. He concluded that Captain Ninehaus would defend Antanas and Jadwyga if he forced himself upon her. He reasoned, therefore, that he must make Jadwyga feel so afraid of him and so guilty that she would give in to his advances and keep their affair a secret.

One day Corporal Schmidt noticed that some cuttings of cotton material were missing from the garments section. He then saw Jadwyga help herself to some of the cuttings and it gave him an idea.

He summoned Jadwyga to his office. When she entered, he yelled, "You've been stealing materials from the Fatherland!" Jadwyga went white. There was an element of truth to his accusations. She *had* been taking discarded cuttings from the supply room. She didn't think that anyone would notice or care. She had seen so many poor German children in Elbing wearing tattered clothes that she had taken it upon herself to make shirts for them from the remnants. The shirts looked like patchwork, but they were clean and intact.

When Jadwyga tried to explain her actions to Corporal Schmidt, he strode forward and placed his face close to hers as he screamed, "You had no right to do this! Those materials are used to insulate sleeping bags for German soldiers on the Russian front. You need my permission to use them for anything else."

Jadwyga stood straight as she faced the corporal. "It's spring. Do the soldiers need warm sleeping bags at this time of year? Do you want me to stop making shirts for the children who need them?"

The corporal's cruel eyes dilated, and he drew his lips taut against his teeth. "No, you dirty thief; continue making them. But you'll give me the cuttings from your unit every day. When you want to use some of them to make shirts, you'll come to my office. Come on Friday, first thing in the morning."

Thereafter, each morning when the corporal walked by her sewing machine, Jadwyga gave him her cotton cuttings from the previous day.

On Thursday morning, he sent for her. When she reached the door to his office, he asked her an odd question. "What are you?"

At first, Jadwyga was surprised by the question, but then she understood. *He wants to know if I'm Polish.* Jadwyga's heart skipped a beat and she fell silent. *Oh, Mother Mary, please make the corporal believe that I'm Lithuanian.*

Major Braunshiedel burst into Corporal Schmidt's office before she could answer. The major had questions of his own. "Corporal Schmidt, why has production of uniforms dropped during the first week of May? What are you going to do to make sure productivity increases during the rest of May?"

Confronted in this embarrassing way by his boss, Corporal Schmidt pointed to the door and barked at Jadwyga, "Get out!"

May 13, 1944

Jadwyga was still thinking about Corporal Schmidt's alarming question when she went to his office the next morning, as he had commanded. She clenched her fists, took a deep breath, and opened the door.

Why is the lighting so dim? she wondered as she entered the office. *Those maps of his tank campaigns on the wall ... they weren't there yesterday. The stuffed wild boar is new,* she thought.

Corporal Schmidt wore a tight-fitting khaki uniform, recently pressed. It was not the uniform he usually wore, but rather the costume of a warrior. He looked handsome, fit, and terrifying.

The corporal stood up from his chair. "Jadwyga, you know that I could have punished you severely for your crimes against the Fatherland. You had no business taking those cuttings from your workplace. I also know that you and your husband live outside the barracks, without permission."

Jadwyga's face went white and she stumbled against the corporal's desk.

The corporal's demeanour appeared to soften. "However, I like you and I could be lenient in your case."

He moved closer to her. She could smell wine on his breath.

He pushed her against the wall and pressed his body against hers. He gently stroked her arm. He looked her directly in the face. "Your eyes are beautiful. Of all the women here in the camp, you are my favourite."

Jadwyga's body stiffened. Corporal Schmidt took a step backwards. "You know, Jadwyga, I can make your life much better, or much worse."

Jadwyga felt paralyzed. But then, she summoned her courage. "What wrong have I done other than try to help German children?"

The corporal folded his arms and glared at her. "You've stolen from the Wehrmacht. You've stolen from me. You've deceived me."

Jadwyga's face reddened and her heart pounded like a sledgehammer. *If he rapes me, I could tell Antanas. He could enlist his boss to avenge such a wrong,* she thought.

The corporal moved closer to her once again and stroked her neck. "Well, little kitten, has the cat got your tongue? Have you nothing to say to your commanding officer?"

Jadwyga's thoughts fluttered. *If Major Braunshiedel were to order Captain Ninehaus not to interfere with Corporal Schmidt's unit, then*

I will be on my own, except for Antanas. She glanced around the room and realized there was no escape. She also realized that if Antanas were to retaliate against Corporal Schmidt, he'd be beaten or killed. If he found out about Corporal Schmidt's sinister deeds and did nothing, he would die of guilt and shame.

Jadwyga offered silent prayers over and over. *Jesus, Mary, and Joseph, pray for me. Jesus, Mary, and Joseph, pray for me.* Suddenly, her fear dissipated. She knew what her oppressor needed better than he did. She stepped towards Corporal Schmidt and said softly, "Corporal Schmidt, I know that you have the power of life and death over me. I also know that you are too much of an officer and a gentleman to abuse that power."

Corporal Schmidt looked stunned. He was unaccustomed to women turning him down, especially when they had no choice. He stepped back from Jadwyga, turned, and sat on the edge of his desk. He looked her slowly up and down. There was something about Jadwyga's behaviour that seemed to please him. She had rejected him, yet somehow her words had made him feel more like a man. He realized that despite her rejection, she might be worth keeping. He pointed to the door. "Go. Get out of here and get back to work."

Chapter 20

What Is Happening?

On May 12, 1944, the Red Army finally liberated Crimea. Allied plans to invade Normandy were nearing completion.

Elbing Work Camp, May 14, 1944

Maria had just finished cleaning the home of her former boss, Captain Harold Edelhoffer. She had scrubbed it spotless and she was now standing on the wooden landing at the top of the porch stairs. There had been a little mud on the landing, but Maria had removed most of it. The morning was warm and sunny, and she had paused to look out over the grounds of the camp. Before she descended the steep stairs, she saw Captain Edelhoffer crossing the street. *Oh, God, it's him. I would recognize him anywhere.* Captain Edelhoffer was a huge brute of a man. He had greasy black hair and his topcoat was wrinkled and stained.

The captain stopped at the base of the stairs, looked up at Maria, and grinned. "Maria, I never see you anymore. Ever since Corporal Schneider and Major Braunshiedel stole you away from me, I don't have the pleasure of your company."

Maria tried to squeeze past her former boss as she made her way quickly down the stairs. As Maria's shoulder brushed against the captain's chest, her khaki-green uniform generated some static electricity. The captain was startled. Maria smiled. "I've been fine, Captain Edelhoffer. But I must go now. I must clean three more houses today."

Captain Edelhoffer reached out and grabbed Maria's left arm as he ascended the steps. He dragged her up to the landing and pushed open the front door. "Oh, please come inside and talk with me for a while. I miss you. I miss your beautiful smile. Come into my house and we can share some brandy."

Maria tried to escape down the stairs, but the captain tightened his grip. Maria resisted. "Captain Edelhoffer, I have so much work to do."

"Nonsense, you can just work a little later this afternoon." He yanked her arm and tried to pull her through the front door.

Maria went cold. Her body became rigid. Her feet would not move. She knew that this man had wanted to have sex with her from the first day she had been assigned to his horrible kitchen. She thanked God that Corporal Schneider had succeeded in transferring her from kitchen duty to his unit of cleaners. In that first week in the kitchen, Captain Edelhoffer had leered at her constantly. Now, she feared that he had stumbled upon a chance to rape her.

"I'll be gentle. You and I will both have some fun," the captain whispered into her ear.

Maria scanned the grounds of the camp. She saw no one. *What can I do? Throw cleaning fluid in his face and run? If I do that, he'll catch me eventually. Then he won't be gentle. But I can't give in. Oh, God, help me.*

At that very moment, she saw Frau Edelhoffer at the top of the street. Captain Edelhoffer saw her, too, and he quickly released Maria's arm. Frau Edelhoffer walked briskly towards her home and soon she stood at the base of the stairs. She glared up at them. "What's this? What are you two discussing? What's your name, young woman?"

Maria straightened her body and smiled. "My name is Maria Paskevicius and I've just finished cleaning your home, Frau Edelhoffer."

"Then why was my husband leading you inside?"

Maria looked innocently at Captain Edelhoffer. "I don't know, Frau Edelhoffer."

"Harold, what were you doing?"

Captain Edelhoffer shuffled his feet, adjusted his collar, and stared at Maria. "I wanted to show her a spot on the kitchen floor behind the stove. She missed it last week and I wanted her to do a proper job this time."

Frau Edelhoffer ascended the stairs. "Harold, you're a fool. You never spend time near the stove. Why would you suddenly be checking the floor behind it? Stop your idiocy and let this poor girl get back to work. By the way, why are you home from work so early?"

Small beads of perspiration appeared on the captain's forehead. "I was working on a report for Major Braunshiedel at home last night. I forgot to bring it to the office this morning. I came back to get it."

Frau Edelhoffer climbed the final two steps until she could look her husband squarely in the eye. She was not a beautiful woman, but she was tall and muscular, with long red hair pulled into a tight bun. When she stared her husband in the face, he seemed to shrink.

"Harold, go into the house, get your report, and go back to work."

Captain Edelhoffer darted inside and quickly shut the door.

Frau Edelhoffer leaned in close to Maria and whispered into her ear.

"I know he's a pig and if he ever bothers you, come see me and I'll make sure he never harms you again. I can promise you I'll hurt him."

"Yes, Frau Edelhoffer, and thank you for your concern."

"I'm not doing this for you. I'm doing this so he doesn't bring more shame upon me and my children. Now, get back to work and remember what I told you."

***

Maria did not usually talk much after work and neither did Antanas. They left all the gossiping to Jadwyga. Tonight was different. Maria was in a rage.

Antanas and Jadwyga were sitting in their small living room when Maria charged into the room. "That pig Captain Edelhoffer tried to have his way with me today. I wanted to kill the bastard. If it weren't for his wife, he would've raped me."

Jadwyga crossed the living room towards her sister-in-law.

"I'm so sorry, Maria."

Tears sprang into the eyes of both women and Antanas clenched his fists.

Maria faced Antanas. "He won't do it again. His wife arrived home just as he was trying to force me into their house. She figured out what was going on; she's smart and she's tough. He doesn't have the guts to try it again."

Antanas placed his hand on Maria's shoulder. "From what I know of Frau Edelhoffer, you're right, but if he does approach you, let me know and I'll talk to Captain Ninehaus. If that doesn't work, I'll talk to him myself in a way that he'll understand."

"Big brother, please stay out of it; you'll only get yourself killed. Frau Edelhoffer will be enough protection for now. What we need to do is get out of this dung heap. I want to go home. I want to see Mama and Papa."

"Going back to Kaunas is impossible right now."

Maria looked at Antanas and Jadwyga thoughtfully. "We need to know as much as possible about our captors. We need to learn more about the guards and how this camp works. And we need to know more about what's happening outside of the camp."

"What do you mean?"

"We need to learn how the war is going. We need to know when we might have the best chance to escape and not get caught."

Jadwyga's eyes sparkled. "Maria, do you want to start a spy ring?"

"It won't be simple. What we have to do will be difficult and dangerous, and if we do it right, most of it will be slow and boring. Still, it's clear to me that this is what has to be done."

"What exactly? And how?" Antanas asked.

Maria turned to face Antanas. "There are a lot of people in this camp, right? We talk to our fellow workers at lunch time, especially you, Jadwyga. These people come from different places that are either occupied or are still engaged in the war. The ones from Belarus know what was going on there before they were captured. The ones from Ukraine know what was going on in Ukraine; the ones from Russia know what was going on in Russia. Do you see what I'm getting at, Antanas?"

"Yes, I do, Maria, but how do we keep our information up to date?"

"The Germans must replace the soldiers killed on the Russian front with German workers. The German workers must be replaced by slave workers like us. There will be new workers coming from all parts of Europe. Each of them will carry a piece of the puzzle. If we keep asking questions, if we keep listening, if we keep analyzing, we will know what is going on in the war."

"I'm good at getting people to talk about themselves," said Jadwyga.

"Yes, you're a very good listener, Jadwyga, and people feel safe talking to you. But you must be careful. Corporal Schmidt is always watching you."

Antanas sat down and cleared his throat. "We must be extremely careful in how we go about this. It must not appear to our fellow workers, let alone the guards, that we are collecting information like spies."

Jadwyga draped an arm around Antanas's neck and gently squeezed his cheek. "I agree, darling husband, but there are two sources of information we haven't yet considered."

"What are those?"

"Maria and I eat lunch on the picnic tables just outside the mess hall. Lately, some of the German guards have been joining us. It's amazing to hear the negative and honest things they say about their superior officers and the whole war effort."

Maria made her fingers resemble a gun and poked her index finger into Jadwyga's back. "The one you have to look out for is Sergeant Erik Schultz; he's a Nazi. He reports to Captain Meyer, but even Captain Meyer seems nervous around him. He hasn't tried to stop the guards from mingling with us. Maybe he wants information about the workers and has a plan similar to ours, but in reverse?"

Antanas nodded. "The trick is to speak less and listen more."

Maria stepped closer to Jadwyga. "You're right; the guards will be useful in that way, but what's your second source?"

"The BBC, the British Broadcasting Corporation. Not their regular broadcasts, but special ones sent to the German-occupied lands. The British want partisans, citizens, and conscripted labourers to know that they've not been abandoned. They want the people who are living under the fist of the Nazis to resist. The best way to make that happen is to feed them hope."

Antanas's eyes widened. "Dear wife, how do you know this?"

"My cousin Wladek; he's very resourceful."

Antanas nodded. "Yes, I agree, but how can he listen to the BBC?"

"I don't know how, but he does."

Antanas rubbed his eyes and looked at his co-conspirators. "This is all very interesting, but what use will it be to us?"

Maria frowned in concentration. "We need to know the moment when the Germans realize that they're losing the war. We need to know this before they surrender. If we run when the Germans feel strong, they'll catch us and punish us or kill us. If we wait until the Germans surrender, the Red Army will take over Elbing and that will be even worse. Our timing has to be precise."

"When the Germans are near collapse, where could we go?" asked Jadwyga.

Antanas sat on the edge of his chair, pulled a piece of paper from his pocket, and drew a map of Germany. He pointed to the southern part of the country. "If Britain, her Commonweath allies, and the U.S. attack from the west and the south, then we need to leave the northeast and flee to the southern part of Germany."

"Maria, you and I have already managed to get some of the privates to have lunch with us and our fellow workers. They like to sing and so does everyone else. It's fun. It helps us forget the bad food and how little of it there is," Jadwyga observed.

"You're onto something. I've noticed a lot of them telling you their life stories. Max Fischer, Lukas Weber, Niklas Wagner, and Hans Muller seem especially open to talking to you," Maria replied.

Jadwyga smiled and added, "Yes, and don't forget the private who likes you."

Maria's cheeks turned crimson. "Who are you talking about?"

"Don't be coy. I'm talking about Private Peter Baur. I see the two of you flirting with each other."

"We aren't flirting."

"Then what would you call it? Maria, I'm not criticizing you. I'm not shaming you. This is a great opportunity. The more he likes you, the more you will learn from him."

Maria hurled a blanket at Jadwyga, but Jadwyga ducked. Both women laughed.

Then Maria cut her laughter short. "One day, we'll know when it's time to escape. We'll run and we'll never look back."

Chapter 21

Building the Pipeline

In May and June of 1944, the BBC had a great deal of hopeful news to report. In late May, they sent a coded message within a poem aimed at the French resistance, alerting them to an imminent Allied invasion.

Elbing Work Camp, April 5–May 20, 1944

The foreign workers' mess hall was built like a low-rise barn. It featured a sloping silver coloured roof and spruce planks painted red. This long structure could comfortably seat 400 people.

There were forty outdoor picnic tables just to the east of the mess hall. At one time, just five tables stood at that site, but Captain Johan Kessel had ordered the carpentry unit to make more. These tables were no works of art, but Jadwyga and Maria loved them.

When Captain Kessel had shared his idea of providing more outside tables with the non-commissioned officers. Corporal Schmidt challenged him, demanding to know why such a project was necessary. Captain Kessel retorted, "With the increased number of foreign workers arriving each day, sooner or later there'll be a riot in the mess hall. Despite staggered eating times, there are 600 foreign workers there at any one time."

Captain Kessel had seen workers get jostled, spilling their food. This was a big problem because there were no refills. Food had become very scarce. He declared, "Workers who lose food become angry and fights break out."

Corporal Schmidt suggested a different solution other than building picnic tables. He sneered and laughed as he asked, "Why cater to these swine? If they want to fight, send them to the hole for a few days. If they still don't behave, shoot them."

Captain Kessel pushed his face up against Corporal Schmidt's and stared him in the eye. "*Nein.* I'm your superior officer. I'm responsible for the physical plant. If I want tables for the workers, there will be tables for the workers. Do I make myself clear, corporal?"

Corporal Schmidt tightened his face and saluted. "Yes, Captain Kessel."

Later that week, Antanas observed Captain Kessel in the mess hall consulting with Captain Edelhoffer, the commanding officer of the kitchen services. Antanas inferred that Kessel had secured Edelhoffer's cooperation. Antanas suspected that the captain hated Nazis—and Corporal Schmidt was a Nazi. He believed that many of Captain Kessel's fellow officers didn't respect the Nazis either, but they were in no position to rebel. *They are in a war with Russia, Britain, and America and they are loyal to the Fatherland.*

The tables were built. The crowded conditions in the workers' mess hall improved, and the slaves enjoyed a bit more freedom and privacy when they ate. *This plays well into the plan hatched by Maria and Jadwyga because it gets them out of range of prying ears,* thought Antanas.

The garage at which Antanas oversaw his crew was on the other side of the camp relative to where Maria and Jadwyga met for lunch. Maria and Jadwyga would skillfully extract information from their lunch mates. Antanas would continue to eat with the mechanics who worked for him. He would also break bread with some of the bus drivers. Occasionally, his commanding officer Captain Ninehaus joined them. The guards rotated positions within the camp, so when a guard was stationed near the garage, that individual often joined the mechanics for meals. Even Captain Daniel Becker, the officer in charge of the bus drivers, dropped by from time to time.

One day, Maria and Jadwyga convinced Tanya Shushekich, Alfred Menthe, and Wladek Szudy to join them at one of the larger outdoor tables.

"None of you has to deal with the Germans as much as I do," complained Maria. "I meet them when they're coming back from work. I meet their wives when they return from the Elbing market.

Some of them say thanks for cleaning their house, but most don't, and a few of them have the nerve to complain that I've not cleaned to their standards. What swine."

Wladek glared at Maria. "Be careful what you say and how loud you say it."

Jadwyga smiled. "Let's not talk about who has the worst job. Let's talk about our homelands and our families."

Tanya sat up straight. "Jadwyga, I told you that the SS killed my parents and my brothers in Belarus, but I didn't tell you the rest of the story. Maybe this isn't what you want to hear?"

"That's okay, Tanya; you're with friends."

"The Germans have no use for Belarusians. They either kill us or drag us off to work camps." Tanya lowered her voice. "I overheard an SS officer in a Minsk bar once. He was talking about something called the General Plan OST."

"What is this plan?" inquired Maria.

"The Germans want the lands in Poland, Ukraine, and Belarus, but they don't want the people living on those lands. This officer was drunk and shared more than he should have. He claimed that the SS would ensure that 80 percent of the Poles and 75 percent of the Ukrainians and the Belarusians would be killed," Tanya reported.

Jadwyga shuddered. "Why so much killing?"

Wladek glimpsed over his shoulder and cast his eyes left and right. He spoke in a hushed tone. "They want the land. Germany is too crowded. They will move Germans into Ukraine and Belarus to farm and create German babies and German cities. They plan to do the same with Poland and even Russia, but this last nut has proved to be too tough to crack."

"Wladek, how do you know all these things?" Tanya probed.

"I just do."

At this point, a whistle blew, signalling the end of their lunch break. Everyone trudged back to his or her respective work station, but Wladek held Jadwyga by the arm and whispered into her ear, "I think that I know what you and Maria are doing, but be careful. You, Maria, and I should meet at one of the outside tables on the west side of the mess hall tomorrow at lunch break."

***

The next day, Maria and Jadwyga were at the appointed spot and at the designated time, but Wladek was not there. "Where is he?" demanded Maria. "If he isn't here in five minutes, I'm moving to the other side with our friends."

Just as Maria said these words, Wladek approached them with George Dyer at his side.

"What's all this mystery about today?" Maria inquired.

Wladek responded, "Maria and Jadwyga, what I'm about to tell you could get us all killed. If you don't want to endanger yourselves, leave now."

Jadwyga and Maria were far too curious to leave.

"Tanya asked me yesterday how I know so much about what the Germans are planning. I couldn't answer her because I don't know her well enough. However, I sense that both of you are gathering information. Am I right?"

"Yes," said Jadwyga with a small laugh.

"It's not funny. If Major Braunshiedel or any of his henchmen suspect what you're doing, they'll interrogate you, and if they don't believe you're being honest, they'll call in the Gestapo."

Jadwyga frowned. "How do you know what the Germans are up to?"

"You answer me first; why are the two of you gathering information?"

"We want to escape," replied Maria. "Before we can make any realistic plans, we need to know where we can run to and when would be the best time. We need to know whom we can trust in the camp and what the guards' routines are."

Maria looked at Wladek with questioning eyes. "What did you want to talk to us about?"

"I've created a simple crystal radio receiver from spare parts that I've collected here in the camp over the past four years. We take it out to one of the storage sheds and listen to broadcasts. I can pick up special radio programs that the BBC sends out to Europe. They have resistance fighters trained to send and receive radio messages. They're in all the occupied countries and even Germany."

Maria was beside herself with joy; she could barely refrain from jumping onto the tabletop and screaming.

Wladek motioned for George to stand beside him. "George is here because he shares the crystal set with me. His first language is German, so he can listen to the BBC programs that are broadcast in German and to the Nazi propaganda radio shows. George is also fluent in English, so he can listen to the English language broadcasts. I listen to the Polish, Belarusian, and Ukrainian programs."

Maria could not suppress her excitement. "What have you learned about the war?"

George fielded her question. "This isn't the time to try to escape. Germany has a grip on Western Europe, except for Sweden, Portugal, Spain, Switzerland, and Great Britain. The Wehrmacht still controls much of Eastern Europe, but they are being pushed out by the Red Army advancing from Russia, Ukraine, and Belarus. Soon the Russians will liberate Lithuania and Poland. The Germans are fighting a tough defensive campaign. They are losing but they have not surrendered yet."

"What about the British?"

"Goering convinced Hitler that he could bomb the British into submission, so between mid-July and November 1940, the Luftwaffe threw everything it had at the Royal Air Force. They tried to blow up and burn as many British planes on the ground or in the air as they could, but the British and their allies flew their Spitfires and Hawker Hurricanes to victory."

"How did the Polish pilots do?" Jadwyga asked.

"They were brilliant. The British acknowledged how skillful, determined, brave, and effective the Polish pilots were. They had battle experience. More importantly, they knew what had happened to their homeland when the Germans conquered it. They hated the Germans."

"What's really happening on the Russian front?" asked Maria.

Wladek answered, "The Russian front has seen the greatest action by far. In 1941, Stalin successfully pulled most of their factories from the western region of Russia and relocated them east of the Ural Mountains. The Wehrmacht sieges of Leningrad, Moscow, and

Stalingrad have all failed. The Germans have been in retreat since 1942. They've fought a brilliant defensive war, but they are vastly outnumbered in terms of men, tanks, artillery, and planes. The Wehrmacht has all but disappeared from the Soviet Union, and now the Red Army is about to liberate the Baltic countries and Poland."

Maria asked, "What about the Americans?"

"The Japanese attacked Pearl Harbor in Hawaii on December 7, 1941. The Americans declared war on the Japanese and within days they declared war on the Germans and the Italians."

Maria raised her arms impatiently. "Okay, Wladek, George—this is all great news, but what does it mean for us poor workers here in the Elbing camp?"

George answered, "It means that now is not the time to attempt an escape unless your goal is suicide. The war will not last forever and the Germans will lose. We just have to get out of northeast Germany before the Germans collapse and the Soviets become the new landlords."

Maria asked, "When do you think we might have a good chance at making a successful escape?"

The whistle blew for them to return to work.

Wladek clenched his jaw. "Maria, your question is both simple and complex. Let's discuss the answer tomorrow."

Chapter 22

A Window on the War

After Hitler attacked the Soviet Union in 1941, Churchill, Roosevelt, and the Polish-in-exile government persuaded Stalin to release Polish military prisoners of war who were being held within the Soviet Union. By 1943, some of these soldiers were assigned to the British army, but most were deployed to fight beside the Soviet Red Army. On May 18, 1944, the Allies pushed the Wehrmacht out of Monte Casino in Italy. The attack was led by General Anders of the Polish II Corps and it resulted in a loss of 20,000 Polish soldiers.

Elbing Work Camp, May 21, 1944

Jadwyga, Maria, Wladek, and George gathered for lunch each day with other workers and with some of the guards. They met every day except Sunday, when the Germans gave them a day off from work. It struck everyone as ironic that the Third Reich gave the workers a day off on the Lord's Day, but no one complained. They laughed and joked and ate the little food they received.

On many days, it was singing that everyone enjoyed the most. Singing was rare among the forced labourers, most of whom were tired, hungry, and depressed. The impromptu songfests owed much to the indomitable spirit of Jadwyga and Maria and the workers whom they claimed as their friends. Marion had a beautiful soprano voice, and the more she sang, the less depressed she felt. Alfred's baritone voice blended beautifully with Marion's. Tanya, Veronica, Maria, and Jadwyga were not professional singers, but they could hold a tune. Pavel had a good bass voice and Natasha was always good for a laugh when a song invited some comic acting. Some of Maria's co-workers filled out the choir. Jurate, Birute, and Agafya were regulars. George and Wladek were not great singers, but Wladek could play the accordion and George was a competent harmonica player. Some of the guards lent them their instruments.

Over time, some guards joined them in their music-making and they were not punished for their participation. Privates Peter Baur, Max Fischer, Hans Muller, Lukas Weber, and Niklas Wagner all attended the singing sessions.

Wladek wondered why the guards were permitted to fraternize with the workers. He assumed that Major Braunshiedel allowed this fraternization for several reasons. Since these sing-song lunches had begun, the overall morale of the workers who participated in them had improved, and so had productivity. The morale of the guards also improved. Wladek sensed that there was an additional reason. Wladek was convinced that at least one of those guards was the major's spy and that this spy reported back to the major on a regular basis.

The core group consisting of Wladek, Maria, Jadwyga, Antanas, and George met every other week on a Sunday. They attended mass each week in the mess hall, which became a Catholic church at 9 a.m. and a Lutheran church at 11 a.m. There was no priest present and therefore no confessions or communion, but a group of Catholics nonetheless met every Sunday morning. They read from the Bible and recited the rosary. The Lutherans met and read from the Bible, and their members took turns giving sermons.

Between the two services, Wladek, George, Maria, Jadwyga, and Antanas met and shared the information they had each gathered about the war. They changed the times of their Sunday meetings to avoid suspicion. There was a great deal of information for the group to share because a crucial turning point in the war was occurring.

It was late May of 1944. Wladek and George were perched on a bench facing Maria, Antanas, and Jadwyga. Wladek welcomed everyone to their meeting and then turned to Jadwyga. "What have you learned?"

"There are many more workers coming to the camp from Poland, Belarus, and Ukraine. German workers are being recruited as soldiers for the Eastern Front at an amazing pace."

Maria was next. "Private Peter Baur told me that some of the Belarusians were imported to build new barracks to keep up with the growing numbers of foreign workers."

Wladek cautioned Maria. "Please don't quote the name of any German source; it could be lethal for your source and for us."

Maria nodded.

"They've built special barracks for us Poles," Wladek explained. "They want to keep us separate and under close supervision. They make us wear these stupid pajama-style uniforms." He pointed to his armband. "We still have to wear a 'P' on our sleeve. I take it as a compliment that they find us Poles to be so dangerous."

George jumped into the discussion. "Since earlier this year, the BBC broadcasts have become more frequent and more encouraging."

Jadwyga spoke next. "Pavel has been talking to some new Russian POWs and he has learned a lot. Events on the Eastern Front have turned out very badly for the Germans. The Red Army is destroying the Wehrmacht."

Maria turned to Wladek. "How is it possible that the Wehrmacht is sending Russian prisoners back to Germany if the Red Army is winning on the Eastern Front?"

"The Soviets are not winning all the battles; the Germans are still making counterattacks and they are still capturing Red Army soldiers."

Antanas added, "There has been an influx of Lithuanian workers into the camp this spring. My mechanics, Jurgis Abraitis and Julius Capas, have spoken to some of them. The Germans wanted them to fight against the Soviets, but they refused, so they sent a bunch of them here to work."

Jadwyga looked at Wladek thoughtfully. "There is something different going on with the Nazis and how they are treating Jews. They have always tried to keep Jews in ghettos, but now they are being much crueler towards them."

"I agree," said Maria. "Our conversations with Marion, Tanya, Natasha, and Pavel are confirming that horrors have been inflicted upon Jews in Ukraine, Belarus, and Russia. They are hearing this from all the new workers from their homelands."

"What are you hearing, Jadwyga?" asked Wladek.

"We keep hearing stories of Jews being killed just for being Jews."

Jadwyga wiped her eyes. "These facts are old, but the Germans kept them secret from those outside of Poland. But recent Polish conscripts are bringing their stories with them. During the 1943 Warsaw ghetto rebellion, the Jewish Combat Organization—the JCO—fought bravely against the Wehrmacht. The SS used flamethrowers to set fire to JCO strongholds, and when the Jewish fighters ran out, the SS troops machine-gunned them. Thousands of JCO fighters died, but tens of thousands of Jewish civilians were slaughtered after the fighting ended."

"What did the Polish Home Army do while this was happening?" Jadwyga asked Wladek.

"They tried to smuggle guns and ammunition into the ghetto, and some Home Army soldiers managed to scale the walls and fight beside the JCO. But most of the soldiers weren't able to get into the ghetto to help. In 1943, they were too few and too inexperienced to be very effective. Much of Poland's former army is either fighting with the British or the Soviets now. The Home Army is younger, fewer in number, less well trained, and not well armed."

Maria interrupted. "One of the new workers assigned to clean the barracks is Jewish and she's from Warsaw. Her name is Sarah Friedman. She witnessed the slaughter of Jews after the defeat of the JCO."

"How did she survive?" George asked.

"One of the SS officers recognized her father, Ralph Friedman. He knew her father to be one of the finest tailors in Warsaw from before the war. They conscripted him to make special uniforms for the Nazi High Command. His wife and son had already been killed in the fighting, but he begged them to spare his daughter and they agreed. They sent her here."

"So, what did she say?"

"She said some Poles tried to help the JCO and the Jewish civilians, but they were beaten back by the SS and the Wehrmacht. Joseph Goebbels duped some of the Poles. He convinced them that many of the Soviet oppressors in Poland had been Jews and that now was the time for Poles to seek their revenge against Polish Jews. Some Poles fell for this lie and joined the SS in killing Jewish citizens."

Wladek exclaimed, "Mother of God! This is a terrible thing for the Jews and the Christians of Poland. May God have mercy on the souls of the dead."

Antanas raised his head and spoke. "It's not only the Poles who have stumbled. When the Germans pushed the Red Army out of Lithuania in 1941, the Provisional Lithuanian Government did horrible things to Lithuanian Jews. They killed them by the thousands."

Wladek asked, "Why?"

Antanas looked down at the ground. "I don't know. At the time, they claimed it was in retaliation for Jewish communists and what they did to Lithuanians when the Red Army was in charge. I doubt that this is the real reason. Most of the Lithuanian communists weren't Jews."

Wladek probed further. "Why, then, do you think this happened?"

Antanas replied, "I think that it was mostly due to fear. The Provisional Government wanted their Nazi masters to see them as allies rather than sending them to concentration camps. Some brave Lithuanians risked their lives hiding their Jewish neighbours in their homes, but most neither harmed the Jews nor helped them."

Chapter 23

Fraternizing with the Enemy?

On June 6, 1944, the Canadian, American, British, Free French, and Free Polish armies invaded Normandy in the largest amphibious military operation in history. In June of 1944, the Red Army liberated Vilnius. Stalin, Roosevelt, and Churchill agreed that the Axis powers were losing the war. What they could not agree on was how to establish boundaries after the war. Stalin wanted Eastern Europe to be under the protection and control of the Soviet Union. Churchill vehemently disagreed. Roosevelt tried to mediate between the two powers.

Elbing Work Camp and Old Town, Elbing, June 1, 1944

Alfred was summoned to join a group of German singers to perform at the concert hall in the Old Town of Elbing. The occasion was ostensibly to celebrate the birthday of Elbing's mayor, but it was really intended as a way to bolster the terrible morale among everyone in the camp and in the town. The audience was composed mostly of the officers and soldiers of the Wehrmacht, the SS, and the Gestapo who were stationed in Elbing. Many of the local business owners and politicians and their families were invited. As one of the star performers, Alfred was permitted to invite four friends of his choosing, and so he approached Jadwyga during lunch time.

"Jadwyga, I have good news. We are performing Handel's Messiah this Sunday, June 4. I know that Easter has passed, but it's a beautiful piece of music and I have four tickets that I want to give to you and Antanas. You can share the other two with your sister-in-law Maria and with Private Baur, the guard who likes her so much."

"Alfred, thank you, thank you so much. Antanas and I will be there for your concert, for sure. Whether it would be safe for Maria to be escorted to the performance by Peter Baur—that is a more difficult decision."

Alfred nodded vigorously. "It was foolish of me to even consider Private Baur and Maria being seen together as a couple in public. It would be far too dangerous. I'll give the fourth ticket to Marion Fedyck. If she were German, she would be part of the opera company; she has a golden voice."

Later that evening, Jadwyga entered their small common room and broke the news to Antanas and Maria.

Maria wanted Private Peter Baur to attend the concert with her; Antanas disagreed. "Little sister, you can't be seen together as a couple at such a public event. It would be suicide for both of you."

Maria stood up and stormed towards her brother. "There are lots of German soldiers who have foreign workers as their girlfriends here in Elbing."

"Not officially."

"What about our mousy Major Braunshiedel? He takes that Gypsy tramp, Magda, to his bed two or three times a week; plus, he has a wife. No one bothers him."

"For one thing, he's a major and not a private. For another thing, he takes Magda to his bed, not to the opera. He takes Frau Braunshiedel to the opera and she pretends not to notice his indiscretions. The Wehrmacht High Command looks the other way when their soldiers have sex with foreign workers, but romances are strongly discouraged. Even sex is *verboten* between Germans and Gypsies, Jews, and Poles."

Maria pressed her index finger to her forehead. "Then what do those genius German generals think Braunshiedel is doing with his Gypsy mistress in his office at night? Reading German literature?"

"They would be more concerned about him teaching her German literature than simply having sex. Also, he passes her off as Yugoslavian and not as a Gypsy. Because he has increased productivity in the camp, his superiors look the other way. You and Peter would not enjoy such good fortune."

"But I love him and he loves me. We've talked of marriage after the war."

Antanas held his sister firmly by her shoulders. "After the war, you can go to a concert together, but not now."

Jadwyga took Maria's hand in hers. "Maria, I see the way the two of you look at each other and sing together. I can't help but see how he holds you and kisses you when he thinks no one is looking. It breaks my heart that you must hide your love."

"Peter's captain has never warned him about us."

Jadwyga gently squeezed Maria's hand. "He probably thinks that Peter is using you."

Maria released Jadwyga's hand and faced Antanas. "We haven't done anything that I'm ashamed of. We won't be intimate until we're married."

Antanas asked, "Are you two engaged?"

"No."

"Why not?"

"We've talked about marriage, but only in general terms. You made it clear that it would be too dangerous to become engaged now."

"Then you admit that it would be problematic for you to be seen as a romantic couple. How about if you go as a couple to an opera attended by hundreds of Wehrmacht soldiers and many of the officers and their wives?"

Maria pounded Antanas on his chest. "You're right, but I hate it! It's not fair. It doesn't make sense."

"What's fair about the Third Reich? If you value his life and your own, you'll be very, very careful."

Jadwyga crossed the living room floor and put her arm around Maria's shoulders. Tears welled up in Maria's blue eyes. "Okay, give Peter's ticket to Marion, but I'll still go to the opera with the two of you. Peter will probably be invited to the concert as well, but he'll sit with the soldiers."

Antanas smiled. "The good news is that we are not likely to be bombed while at the concert. I overheard Captain Ninehaus talking with his friend Captain Becker. It seems that this date was chosen for the concert because Luftwaffe intelligence has it on good authority that Allied bombing will be restricted to France and the Ruhr valley that day. Nobody knows why."

***

On the day of the concert, sunshine splashed down upon the brass railings of the balcony seats. Outside, the concert-goers inhaled the fresh scent of spring flowers and admired the spendour of the maple trees.

The Elbing concert hall could not compete with the opera houses in Munich and Berlin, but it was beautiful and, thus far, it had been untouched by Allied bombing. Its large windows let in light from all directions. Its spacious interior could seat more than 500 people, not the thousands that Berlin and Munich could host. Still, the hall was large enough to accommodate half of the armed forces leaders stationed at Elbing. For security reasons, the other half would not attend the performance. As an added precaution, four extra anti-aircraft guns encircled the building at a radius of one kilometre.

Maria, Jadwyga, Antanas, and Marion sat together in the middle of a side balcony. Although they were not close to the stage, the view was excellent.

Alfred performed with great skill and passion and the opera was a huge success. Jadwyga could not help but notice how moved Marion was each time Alfred sang. Antanas and Maria may not have noticed, but Jadwyga was sure that Marion was in love with Alfred. She wondered if Alfred knew.

June 10, 1944

Peter had invited Maria, Antanas, and Jadwyga to meet in the courtyard behind the garage where Antanas worked. It was 6 p.m. and the mechanics had left for the day. Maria finished her housecleaning duties about 5:30 p.m. Peter had been on guard duty for the morning shift and he entered the courtyard through a side gate.

It was a beautiful June evening with radiant sunshine and hardly a cloud in the sky. Yellow climbing roses clung to a metal fence bordering a small patch of ground on the edge of the gravel yard. Some tiger lilies somehow managed to flourish on the other side of the fence. The courtyard was littered with discarded tires, oil drums, and broken-down vehicles. An old bus had been dumped there for some time, and a broken-down Mercedes-Benz sedan had been stripped for its parts.

The courtyard was both a mess and a delight. It was a great place to visit, catch some fresh air, and escape the noise of the garage. It was also remote and safe from prying eyes, so when Peter told Antanas he had important news, Antanas suggested that they meet there.

Maria entered the courtyard through the back door of the garage. She saw Peter waiting for her and strolled up to him. He placed a tiger lily in her hair and they kissed.

Antanas entered the courtyard through the same door, wiping soap from his hands. When he saw Peter, he greeted him affectionately.

"Where's Jadwyga?" Peter asked Antanas.

"The fewer people we assemble the better, but I know that you two lovebirds want to see each other as often as possible, don't you, little sister?"

Maria jabbed her brother in the ribs and smirked.

"So, what's the news?" Antanas asked Peter eagerly.

"The British, Americans, Canadians, Free French, and Free Poles have successfully landed in Normandy in France. There are a lot of them—hundreds of thousands. They landed on five beaches but they've moved off the beaches and have moved steadily inland. Even General Rommel couldn't stop them."

"What does this mean for us?"

"It means that the Wehrmacht is facing a scenario that no army, no country, wants to face: a war on two fronts."

"How do you know these things?"

"Our cowardly Major Braunshiedel had to get this terrible knowledge out of his head and share it with his captains. I was on my way to our barracks when I heard him yelling at his officers in his office on the second floor. I ducked into the stairway and climbed the stairs, where I met my comrades Hans and Max who were guarding the offices. They were as stunned and curious as I was, so they made no fuss when I crouched down on the top step. We all listened.

"The major sounded like he was about to cry. Then he got angry and he ordered everyone to look harder for spies in the camp. I'm sure that he'd been drinking."

"What does this do for our chances of escape?"

"In the short term, it will be even harder, because the major has doubled the number of guards. Normally the guards patrol the perimeters of the camp every hour on the hour. Now the major has turned some office workers into guards and he's increased the frequency of the patrols to every half hour. I'm certain, though, that after a couple of months he'll miss his paperwork and he'll send those office workers back to their desks and the patrols will go back to normal. For now, however, things will be very tight."

Peter slowly turned to gaze into Maria's eyes. "Maria, we'll have to see less of each other until we observe which way this thing goes."

Maria's eyes flashed. "What do you mean?"

"Major Braunshiedel and his Nazi lackeys will be watching for any hint of espionage. They just might start to see the two of us as spies. It will be too difficult to see each other until their fears are lessened."

"Will you still be able to visit us at our flat in Old Town?"

"Not right away, but Braunshiedel will calm down eventually and then I'll start to visit again. Even Hitler could not keep me away forever."

"What do you think will happen on the battlefields?" asked Antanas.

"Well, as I see it, the Allies could break through on the West, the Red Army could break through on the East, or Jodl and Rommel could drive the Allies back into the Atlantic like the blitzkrieg did in 1940."

"What are the chances of the Wehrmacht pushing back the Red Army?"

"It will never happen. The Wehrmacht is still winning some battles, but the Soviets are winning the war. The Red Army is moving steadily west."

Peter cast his eyes down. "God help Germany and anyone standing next to Germans when the Reds get here."

Maria held Peter's arm. "Surely, they'll not seek revenge upon foreigners like us? We were forced to work for Germany."

Peter shook his head. "They'll seek revenge against everyone."

"What can we do?"

"You must escape as soon as you have a good chance to get away. But now isn't the time. However, you need to start planning your escape. I'll keep you posted on changes involving the guards. Antanas, you'll have to find a truck and diesel from your garage."

"All right," replied Antanas.

"You'll need help getting past the checkpoints without the guards shooting at you. I'll ask my friend Walter Merkel to think of possible travel papers that could explain why you're leaving Elbing. You'll have to tell me your destination point and then we'll dream up a reason for why you need to go there."

Antanas raised his eyebrows. "Can we trust this man?"

"Walter and I grew up in the same village in Bavaria and we've been friends all of our lives. I trust him with my life, and he knows my feelings towards Maria."

Maria laughed. "I've met Walter several times. He's a sweet man and he's completely loyal to Peter."

"What gates are best to use?" Antanas asked.

"Our company guards the south and west gates, so you will need to use one of those. The guards who'll trust you the most and who will help you are Privates Hans Muller, Max Fischer, Lukas Weber, and myself. The ones who will be more suspicious are Corporal Erik Schultz and Private Niklas Wagner. I'll alert you as to when the friendly guards are on duty."

Maria wrung her hands. "So, for now, we just wait?"

Peter reached for Maria and pulled her to his chest. "Yes."

Chapter 24

Mastering the Tango in Elbing

From August 1 to mid-October 1944, the Polish Home Army battled the SS to liberate Warsaw. Meanwhile, a massive Red Army stood idly by at the Vistula River despite desperate cries for help from Polish resistance fighters. The Wehrmacht and the SS outnumbered and outgunned the Polish Home Army and, after sixty-three days, it defeated them. In the aftermath, the SS killed tens of thousands of Warsaw citizens and sent even more to concentration camps or work camps. The Red Army did not attack the Wehrmacht in Warsaw until January 14, 1945, but by January 17, 1945, it had pushed them out of the city.

The Red Army launched Operation Bagration on June 23, 1944; it ended on August 29, 1944. During this period, Belarus and the Baltic countries were liberated from Nazi occupation. In June of 1944, the SS and the Gestapo destroyed what was left of the Jewish Ghetto in Kaunas. They killed 2,500 Jewish men, women, and children and sent another 7,500 to concentration camps. Kaunas was liberated by the Soviets in July of 1944.

Old Town, Elbing, December 24, 1944

At 4 p.m. on Christmas Eve, Maria and Jadwyga were stuffing a goose with bread crumbs. Food was getting more and more scarce, but Antanas had managed to secure a goose for Christmas dinner from his boss.

Suddenly, there was pounding on their door. All three of them froze. Maria crept to the door, her heart thumping. Had the major discovered their spy ring?

When she opened the door, she saw Peter. He laughed and she pushed him playfully in the chest.

"How did you get here so early?"

"I traded shifts with Hans. He's working extra hours for me tonight and I'll do the same for him on New Year's Eve."

"You scared us half to death."

"I know. It seemed like a good joke at the time."

Antanas stepped up and slapped Peter on the back. "You're forgiven; come in and join the table."

Before sitting down, Peter gave Antanas and Jadwyga a gift: a small tin of cigarettes. "I wanted to thank both of you for all that you've done for Maria and me. You've risked your own safety by inviting us to your flat on so many Sundays."

Jadwyga accepted the gift graciously. "We're glad to help you both. Merry Christmas."

Peter then presented a gift to Maria. It was a set of small amber earrings. Maria took them from Peter, smiled, and put them on her ears.

She embraced Peter and kissed him. "These earrings will always make me think of my homeland and of you, Peter. They must have been difficult to find."

"I had to search for them, but I made friends with a jeweller in town and he set them aside for me months ago. I paid him a little every week. Merry Christmas."

"I have something for you too, Peter," Maria said as she opened the box and took out a pair of woollen mittens. She fitted them gently onto Peter's hands. "I knitted you these warm woollen mittens to wear when you're on guard duty."

Peter embraced Maria and gave her a kiss. Maria smiled. "Jadwyga deserves credit, too, because she smuggled the wool out for me in her bra."

Peter grinned. "Jadwyga, I'm shocked. You realize that I'll have to report you to Corporal Schmidt."

"Yes, and he'll be ruthless this time because I'm a repeat offender," Jadwyga replied.

"But you have already been disciplined," Maria commented. "That wool in your bra must have been a cruel and unusual punishment."

They all laughed and again wished each other a Merry Christmas full of good health and hope.

But sadness took hold of Antanas. *When will I see my family again? Is my dog Nero still alive? Has Nero died of a broken heart?*

Sunday dinners were the only times during which the Paskevicius family could eat anywhere but the mess hall. These were cherished moments. After dinner, Jadwyga and Antanas washed the dishes, while Peter and Maria took a walk through the Old Town. They hoped that the darkness and the fact that Peter was not wearing a uniform would conceal his identity. Spending time together in Old Town rather than the camp was safer for them, but it was not a foolproof strategy. They always walked on the dark side of the street, but it still did not give them as much privacy as they desired. In the winter, it was often too cold to walk very far.

As they strolled along the cobblestone road on this Christmas Eve, Peter observed that at this end of Old Town the effects of the Allied bombing were obvious. Although the bombers' primary target had been the industrial part of Elbing, it was clear that British and American bombers had bombed this neighbourhood several times. Many of the houses that they passed were untouched, but other homes had been shattered so badly by bombs that their owners had abandoned them.

Maria squeezed Peter's arm. "How come you're so quiet?"

"I was wondering where the people who used to live in these houses are living now. I was also thinking about our future. I pray that we can share Christmas together again next year."

"I feel the same."

"I'll continue to see you as often as I can, but we'll have to separate soon."

Maria stopped, turned, and held Peter's hands as a look of anguish passed over her face. "Why?"

"Because you, Jadwyga, and your brother must flee, and I won't be able to follow. Once the war is over, if I'm still alive and not mutilated, I'll find you, no matter where you are."

"I love you and I want to be with you."

"I love you, too, Maria. I wanted to ask you to marry me tonight, but the stars are still aligned against us. It would be too dangerous to become engaged now. It would not be fair to you if we promise to wed and then I'm killed or become so mangled that you can't recognize me."

Maria hugged Peter with all her might and then whispered, "How will you find us?"

"I'll find you. Not even Stalin and Hitler combined could stop me."

Peter held Maria in his arms, and they kissed on the street for a dangerously long time.

Chapter 25

Bombs Away

Allied bombing was killing tens of thousands of German citizens as well as conscripted foreign workers. Large industrial centres such as Hamburg, Berlin, and Dresden were levelled by blanket bombing, and medium-sized centres such as Elbing were not spared.

Old Town, Elbing, January 14, 1945

Jadwyga bolted upright in bed. "Mother of God! What was that sound?"

Antanas crawled over Jadwyga to her side of the small bed and stared out the window into the night. He saw flashes of yellow and red followed by ear-splitting explosions. "It must be the British; they're bombing the factories again."

"But it sounds so much closer."

"You're right; they're also targeting the homes in Old Town."

As Antanas spoke these words, a blast of tremendous strength shook the whole house. It threw Jadwyga out of bed and onto the floor. Antanas fell backwards onto the mattress. They heard Maria scream, apparently from the first floor. Antanas rushed downstairs and into Frau Brewer's living room, where he saw Maria sprawled on the couch.

Antanas ran to Maria's side and pulled her to her feet. "Are you okay?"

"I heard the bombing. I came downstairs. Then a bomb exploded, very close. The blast knocked me off balance. I stumbled into the living room and landed on the couch."

Jadwyga raced into the room and peered through the window in the front door. "Look outside. The entire sky is blazing."

Maria joined Jadwyga by the window. Together, they stared at the crimson and yellow horizon. "We've been slaves for the Germans for so long and we've managed to survive—but now the British might be the ones who kill us."

Another blast blew out the glass in both bedroom windows upstairs. They could hear their landlady and her children screaming.

"Antanas, go and comfort them," Jadwyga implored her husband.

"Dear Jadwyga, what can I possibly say to take away their fear?"

"Antanas, just showing them they aren't alone will be enough."

As Antanas started down the hallway towards the Brewer's sleeping quarters, a bomb hit a house close by; the impact was so violent that Antanas hit his head against the wall before landing on the floor.

Jadwyga ran and knelt beside him. "Antanas, are you all right?"

"Yes, I'm okay," he answered weakly.

Frau Brewer staggered into the hallway and knelt by Antanas's side. "No, he's not okay. Look at the huge bump on his head. And he's bleeding."

"Thank you for your concern, Frau Brewer, but I was on my way to help you and your children. I don't need medical aid," insisted Antanas.

Frau Brewer got a wet towel from the bathroom and soaked up the blood on Antanas's face. "You're very kind, Antanas, but we'll manage, as long as those damn Brits don't kill us with one of their bombs."

When the bleeding was under control and his strength had returned, Antanas could not resist stepping outside the front door to survey the damage. He peered to the west, where most of the attack was taking place. He saw flames and smoke, a fog of fire and dust, and people running and stumbling in the street.

Antanas suddenly thought of his mechanics. Their barracks were much closer to the centre of this bombing raid. He turned his gaze towards the downtown area. It was ablaze. The factories and warehouses resembled a giant bonfire.

Antanas could sense the heat from nearby burning buildings. He returned to Frau Brewer's home. Jadwyga and Maria met him just inside the doorway. He shut the door and then his sister interrogated him.

"Are firemen fighting the blaze?"

"I'm sure there are firemen everywhere. I saw a few down at the end of our street. They look to be ill-equipped and exhausted. There are hundreds of women and children and old men in the streets. They look scared, cold, and lost."

Maria opened the front door and stared towards the camp. "Do you think that many Wehrmacht soldiers have been enlisted to fight the blaze?"

"I'm sure that most of them have been ordered to do so."

"So ... Peter may be in danger?"

"Well, he's a brave man; he probably volunteered to help."

"Do you think our work camp was hit?"

"Yes, certainly."

"Then Peter will be fighting fires there. Let's pray for him and for all those who have lost their homes."

January 15, 1945

The camp had been hit hard the night before. Many of the manufacturing sites and warehouses within the camp had sustained significant damage, but the sewing and tailoring shop had been spared. The cleaning depot had not been hit directly, but some buildings bordering it had been destroyed. Peter and the other soldiers fought the various blazes throughout the camp until the flames were finally extinguished by morning. Although exhausted, before he returned to his barracks for some much-needed sleep, he paid a short visit to the cleaning depot to make sure that Maria had survived the bombing the night before. Maria was elated to see that Peter was alive.

January 27, 1945

Maria was surprised to see Peter at the officer's home that she was scheduled to clean that day. He called to her and she dropped her pails, mop, and broom and ran to him. He held her by the arms and spoke softly into her ear. "Maria, Major Braunshiedel is ordering all foreign workers to assemble in the courtyard immediately. Don't delay. He means business."

"Peter, what's this about?"

"It's about Wladek. They found his crystal set hidden in the wall, beside his bunk."

"Is he all right?"

"No, he's in terrible shape. Major Braunshiedel and the Gestapo agent have been torturing him all night."

Maria stumbled and sat down on the steps in front of the cleaning depot. She gulped. "What do they want from him?"

"They want him to confess that the crystal radio set was his. They want to find out what he was using it for and to learn who else was working with him."

Maria's face turned pale. "Do you know what he said?"

Peter lifted Maria to her feet. He spoke slowly. "I was one of the guards assigned to the jailhouse while they performed their butchery. It was the worst thing I've ever had to endure. Even worse than pulling burned bodies out of bombed buildings."

Maria gasped. "What did they do to Wladek?"

"They beat him, they cut him, and they burned him for hours. He screamed, he cried, he begged, but all they could get from him won't endanger any of us. He finally admitted that the crystal set was his and that he was listening to BBC programming, but he denied that he was working with anyone else."

Maria remained silent for a moment and then asked, "Did they believe him?"

"No, but the Gestapo agent was called away to the front and he told the major that he didn't think that Wladek would ever give names and certainly not in a short time. They almost killed him trying to get names. They failed, but now they'll need to make an example of him before he dies."

"What more awful things can they do?"

"That is what they're making everyone gather in the courtyard to watch. The major will accuse Wladek of being a spy and then shoot him. Everyone will see from his wounds that he's been tortured and they'll witness his execution, up close."

Maria closed her eyes tight. "Why are they doing this?"

"Because they're afraid that all the foreign workers will revolt if they think they might escape with their lives. They want to terrify everyone into submission. They feel compelled to uphold the myth of Nazi supremacy."

"What should we do?"

"For now, get over to the courtyard. Don't display any emotion or the major will suspect you of working with Wladek. Then, when this gruesome show is over, go back to work. Tell your brother that security will get tighter for a few days, but then it will likely slacken again. That will be the time for all of you to get the hell out of here."

"Peter, what about you?"

"I'll find you after the war if the Soviets haven't killed me, crippled me, or sent me to a camp."

Maria's eyes widened. "Why don't you escape with us?"

"You know that would be far too dangerous for both of us."

"Peter, you're telling me that if you stay, the Soviets will kill you, and if you try to escape, the Wehrmacht will kill you. I think that escaping is the less dangerous option."

"At least if I stay, I'm only risking *my* life. But if I run away with you three, then I'll risk all of our lives."

Maria shook Peter gently by his shoulders. "You're wrong. If we plan it well, we can all run from here. Will you at least think about what I've asked?"

Peter stroked Maria's face. "Yes, I'll think about it, but that's all I'm promising. Now get over to the courtyard before Major Braunshiedel comes looking for us both."

***

Peter stood on the north side of the courtyard with the guards, while Maria, Antanas, and Jadwyga stood on the south side. There were 300 foreign workers present, twenty heavily armed guards, and four guard dogs. The courtyard was covered in snow. Buildings bordered the courtyard on two sides; on the other two sides lay piles of rubble where the warehouses had once stood, before the bombing raid.

About half the camp was in ruins now. The major factories and warehouses on the west side of town had been turned to ashes. Some of the homes in the Old Town had been destroyed as well.

As they all gathered amidst the scarred landscape, Major Braunshiedel stood in his dress uniform, surrounded by armed guards and vicious dogs.

"You see before you Wladek Szudy. He was a sergeant in the Polish Army, but the Wehrmacht had mercy on him when he was captured. We let him fix shoes instead of killing him. He should have been shot when we captured him in France. Instead, we let him live and he has repaid us with treachery. He's been listening to lies about the war broadcast by the British on their radio programs. We have found a crystal radio set in his possession. He denied at first that it was his, but eventually he confessed."

Jadwyga thought that she was going to vomit. She could see cuts, bruises, and burns on Wladek's face and body. His left eye was swollen shut. Blood was streaming from his mouth and it appeared that he had lost a lot of teeth. He was on his knees in the snow, wearing only pants. He wore no shirt or shoes so everyone could see the Gestapo's handiwork.

Maria leaned into Jadwyga's ear from behind and whispered, "You can't show any emotion. Wladek didn't give names, but the major and his men will be reading faces. Be strong."

The major continued, "This fool claims to have been working on his own, but we know that's a lie. You might think that he's brave for not giving us names, but he's merely stupid. We'll find out eventually. He could have saved himself a lot of pain, and now he'll lose his life." With that, Major Braunshiedel drew his Luger pistol from his holster. He pointed it at Wladek's temple. "One more time I ask you, who else was working with you?"

Wladek screamed out, "Long live Poland!" Major Braunshiedel pulled the trigger and brains, blood, and bone exploded onto the snow.

The major replaced his revolver calmly into its holster. "If you were working with Sergeant Szudy, come forward now and we will be merciful. But if you try to hide, we'll find you and you'll suffer the same fate as this wretched Polack. Now, get back to work."

If the major's intention was to terrify all the foreign workers, he succeeded. If he was hoping to force them into submission, he failed. When Maria, Antanas, and Jadwyga met that night back at their flat, they were shaken to the core. But Antanas and Maria were unanimous in their decision. "We must leave."

"Peter said to forego any escape attempts for a few days because security is at a maximum, but time will wear down the guards' vigilance," Maria stated.

Antanas frowned. "Okay, but we can't delay much longer. The major has gone mad."

Jadwyga reached out to both Antanas and Maria and held hands with them. "Before we go to bed, we need to thank Wladek for enduring such hellish pain to save our lives. Let's pray for him. Let's say the rosary together."

Antanas shook his head. "We need to sleep and then we need to start putting the pieces together for our escape."

"Yes, but before we do that, we need to pray."

"I agree with Jadwyga, big brother; no one is going to sleep right away. We need to thank Wladek and we need to thank God. Let's pray for Peter and George, as well."

"Okay," relented Antanas. "Our Father, who art in heaven...."

Chapter 26

Exodus Part 2

The Red Army entered Germany. The Wehrmacht fought with skill and determination, but their efforts were not enough. The battle for Elbing that had begun in the city's outskirts on January 23 was still raging in February, but now it was much closer to the city.

West and South of Elbing, February 5, 1945, 12:50 a.m.

Maria was still struggling to hold Jadwyga upright in the cab of the truck when the German sergeant approached them. Antanas rolled down the window and the sergeant thrust his head through the opening.

"Where are you going?"

"We're going to Bavaria to prepare for the spring planting. I'm a mechanic. I'll be getting the tractors ready. These women beside me and those in the carriage will be planters."

"Show me your papers."

Antanas complied.

As the corporal checked their forged papers, Maria noticed something. *These soldiers are boys. This sergeant can't be more than fifteen years old. He's blond and still has no beard to shave. The other four soldiers look even younger. Their helmets are too big for them.*

"Your papers seem to be in order, but we have a request."

Antanas swallowed hard. "What is it?"

The sergeant pointed to his men. "The five of us are in the Hitler Youth Eagle Company, Number Eight. With the Red Army pushing into the Fatherland, the Führer mobilized all Hitler Youth companies. The Wehrmacht gave us guns, ammunition, uniforms, helmets, and an armored car."

"Where's your vehicle?" Maria asked.

"It's hard to see in the dark, but it's just about thirty metres behind your truck. You passed it just now. When we saw your truck, we flagged you down. We didn't think you were going to stop, but finally you did. That's good, because if you hadn't pulled over, we would've shot out your tires."

"I didn't see your vehicle, but I'm glad we saw you in time," remarked Antanas, without a hint of a smile.

"We're out of fuel. Can we siphon some diesel from your truck so our armored car can get us to Elbing?"

"Yes, let me help you. Do you have a diesel can?"

"We have two cans of ten litres each."

"Have you ever siphoned diesel before?"

"No, but I've seen Wehrmacht instructors do it."

"Do you want to try?"

"Yes," the sergeant replied as he turned towards two of his privates.

"Eric, bring the cans here. Ludwig, bring the hose."

The two privates fetched the equipment. Maria could not help but notice how afraid the privates appeared.

The sergeant removed the fuel cap from their truck, placed the hose inside the fuel tank, and inserted the other end in his mouth. He sucked hard on the hose and then spat out some diesel. He quickly placed his end of the hose into the fuel can. While he performed these operations, he gasped for air and spat the residual diesel out of his mouth unceremoniously.

Antanas and Maria suppressed laughter.

Antanas told the sergeant, "Don't worry; the first time I siphoned diesel, I swallowed a mouthful. You did well."

The boy-sergeant beamed. "Thank you," he said. He filled the first can to the brim and then repeated the procedure for the second can.

When she was sure that the young soldiers were out of earshot, Maria whispered into Antanas's ear, "Why didn't you show them the spare can of diesel we have in the back of the truck?"

In a muffled voice, Antanas answered, "Two reasons: it has twenty-five litres in it. I was afraid they would take the entire can instead of the twenty litres that they asked for. Also, by getting their sergeant involved in siphoning the diesel fuel, it diverted their attention from examining our cargo of people. It made it less likely that they would interview our passengers and challenge our papers."

"Very smart."

When the sergeant was finished, he thanked Antanas and Maria one more time, but then he paused. "Who is that woman between the two of you, and why is she sleeping so soundly?"

Maria responded with the answer that she had been preparing for the past five minutes. "She's Antanas's wife and she's pregnant. She's in the first trimester and she has been nauseated and vomiting all day. The truck ride didn't make her feel any better, but she finally fell asleep about thirty minutes before you pulled us over."

"Oh, I see," the sergeant replied.

"Please do not wake her," Antanas implored him.

"No, we won't," the sergeant stammered, and then added, "Safe journey, and *Heil Hitler!*" The sergeant and his boy-soldiers all performed the appropriate salute and Antanas and Maria replied with their own "*Heil Hitler,*" but more quietly and without the salute.

Antanas turned on the ignition and they thanked God that the truck's engine started the first time. Antanas slipped the truck into first gear, pulled away slowly, and drove down the road.

After a few minutes, Antanas asked Maria, "Where did you come up with that lie to explain why Jadwyga was unconscious?"

"I thought that the mere mention of morning sickness, nausea, and vomiting would dampen the sergeant's curiosity and end his line of questioning."

"You handled him well."

Just then, Jadwyga awoke and asked, "What did I miss?"

Antanas and Maria both laughed, and over the next ten kilometres Maria described for Jadwyga their interaction with the Hitler youth patrol.

Chapter 27

Feeding the Beast and Feeding Themselves

Despite its mounting losses, the Wehrmacht still fought hard against the advancing Red Army. They were outnumbered five to one in terms of soldiers and six to one in terms of tanks. Most of Elbing's citizens had begun to flee.

Central Germany, February 6, 1945

Antanas stopped the truck beside a field, where he emptied all but one litre of their reserve fuel into the truck's fuel tank. The women and children relieved themselves in the field.

Antanas was pondering their route strategically. He knew that the fastest way would be to take the highway running near Berlin, but he concluded that that would be far too dangerous. Instead, they could take a slower, less efficient route through smaller centres. This would take more time and it would consume more fuel. The fuel gauge had been functioning well in the garage, but now Antanas suspected that it had seized up in the cold at the one-quarter mark.

Jadwyga looked at her husband. "Antanas, you seem worried."

"This is an old truck and we're fully loaded. I knew that it would burn diesel quickly, but this beast is gulping diesel even faster than I estimated. We need to steal some fuel soon. It's 2:15 a.m.; let's keep driving until we find an unattended truck or a farm."

Despite their deep fatigue, Jadwyga and Maria kept watch as Antanas drove. They were travelling through beautiful farmland with rolling hills, but due to the time of day and the cold, they did not see any people, cows, or horses. At 3 a.m., Jadwyga spotted a farm up on a hill to the right. Antanas had to gear down to make the turn, and then he took a run at the incline. As the hill steepened, the tires started to spin in the snow.

"Everybody out of the truck. We have to lighten our load," he called out.

All the passengers climbed out and Antanas backed up to the flat stretch of the long driveway leading to the farmhouse. He shifted into first gear, then second, and then third before the snow and gravity could stop him. The truck began to slow down near the crest of the incline, but it had gathered enough momentum to make it all the way. Antanas drove another twenty metres and parked in front of the farmhouse. Jadwyga and the rest of the group soon caught up with him. The farmhouse sat silhouetted against a dark sky with a few bright stars.

Antanas shouted, "Jadwyga, you and Maria check to see if the farmers still live here. If no one is around, look for food and places to sleep. I'll look for diesel."

The exhausted travellers knocked on the front door but there was no response. It was an old farmhouse constructed of solid pine and cedar shingles. Thirty metres from the house stood a large barn made of spruce. On the near side of the barn was a chicken coop and a wooden shed.

"Where is everyone?" Maria wondered aloud.

Tanya answered. "I think I know where the farmer and his family went. I saw this in Belarus in 1941 when the Wehrmacht and the SS were chasing the Red Army. The Soviet soldiers warned the farmers to run for their lives."

Birute opened the farmhouse door and shouted back to the others. "It looks like this family left just a few hours ago. There are still embers in the pot-bellied stove."

Maria placed her hand up to her ear. "Listen. I can hear the squawking of chickens from that coop over there."

Tanya and Agafya lit the kitchen lantern and ran to the chicken coop. They shrieked in delight. "There are chickens and eggs in here. We can eat."

Veronica yelled through the kitchen window. "I found some rye grain in the pantry. There are candles and candlesticks. We have matches, so we can have some light."

Carola carried Katrina while little Sebastian ran into the yard in front of the farmhouse. "There are apples in the cold cellar," shouted Carola.

Maria lifted the broom she had found and twirled it in the air. "Okay, let's draw straws to see who kills the five chickens and who plucks their feathers. Then we can cook the chickens and their eggs."

They were all cold and terribly hungry. To Jadwyga, this farm seemed like paradise.

Antanas opened the front door and dusted the snow from his boots. "I found a tractor in the barn and I siphoned twenty litres from it. Plus, I found a five-litre fuel can full of diesel. Now we'll have some diesel in the tank plus a few litres in reserve."

Marion swung open the front door and stepped inside. "There's lots of dry wood in that shed over there." Sarah and Johanna raced to the shed and picked up as much wood as they could carry. They promptly brought their treasure into the farmhouse and loaded it into the stoves in the kitchen and living room.

Maria added some kindling and set the wood ablaze. "Our meal is coming soon!" she cried excitedly. "Veronica and Tanya killed the chickens with an axe they found in the barn. Jurate and Birute plucked the feathers."

Maria and Jadwyga did most of the cooking, but everyone did the eating. Little Sebastian devoured his piece of chicken and they all chuckled when he licked his lips in satisfaction. All the women helped to clean up afterwards. Sarah and Jadwyga found bags in the cold cellar. They used them to store what was left of the grain and the apples. Then they stashed the bags in the back of the truck.

Not long after their feast, Antanas and all the women began to yawn. Jadwyga saw that they all felt safe enough to rest, at least for now. Carola, Katrina and Sebastian got to sleep in the farmers' bed and Veronica, the oldest, got to share a bed with Sarah, who was freezing. Birute and Jurate were the next coldest pair, so they got to share the remaining bed.

Jadwyga stood on a chair and addressed the party of refugees: "The rest of us will sleep around the wood-burning stoves in the living room and the kitchen. We'll take turns standing on guard, except for my husband, Antanas. As the driver, he can sleep without interruption. Marion, you can be on first watch."

"Let's pray that the Wehrmacht holds off the Red Army for another week!" shouted Tanya.

"Amen," everyone responded.

Everyone finally got to bed around 6:30 a.m. It was mid-afternoon before the early risers woke up and made breakfast from the remaining eggs and the rye.

By about 6 p.m. they were on the road again. Although it was harder for Antanas to see the road at night, everyone agreed that it was safer to drive during nighttime when there would be fewer Wehrmacht patrols. The night sky was very dark, but a sliver of moon was beginning to appear.

About an hour and a half later, it was snowing hard and Antanas had to stop the truck a few times because some of the snow-covered hills were too difficult to climb. The women took turns wielding the two shovels to clear the snow so the truck could take a run up the hill. For some inclines, one attempt was enough, but sometimes it took two or three attempts. On one try, the truck almost made it to the top of the hill before the tires began to spin and the truck started to slide backwards down the hill. The women and children had already disembarked to lighten the weight of the truck.

"Watch out!" shouted Jadwyga.

Maria, Carola, Katrina and Sebastian, Tanya, and Marion were standing in the direct path of the out-of-control truck.

"Jump!" Maria screamed. Soon all those in the trucks path found themselves up to their shoulders in the snow-filled ditch. Katrina cried but Sebastian thought that jumping into the snow was some kind of game.

Antanas continued to fight with the heavy truck as it slid backwards. He had to correct the steering to counteract the skid, but each time he did so, the truck would skid again. *Get them out of the way*, he pleaded with God. Eventually, the skids grew smaller and Antanas regained control of the vehicle.

Once he had stopped, Jadwyga approached him on the driver's side. "Antanas, rest," she pleaded. "We'll clear the road behind us. That will give you a longer run at the slope."

Jurate and Veronica shouted, "Let's get to it! We can all take turns."

Antanas leaned out the window. "Thanks. You only need to shovel a space on the road half a metre wider than the truck."

Jurate and Veronica started shovelling. It was hard work, as they had to clear a thick layer of snow and a thin layer of ice beneath it. Due to her age, it was not long before Veronica was sweating, despite the cold air and the stiff wind. Then she stumbled and fell face-first into the snow. Tanya rushed to her side.

"You've shovelled long enough; let me take your place."

"I'm okay; I can do it," Veronica replied.

"No, you can't," Tanya said, and she took the shovel from Veronica and started to dig.

Jadwyga stepped in for Jurate. All eleven women took turns employing the two shovels to clear the road. Even Carola shovelled while Jadwyga and Johanna cared for her children. The pace of the work was swift and constant.

After a while, Antanas shouted, "Enough. Let's try again."

He backed up over the newly cleaned, flat stretch of road. He accelerated the truck to maximum speed. As the steepness of the hill increased, the truck began to slow down. Soon the vehicle was doing only fifty, then forty, thirty, twenty, ten, and finally five kilometres per hour. By this time, Antanas was almost at the crest of the hill. The truck began to slide to the right, but Antanas corrected the skid without veering off-track. Sweat broke out on his forehead.

"Look, he's almost reached the top," called out Veronica. All the women shouted in unison, "Keep going." The truck chugged to the summit, and Maria and Jadwyga cried out, "Three cheers for Antanas!"

All the women joined in the cheering and pumped their fists skyward. Then everyone climbed back into the vehicle and they drove down the other side of the hill.

Antanas stared at the fuel gauge and frowned. "The good news is that the fuel gauge is working again. The bad news is that all this driving up snowy hills is burning diesel at a fast rate. We are one-quarter full and the last time I added fuel from the reserves, there were only two litres left in the can."

"Well, husband, we have no choice. Stop and add the last of the diesel. But if you look to the southeast, you can see some light on the clouds. Maybe there's a village or a town on the other side of those hills."

"I hope you're right. Keep praying."

When they reached the top of the third hill, they saw the lights of a town. It was named Prenzlau. *This town had better have some diesel*, thought Antanas grimly. It was almost 4 a.m.—a good time to siphon diesel. As they drove slowly down the main street of the town, Jadwyga spotted a truck in an alley parked behind a store. Antanas turned and coasted towards the truck.

"Damn! I can't get the trucks close enough to each other. The hose isn't long enough. I'll have to be content with filling the reserve tank."

Antanas stopped the truck and everyone got out. Then he walked over to Jadwyga and Maria and said, "Please take care of Carola's infant and her son."

Carola overheard Antanas's request and asked, "Why should your wife and sister look after Katrina and Sebastian?"

"Because I need you and your friend Johanna to act as lookouts in case any Wehrmacht soldiers or the owner of the truck appear. Maria and Jadwyga speak excellent German, but German is your mother tongue and you have no accent. We'll need a perfect diversion if someone shows up in the alley."

"What should we say?"

"Flirt with them. Be shameless. Your lives, our lives, and the lives of your children will depend on it."

"Okay. Come on, Johanna, let's get over there and keep watch where the main street meets this alley."

Johanna followed Carola to the lookout spot.

Antanas walked around to the back of the truck and pulled out the twenty-five-litre fuel can and the rubber hose. He walked down the dimly lit lane, followed by Maria. They stopped behind a two-story red brick building.

Maria sniffed the air. "Hurry, brother. If this is a bakery, then the bakers will be here in less than an hour to begin their day."

Antanas nodded and removed the fuel cap from the truck, placed the hose into the fuel pipe, and sucked strongly on the other end of the hose. The truck was an old Fiat. The fact that it was a Fiat seemed strange for a German town, but it reminded Antanas of his old car, Zabka. *I wonder how Zabka's doing. I wonder if Dad managed to keep her out of the hands of the Germans. I hope that Mom and Dad and the family are still alive.*

"Antanas, what are you staring at? This is no time for daydreaming," said Maria.

Antanas ordered. "Bring Carola and Johanna back here and let's get rolling. Tanya, help me drag this fuel can to our truck and then help me pour the contents into the tank."

"*Jawhol, Mein Capitain,*" laughed Tanya. Together, they hauled the fuel can to their truck and filled the tank.

Everyone boarded the truck and they drove stealthily down the main street and back onto the road heading south long before the sun rose.

Birute sat beside Tanya and Marion in the carriage of the truck. "While you were busy stealing diesel from that bakery truck, I looked in the back of it. I found ten stale loaves of bread." She opened the bag and began to share the bread with everyone.

"Be sure to save some for Antanas, Jadwyga, and Maria," Tanya reminded her.

"Don't worry; I won't forget our fearless leaders."

Everyone laughed so hard that Antanas, Maria, and Jadwyga could hear them up front in the cab. "What's so funny back there?" Maria wondered aloud.

"Who knows?" Antanas replied. "At least they're happy."

After another hour of driving, a howling snowstorm surrounded them. After battling the storm for another hour, Antanas pulled off the road as far as he dared. Steep ditches bordering the road could easily trap the truck.

"We'll have to sleep in the truck," Antanas told everyone. "It's too dangerous to drive any farther tonight."

Birute reached into her bag and pulled out one of the stale loaves of bread. She handed it to Antanas. "Here's your share of the bread that I liberated. Share it with your sister and your wife. We still have some in reserve."

Sarah had started to shiver violently.

"It's freezing in here and Sarah could go into shock," Tanya warned.

"Sarah needs special attention," responded Antanas.

"Let's eat half of our bread now and then sleep," Veronica said to Tanya.

Veronica and Tanya pulled out the blankets that Peter Baur had stolen from the Wehrmacht. She spread them over all the travellers. They placed Sarah between Marion and Birute to give her extra warmth. At around 7:30 a.m., they all fell asleep.

***

When they awoke, it was 3 p.m. The sun was shining and the sky was clear. The temperature had risen to zero and Maria, Jadwyga, and Antanas felt much warmer. The sun was bestowing heat upon them through the windows of the truck. The others in the back of the truck did not benefit as much from the sunshine. However, because they had absorbed one another's body heat, no one had frozen to death in the night.

Marion sat up and stretched. "Let's have breakfast. We can eat the remaining loaves." No one disagreed with her suggestion and Veronica began to break up four loaves of bread and divide them up among the passengers. She kept one loaf in reserve.

Jurate grimaced. "These loaves are as hard as rock and tasteless."

"I'm surprised you're complaining," Maria jested. "This is the same delicious bread they fed us in the camp at Elbing for the past year. It's half rye and half sawdust."

"Everyone had enough?" asked Antanas.

Johanna held up the small bags of apples and grain. "No, but we had better save the rest of this food."

Antanas pointed to the field bordering the road. "Everyone goes to the toilet in the snow by the road. I promise not to look. Then we'll get back on the road. It's almost 4 p.m."

They experienced good travelling time, but their fuel began to run low again. Towards 6:30 p.m., Antanas calculated that they were about 110 kilometres to the northeast of Brunswick. That meant that they were about 600 kilometres from Nuremburg in Bavaria.

Antanas confided his concerns to Maria and Jadwyga. "We don't have enough fuel to make it to Brunswick. We have to steal some fuel—and soon."

At about 7 p.m., Jadwyga spotted a Wehrmacht truck parked outside an inn located just off the road.

Antanas slowly braked, pulled into the driveway, and coasted up behind the Wehrmacht vehicle. "Carola and Johanna, I need you both to go into the inn and find out if there are any soldiers around. Be creative, but please be careful."

Carola and Johanna jumped out of the truck, crossed the snow-covered parking lot, walked up the stairs, and entered the old building. The exterior of the inn resembled a ski chalet, but it was in disrepair. Inside was a small foyer that smelled of cedar. There was a fireplace to the left of the desk.

"How much are your rooms?" Carola inquired.

"More than you can afford from the look of you," answered the blonde middle-aged woman sitting behind the desk. "We have only five large bedrooms and they're full of sleeping soldiers right now. They've been driving for hours. They came from Bavaria. When they wake up, they'll be heading for the Oden River. They've been sleeping for six hours but I don't have the heart to wake them."

"Let our fine soldiers sleep because soon they may be sleeping forever," said Carola sombrely.

"Don't say that. These are our boys; pray that they save us from the Red Army."

"My sister, we join you in that prayer."

Johanna and Carola returned to Antanas and reported their findings.

Antanas removed his hat and ran his hands over his bald head. "If we get caught stealing diesel from their truck, they'll kill us; but if we don't, we'll run out of fuel again very soon and we'll freeze to death…. So let's do it."

Antanas pulled the truck up beside the Wehrmacht truck and connected the hose between the fuel intake pipes of both trucks.

"Johanna and Carola, go keep a lookout."

"*Jawhol, Mein Capitain,*" they replied with a smile. They stood on the steps of the inn watching out for any Wehrmacht soldiers who might have awakened from their slumber.

Wasting no time, Antanas almost drained the Wehrmacht truck of fuel. "Johanna, Carola, get in the truck; we're pulling out of here— now!"

They got back on the road and headed southwest.

"Those soldiers won't get far on the fuel you left them, Antanas," Jadwyga laughed.

"No, they won't drive many kilometres on fumes, but maybe we saved their lives. Only death will await them at the Oden River."

Chapter 28

The Road Gets Tougher

Joseph Stalin, Franklin Roosevelt, and Winston Churchill met at Yalta, a town on the Black Sea, from February 4 to 11, 1945. Their objective was to restore Europe to long-term peace once the war was over. Roosevelt and Churchill advocated that the Nazi-occupied countries be re-established as free and independent nations. Stalin demanded a Soviet political influence in Eastern Europe. Given that the Red Army had three times more military power than the combined strength of Britain and the United States in continental Europe, Stalin got what he wanted.

North of Erfurt, Germany, February 7, 1945

Antanas covered over 250 kilometres after heisting fuel from the Wehrmacht truck. They saw no abandoned trucks or cars over all that distance and the fuel metre was soon at empty again. The truck rumbled on for a few more kilometres. It sputtered, and then the engine died. Antanas steered the coasting truck onto the shoulder of the road, where it came to a full stop. It was just after 2 a.m. and the temperature had dropped to minus twenty degrees Celsius.

Maria, Jadwyga, and Antanas shared a blanket in the cab while the rest of the women and children in the back of the truck pulled out the blankets and huddled together for warmth. Jadwyga looked back at them through the window that joined the cab to the carriage. She could see their breath forming little clouds in the frigid air. *I wonder how long they can survive in this cold without food?*

After a fitful sleep lasting five hours, Maria spotted a man leading two plough horses down the road. She shook Antanas gently and he opened his eyes. "What is it?"

Maria pointed down the road. "Look, brother, there's a man leading horses in our direction." Antanas jumped out of the truck and walked towards the man. He spoke with the stranger for a few minutes and then he pointed at Jadwyga. He motioned to her. She ran up the road to join them and Antanas introduced the man, Jan, to his wife. Jan told them that he was originally from Krakow and that he had been working for a local German farmer for the past three years. "The farmer I work for lives five kilometres to the northeast, but the town of Erfurt is very close to our village. My master, Herr Bachman, will be angry with me for returning the horses late, but I'll let you use them to tow your truck to the next farmhouse. You can take shelter there. It's just over that hill, less than a third of a kilometre from here."

Antanas gathered the thick ropes he had packed from his garage along with the blankets from the back of the truck. Antanas and Jan fashioned the ropes and blankets into harnesses for each of the horses. The blankets prevented the ropes from cutting into their flesh. Jan introduced his equine friends as Max and Eva.

"Max is the beautiful black Clydesdale. He's in the prime of his life."

Jadwyga was impressed that Max's shoulders were taller than Antanas's full height.

"Eva is a chestnut-brown mare. She's shorter than Max but she's almost as strong as he is. These are two fine horses, but they will need help towing this truck up that hill. It's a gradual incline, but it's still a hill."

"Don't worry," Antanas replied. "Our crew has experience pushing this beast." Antanas gestured towards the passengers in the truck. "I'll steer while the rest of you push the truck from the sides and from behind. Jan will guide Max and Eva and they'll pull from the front. When we get to the top of the hill, we'll untie the horses and I'll use gravity and the brakes to coast down to the farmhouse."

All these people and horses labouring together made Jadwyga think of Egyptian slaves building the pyramids. The horses were strikingly impressive as they strained against the ropes. Despite the cold, their sleek bodies became drenched with sweat.

When the truck reached the flat summit of the hill, Jan yelled, "Max and Eva, halt!" The horses obeyed. Jan and Antanas removed the ropes that harnessed them and Antanas hopped back into the truck. Except for Carola and the children, everyone pushed the truck along the flat crest of the hill until it started to coast downwards towards Erfurt.

Maria, Jadwyga, and Jan accompanied Max and Eva down the hill. Maria expressed surprise that the hill was so much longer on the descent, but Jan explained. "The farmhouse that you're heading towards is in a valley. Aren't you glad that you're going down and not up this part of the slope?" Jadwyga and Maria both agreed with Jan.

"Where, exactly, is my brother headed?"

"I told him to pull into the driveway of that big house over there with the red roof."

Maria raised her eyebrows in disbelief. "Do you think that he can coast into that driveway? It's long and it's uphill."

"Well, it depends on how good a driver your brother is on a snowy road. He has to go fast enough to coast up the incline of the driveway, but not so fast that he flips the truck as he turns off the road."

Maria grinned confidently. "He can do it."

Antanas glided down the hill, then used his brakes to reduce his speed. He released the brakes and turned right into the driveway. The truck's back wheels began to slide to the left and towards a snowbank. Antanas turned the front wheels to the left and he straightened the truck out as it rolled up the driveway. The truck had almost reached the house when Antanas pumped the brakes and came to a full stop.

Maria and Marion opened the front door of the two-story brick farmhouse and stepped inside. The rest followed. After a brief search, they concluded that this large home had been abandoned.

The house had a spacious living room with a comfortable couch and two plush chairs. It had two lamps, an overhead fixture, and a long table in the centre of the room. Along the back wall was a large brown piano with a bench. In the far corner, a pot-bellied stove still had streaks of ashes on its door handle. Except for the voices of the women and the children, the building was silent.

Maria asked Jan, "Have the owners fled?"

"Yes. This was the home of the burgermeister of this village, but he and his family bolted southwest to stay well ahead of the Reds."

"And what about the rest of the village?"

Jan smirked. "When the villagers saw their cowardly burgermeister and his family run away, they did the same thing. Not many people are left, except for my master, Herr Max Bachman. He's a wealthy farmer who has done well by the Nazis and he has some crazy loyalty to them. He and Hitler must be the only ones in all of Germany who don't know that the war is over for the Third Reich."

"What are you going to do?" Jadwyga asked gently.

"Don't worry about me. As soon as I hear the Reds coming, I'll saddle up Max and Eva and we'll escape through the forest trails to a safe village. Herr Bachman can fight the Red Army without my help."

It was late morning and everyone was very hungry, so they all searched the farmhouse for food. In the house, they located cabbages, carrots, beets, and cheese.

About five minutes later, Jurate and Birute came running into the kitchen screaming, "Eureka! We found a treasure trove. You should see the wine cellar this fat burgermeister left us. We'll drink well today." They all ate and drank and by mid-afternoon most of the group were overcome with drowsiness.

Maria stood on the piano bench in the living room and announced, "Carola—you, Katrina, and Sebastian get the burgermeister's bed." The other women huddled together waiting to hear their assigned sleeping arrangements. "Veronica and Sarah, you two are the most exhausted, so you get to share the children's bed."

Jadwyga stepped up onto the piano bench beside Maria. "Marion and Tanya, you haven't slept in a real bed since we left the camp, so you get the last bed."

Maria jumped down from the bench. "Agafya, you haven't slept well since we left camp, so you get the couch. The rest of us will sleep on the floor here in the living room. There are some blankets in the hope chest that we can add to those in the truck. Share them as best you can."

February 7, 1945, 7 p.m.

It was dark when they heard the Wehrmacht soldiers barge into the house. The soldiers were dirty and shivering and their eyes were bloodshot. Two of them pointed their machine guns at the sleepers on the floor, while their sergeant aimed his pistol at Antanas.

The sergeant waved his gun. "Who's the driver of the truck?"

Antanas slowly rose to his feet. He raised his arms above his head. "I am."

The sergeant was a tall man and when he walked up to Antanas he towered over him. But Antanas held his ground and stared the young man in the face. "What do you want?"

"Our general's car slid off the road into the ditch and you will tow his vehicle out of it."

Antanas walked past the two machine gunners and stared out the window towards the road. "We can't help you unless you can bring us some diesel. We're bone dry."

"Stay here; we'll be back within the hour."

The sergeant and his men were true to their word. They returned with a can holding five litres of diesel. The privates went out to the truck and poured the diesel into the fuel tank. Then the sergeant barked an order: "It's time to go."

Maria and Jadwyga rounded up all the women and children and helped them to board the truck. The sergeant and the privates stood on the running boards of the truck and grasped the tarp for dear life.

Antanas drove slowly. In ten minutes, he spotted the general's armoured car in the ditch. He slowed to a halt. The Wehrmacht soldiers jumped off the truck and the sergeant ordered Antanas to get out.

Antanas positioned the truck to face the military car stuck in the ditch. Maria and Jadwyga helped the women and children to disembark. Antanas gathered the ropes and threw them at two of the privates. "Tie them to the chassis of your officer's car and I'll tie my ends to the undercarriage of the truck." The soldiers did as they were told and, after securing the ropes, Antanas got back into the cab and started the engine. He put the truck into reverse and, as he backed up, he could see the black sedan starting to rise out of the ditch. Snow slid off the roof and the hood and soon the car was back on the road. Now that they had liberated the general's car, Antanas wondered what the soldiers would do with them and their truck. The general was nowhere to be seen, but Antanas concluded that he was probably in a warm bed in Erfurt.

The sergeant ordered the women and children back into the truck. He motioned to Antanas and one of the privates to climb onto the side of the truck and to hold onto whatever they could to keep from falling off. He told the other private to drive the truck while he got into the general's car. He turned the ignition and, miraculously, the car started, and he headed the newly rescued vehicle towards Erfurt. The private and the truck and its occupants followed closely behind, making a small but interesting convoy as they drove into town.

It was almost 11 p.m. when they rolled into Erfurt. The sergeant drove the general's car up behind a grey one-story warehouse. The private stopped the truck just behind the car. The sergeant exited the sedan and marched to the back of the truck, peered inside, and ordered everyone out. After helping Carola, Katrina, and Sebastian from the truck, he asked, "Why are you travelling with your children? The weather is terrible and the roads are dangerous."

"Because we fear the Red Army. We're heading for Bavaria."

"Do you have business there?"

"We're crop planters and Antanas is a tractor mechanic."

"We need this truck for our own purposes. If we can't stop the Red Army, then the spring crop will be their problem," said the sergeant.

The sergeant could not detect an accent when Carola spoke, yet he asked her, "Are you German?"

She shifted her infant Katrina in her arms. "Yes, I am."

"What about the rest?"

Carola pointed to her friend Johanna and said, "She's my friend and she's German."

"And the rest?"

"They are my friends, too, and they have risked their lives to protect Johanna, my children, and me."

"That's not my question. Are they German?"

"No, they're not. They are foreign workers who were stationed in our town, Elbing."

"Come with me. I'll wake the burgermeister of Erfurt and he'll find you some families that will take you into their homes."

Carola put her face right up against the sergeant's. "What will happen to my fellow refugees?"

The sergeant scowled. "I don't care. You can save yourself, your children, and your friend and come with me, or you can stay here with your foreign friends and freeze to death. You decide."

Carola motioned to Johanna to join her and she took Sebastian by the hand.

The sergeant helped Carola, Johanna, Katrina, and Sebastian into the general's car. He ordered the privates to load their suitcases as well. Then the sergeant pulled away and pointed the sedan towards the main street. Carola looked down from her seat in the car as they drove past Maria and Jadwyga in the courtyard.

Maria shouted, "Traitors!"

Jadwyga whispered, "Don't be so quick to judge. Her children wouldn't last long in this bitter cold."

Maria spat on the ground.

After their sergeant drove off, the two privates looked confused. Antanas strode up to them with his breath flaring from his nostrils. "Where are these women and I going to sleep and stay warm?"

A walkie-talkie crackled in the hands of the taller private. He looked at his comrade. "It's our sergeant. He wants us to drop the truck off at the garage. He wants us to do it right now."

"What about us?" Antanas repeated.

"What about you? You can all go to hell as far as we're concerned. Get moving." Having delivered this command, the private shot two rounds from his machine gun into the air. He aimed over the heads of Antanas and the remaining women. They all fell to the ground, then picked themselves up and ran down the street. Once they were out of sight, they ducked into an alley. Everyone was panting. Veronica looked pale and could not catch her breath.

As their breathing slowed, they heard the truck pulling away. "Bastards!" shrieked Maria. "They took the truck and all our belongings. The only ones they cared about were their fellow Germans."

Jadwyga stepped out of the alley and peered down the road. "Look, Maria, I think they dumped our stuff onto the street."

They all hiked back to where the truck had been parked. There, they found their luggage tossed into the snow. "Maybe they're not as bad as you thought, Maria?"

"Not much better. Without shelter, we'll freeze to death. Veronica can't stop shivering and coughing."

Antanas stepped into the middle of the street and spoke in a trembling voice. "This is the end of the line for us as a group. It's too far and too cold to walk back to the farmhouse. If we're going to survive in this town, we'll have to split up and go door to door begging for food and shelter."

"Brother, do you think these German townspeople are going to open their doors to foreign workers in the wee hours of this frigid morning?"

Antanas took hold of his sister's shoulders. "We have to have faith. What choice do we have? If we stay outside, we'll freeze."

"Most of them will pretend not to hear or see us, but some might have pity," Jadwyga said.

"If we are to have any chance of finding shelter, we have to split up into small groups. We'd have much better odds of being allowed into these homes if we're in groups of twos or threes. No one will welcome ten of us into their home," Antanas pointed out.

Sarah stepped forward. "I'll go with Veronica. I pray that they'll see how cold she is and show us some mercy." Veronica said nothing as she continued to shiver.

Jurate and Birute locked arms and Jurate said, "We've been friends since we were three years old, so we'll stick together."

Tanya took Marion by the arm. "Well, my Ukrainian friend, do you want to start scrounging with me?"

"What about me?" implored Agafya.

Tanya took Agafya by the hand. "Well, you may be a Russian, but you're still our friend. Marion, shall we let her beg with us?"

Marion lowered her hands and held them together with the palms facing upwards. "Yes, my Belarusian friend; let's join our Russian comrade and start to beg."

"Antanas, Maria, and I will stay as a team of three," Jadwyga announced. "We'll miss you. May God be with all of you." Jadwyga solemnly bade farewell to all the women, one after the other.

Antanas began to walk down the street carrying his one piece of luggage. He turned and waved at his former passengers and friends. Jadwyga and Maria pulled their bags with the ropes that were still attached to them. When they caught up to Antanas, they divided themselves up and each one knocked on the front door of a different house.

Each of them moved down the street three houses at a time, so that they did not double up or triple up on the same house. They knocked on doors from around 11:30 p.m. until close to 2 a.m. By this time, Maria was shivering uncontrollably and she had begun to cough violently. They stood huddled together on the same porch to give each other warmth.

Antanas pounded harder on the door facing him than he had any other. To their amazement, they heard someone rustling inside and a light came on in the hallway. The door opened a crack, but the latch was held firmly in place. They could see the outline of an older woman through the opening. She had grey hair, a wrinkled face, and bright blue eyes. She was short and slim and she was wearing a coat over her nightgown. "What do you want?"

Antanas answered, "We're running from the Red Army. The Wehrmacht took our truck and dumped us into the street. My sister and wife are freezing. Please take us in or we'll die."

The woman hesitated, and then stammered, "I'm alone here; I can't take such a chance." Maria turned her back and began to descend the stairs. As she did, she started to cough. Her body shook from the coughing and her shivering grew worse. Jadwyga held her and rubbed her back. To their astonishment, the woman fumbled with the latch and opened the door. "Come in before you all freeze to death," she said.

"Thank you, thank you!" exclaimed Jadwyga. She knew that they would have collapsed in the cold and died were it not for this woman's compassion. Once inside the house, Jadwyga detected a pungent combination of mould, wood smoke, and dust in the air. *I wonder where her family is? Maybe she needs us as much as we need her?*

"My name is Helga Hartmann and I don't have much, but I'll share what I do have with you."

Antanas held up her right hand and kissed it. "You've saved us from freezing to death and we don't want to bring you any harm."

"You remind me of my sons, Horst and Kurt. They're gentlemen, too," Helga beamed.

"Where are they?"

The woman's blue eyes became teary. "Horst was killed in Ukraine in 1941 and Kurt's still fighting the Red Army."

Jadwyga touched her shoulder. "We'll keep him in our thoughts and prayers."

The woman nodded. "Young man, you can have Horst's old room. It's up the stairs and to the left. You two young women can sleep in Kurt's room to the right of the stairs."

Jadwyga took Frau Hartmann's hand into her own. "Thank you. I'm Jadwyga and this is my husband Antanas and his sister, Maria."

"Sleep well."

Antanas slept for twelve hours and did not awaken until almost 3 p.m. The smell of a wood stove, oatmeal, and tea enticed him out of bed. Maria arrived not long after him in the kitchen.

"How was your sleep?" Frau Hartmann inquired.

Maria beamed at her. "It was wonderful."

Antanas stretched his arms. "My sleep was so good that now I can take on the world again."

"Where's Jadwyga?"

"She was still sleeping soundly when I awoke," Maria answered.

Frau Hartmann stirred the oatmeal and then asked Maria, "Can you stir this pot while I go upstairs to check on your sister-in-law? Antanas, can you go into the back yard and bring in some wood from the shed?"

"Yes," replied the Paskevicius siblings.

Frau Hartmann lumbered up the wooden stairs. When she reached the bed where Jadwyga and Maria had spent the night, she saw Jadwyga curled up in her sheets and blanket.

She whispered, "Jadwyga, it's time to eat."

Jadwyga did not stir.

Then Frau Hartmann repeated her words more loudly. She tried a third time. *She doesn't seem to be breathing.* She put her hand on Jadwyga's forehead and gasped. *Her head is cold. Maybe she's ill. Is she dead?*

"Oh, my God! Antanas, come here right away." Frau Hartmann shouted.

Just at that moment, Antanas had stepped into the back room carrying two armfuls of cut maple wood. He had set the wood onto the floor in the kitchen and was dusting off the snow when he heard Frau Hartmann cry out for him. He sprinted up the ten steps in three bounds.

Frau Hartmann met him at the bedroom door. "Please check her breathing. I'm not sure if she's sleeping or dead."

Antanas placed his hand by Jadwyga's nose and mouth and felt her breath. Then he swept Jadwyga up into his arms and started to dance while singing the German song, "Underneath the Lamp Light." Jadwyga woke up and smiled until she saw Frau Hartmann standing in the doorway.

"Put me down, silly man." Jadwyga shrieked.

Relieved, Frau Hartmann laughed and said, "Breakfast is ready."

At the kitchen table, everyone kidded Jadwyga about sleeping like the dead. In time, however, the mood became more sombre. Antanas asked how far away the railroad station was. Frau Hartmann gave him directions.

"What's happening at the station?" Maria asked.

Frau Hartmann placed both her hands on the table. "The citizens of Erfurt are terrified that the Wehrmacht will collapse and that the Russian bear will seek his revenge. Many people are trying to get out of here and are heading to Bavaria, Rhineland, or Stuttgart."

"How are they travelling?" Maria queried.

"Any way they can. Some by car or truck; some by walking; even more are boarding the trains. Most people can't afford to leave by any means whatsoever. Still, the train station was overwhelmed with people yesterday. My neighbours were disgusted by all the pushing and shoving they saw at the station."

Frau Hartmann shook her head. "This isn't the Germany that I've known."

Jadwyga held Frau Hartmann's hand. "When is the last train going south?"

Frau Hartmann shrugged but offered a guess. "I think about 8 p.m.? You'd better hurry because the train will be packed hours before it leaves the station."

Antanas stood up from the table. "Maria and Jadwyga, please gather your things; we're heading for the train."

Luggage in hand, Maria and Jadwyga approached Frau Hartmann. "We wish safety and health for you and your son."

Antanas put on his coat and slung his bag over his shoulder. "Thank you, Frau Hartmann, for shelter from the cold."

Frau Hartmann could not speak but she smiled at her guests and waved farewell.

Chapter 29

All Aboard

By January 25, 1945, it was clear that the Wehrmacht's Operation Nordwind had failed. This was the final major German offensive on the Western Front. Hitler and his mistress Eva Braun ensconced themselves in their Berlin bunker. Hitler ordered his generals not to retreat on any front without his personal approval, and never to surrender. Morale was crumbling in the German armed forces and fear mounted among German civilians.

Erfurt Railroad Station, February 8, 1945, 5:30 p.m.

The train station was even more chaotic and violent than Frau Hartmann had described it. Men were fighting with one another, and women were struggling to protect their children from the surging crowd. The station smelled like an unholy blend of sweat, urine, blood, fecal matter, and smoke. To Jadwyga, the Wehrmacht soldiers appeared confused, exhausted, and terrified.

Antanas stood behind a tree on the outskirts of the station and dug into his bag. He pulled out a tightly wrapped handkerchief. Inside the handkerchief, he had stashed about 200 cigarettes. These were infinitely more valuable on the black market compared to the official German currency. The Reichsmark had lost 80 percent of its value over the past year. He took out the cigarettes and divided them into ten smaller napkins holding twenty cigarettes each. He tied up the napkins, put them back in his satchel, and then walked towards the caboose of the train. He got to within three metres of the car when a burly soldier pointed his rifle at him.

"Halt!"

"I have something for you," said Antanas.

"What could you have that I would want?"

Antanas knelt down and opened two of the napkins. "These."

The private relaxed and smiled. "What do you want?"

"Where is this train going?"

"Nuremburg."

Antanas glanced at his new friend. "There are forty cigarettes here. Find another soldier to help you get us onto this caboose and I'll give you these forty cigarettes plus another forty for your comrade."

The private stared at the ground. "Forty cigarettes each?"

"Yes, forty each."

"Wait here," the private ordered.

The soldier soon returned with an older man, a corporal.

"Do you have tickets?"

Antanas did not see them approach, but Maria and Jadwyga were standing right behind him. Maria stepped up to the corporal. "No, but we have cigarettes for you and your friend. Just think what you could buy your wife or girlfriend with these."

The corporal's eyes bored into Maria's. "Have you seen how angry this crowd is?"

Jadwyga lightly touched his arm and Maria stepped back. Jadwyga looked the corporal in the eye and said, "Think how happy your sweetheart will be if you do this for her. If she knows how much danger you faced for her, just imagine how grateful she'll be."

"Okay, private, we let them in but not through the door," the corporal commanded. "Go into the caboose and open two windows on the opposite side of the crowd. You three follow him and push your luggage through the open windows, then climb in yourselves."

"Thank you," said Jadwyga.

The corporal waited for the private to exit the caboose and then they both stood guard by the door while Antanas, Jadwyga, and Maria approached the side of the caboose where the crowd was not permitted. After a few minutes, the corporal left the private to stand guard while he went to collect his reward. He saw Jadwyga, Maria, and Antanas inside the caboose. They placed their things up on the luggage rack and then flopped into their seats. He poked his head through the open window and growled, "Where is our payment?"

Antanas walked over to the window and handed the soldier four napkins. "Open them and count them. You'll find forty cigarettes for each of you."

"Make sure you have some cigarettes for the conductor, or he'll throw all of you off the train."

"Don't worry; I have a reward for him too."

For the next two hours, the three refugees tried to stay calm while the surging crowd yelled and screamed at the corporal and the private as they guarded the train. "How did they get into the caboose? Are they Hitler's pets?"

Undeterred, the corporal and his private stood their ground. The crowd calmed down somewhat. At 8 p.m., the diesel engines roared into life and the conductor and the soldiers let the people who had bought tickets board the train. They let thirty ticket holders into the caboose. The people who were not allowed onto the train became frantic and angry and they began to push forward. The captain of the Wehrmacht soldiers fired his pistol three times into the air and ordered his men to aim their rifles at the angry mob. "If anyone moves past the yellow line, we shoot. Do you understand?" he yelled out. The crowd ceased moving forward.

On board the train, the conductor checked tickets and then pulled a cord just below the luggage rack. Once the engineer heard this signal, he released the brakes and the train began to roll south towards Nuremberg. Antanas felt fortunate that the conductor had been too busy checking the other passengers' tickets to challenge them. But he knew he had to get to the conductor before he did another round of checks or they would be dumped off the train.

When Antanas spotted the conductor re-entering the caboose from the adjoining car, he jumped to his feet and walked quickly towards him. He had two cigarette-filled napkins in his coat pocket and two more in his pants pocket. "Herr conductor, may I speak with you for a moment?"

"Hurry; I don't have much time."

"I would like to give you a small gift to thank you for the great work you are doing for the Fatherland as the train's conductor." As he spoke, Antanas removed the napkins from his pants pocket and placed them in the conductor's hand. The conductor did not unwrap the gift but he used his fingers to determine the contents. "How many?" he asked.

"Forty."

"You have no tickets?"

"No."

"How many of you are there?"

"Three." Antanas pointed to his sister and his wife.

The conductor smiled. "This isn't enough. The Fatherland can't afford freeloaders like you."

Antanas reached into his coat pocket, removed the remaining two napkins, and gave them to the conductor. "This is all we have."

The conductor tucked both napkins inside the jacket of his uniform and said, "It's not enough, but I feel generous today. You three can stay on the train. How far do you want to go?"

"We want to go to south Bavaria, but we have not yet chosen a town."

"This train only goes to Nuremberg because the tracks change for those going farther south. You must disembark there."

Antanas agreed that they would do so.

Antanas joined Maria and Jadwyga on a bench seat. The caboose was small but it had been converted from the usual style of caboose into a small passenger car. It had bench seats and luggage racks and could comfortably seat fifteen people, but the soldiers had let thirty ticket holders on board plus the three of them. Most of the passengers had to stand in the aisles. It was so crowded that there was little danger of falling when the train lurched. Antanas spotted a woman holding a baby and he gave her his seat. Jadwyga and Maria were already asleep on their bench.

After a four-hour journey, the slow-moving train finally pulled into Nuremberg station and all the passengers prepared to disembark. As Jadwyga passed the conductor, she said quietly, "Thank you."

The conductor whispered into her ear. "Go to the south end of the station. Look for the freight trains and try to board one of the cars. Most of them don't actually stop in Nuremberg but they slow down while passing through the station. Boarding a moving freight train is dangerous and if you're caught, you'll be arrested. Still, there are not enough soldiers patrolling Nuremberg station to prevent stowaways from jumping onto the freight cars. Most freeloaders try to sneak onto the passenger trains, but they fail. You should be safe."

"Thank you," Jadwyga said again.

When they disembarked, it was almost 12:30 a.m. Jadwyga, Maria, and Antanas were amazed by Nuremberg station. It was much larger and grander than anything they had seen before. True to the conductor's warning, there were thirty or more Wehrmacht soldiers patrolling the passenger cars. Jadwyga shared the conductor's advice with Antanas and Maria. Antanas concurred that boarding a moving freight train was their best bet. They walked to the south end of the stockyards, where the smell of cattle, pigs, and sheep manure was ripe.

Suddenly, in the faint starlight, Antanas spotted a freight train crawling out of the stockyards. One of the cars had a huge sliding door that was slightly ajar, and it seemed to be full of crates rather than livestock. They knew that, for security reasons, it was safer to try to board a moving freight train than a parked train, but chasing a moving locomotive was a terrifying prospect. The three refugees ran hard while grasping their luggage. The crescent moon gave them some light, but there was a real danger that they could trip on something that they could not see in the dim light.

In less than thirty seconds, Antanas caught up to the train and threw his luggage through the freight car door. Then he hopped onto the train. He pulled the heavy door open while Jadwyga and Maria continued to run. He jumped off the train again and took Jadwyga's suitcase from her hand and heaved it into the freight car. Then he did the same with Maria's luggage.

The train's speed was increasing.

"Maria, run and jump onto the freight car before it picks up too much speed," he yelled. Maria had been an athlete in high school and she easily caught the side of the car and simultaneously jumped and pulled herself up onto the ledge.

"Now it's your turn, Jadwyga," she called.

Jadwyga was not as fast as Maria and the train was accelerating. She was just quick enough to jump up and fling her upper body onto the floor of the freight car, but she was too exhausted from running to pull herself up the rest of the way. Maria dragged her by both arms into the car. Meanwhile, the train had picked up speed significantly, and now it was all that Antanas could do to keep pace with it. He forced himself to run faster than he had ever run in his life. He pulled up beside the open door and leaped onto the car. His arms and chest were inside the train, but his legs dangled dangerously over the edge. His feet were just centimetres above the track. He grabbed onto the wooden floor with all his might. There was nothing much to hold onto to prevent him from falling out of the train. Maria and Jadwyga each took an arm and pulled him into the boxcar.

"Safe," yelled Maria.

"Thank God," cried Jadwyga.

"Where is this train going?" Maria asked.

"Who knows?" Antanas laughed. "But from the stars I can tell that it's going south, and south takes us closer to where we want to go."

The train made frequent stops to take cargo on or off, and by 6:30 a.m. they had travelled only seventy-five kilometres when Antanas spotted a tall church tower. They did not know it at the time, but they were entering the town of Walting in Bavaria. While Maria and Jadwyga slept from exhaustion Antanas viewed the small village in the dawn light. He concluded that it looked like a good village to live in while they waited for liberation.

Antanas shook the shoulders of both women. "Wake up, Jadwyga. Wake up, Maria. This is our new home."

Maria wiped the dreams from her mind. "What's it called?"

"I don't know yet, but the train has slowed to a crawl and it looks like there are soldiers at the upcoming station. We need to get off this train now."

Maria threw her suitcase onto the snow beside the tracks and Jadwyga and Antanas did the same with their luggage. Maria jumped off the train and Jadwyga and Antanas followed her in quick succession. As each person landed, they tucked in their arms and rolled in the snow to avoid breaking limbs. This was a trick that Jadwyga's cousin Wladek had once told them about when they used to have lunch at the camp together. Jadwyga reflected sadly, *Those days at the work camp seem like a century ago. I really miss Wladek.*

"Everyone all right?" Antanas called out.

Maria stood up and brushed the snow off her mitts, coat, and hat. "I've had better landings, but nothing's broken."

"I'm alive," said Jadwyga.

"The station is about three hundred metres away," observed Antanas. "Let's not walk in that direction. We don't want to meet nosy police or soldiers. Let's head this way."

Antanas pointed to the west and Jadwyga and Maria followed him. They found themselves in a large empty field where they had to trudge through deep snow for about half a kilometre. They used the church steeple as a beacon. Finally, they arrived at the doors of the largest church in Walting. It was St. Agnes, the town's Catholic church. The three of them had been allowed to meet for prayers on Sunday mornings in the work camp in Elbing, but they had not been allowed to enter a church, talk to a priest, or receive confession or communion since 1942. They walked up the steps of the church dragging their luggage behind them. Maria opened the large wooden doors. When they stepped inside, they could smell incense. They looked up and saw paintings on the walls above the windows depicting the stations of the cross.

It was a church that served a small town, but the long, dark wooden pews could have held as many as 300 people. At the back of the church was a wooden balcony with a large pipe organ and space for the choir. At the front of the church was the altar with the tabernacle containing the wine and the hosts. Above it was a large wooden cross depicting a crucified Jesus. All three refugees fell to their knees and prayed for the same thing: *Please help us to be accepted in this town.*

A tall, middle-aged man with blond hair, brown eyes, and high cheekbones was praying near a statue of the Blessed Virgin Mary. He stood up, put a few coins into the metal box by the candles, and lit one of the candles. He made the sign of the cross, genuflected, and then approached Antanas. "Hello, I'm Ade Muller. I'm the burgermeister of Walting. We are a very small town, so I know that you're not a citizen here. What brings you to Walting?"

Antanas was startled, but something made him trust this man, at least a little.

"We're running from the Red Army. We've been travelling for days from Elbing in the northeast."

"That's a long journey. What do you seek?"

Jadwyga and Maria stood up from their pews and joined them. Antanas made introductions. Maria spoke for them all. "We want food and shelter. We are happy to work for these things."

"Welcome to Walting. I think that this town can help you. What kind of work can you do?"

Maria replied, "My brother is a fine mechanic and he can fix anything. Jadwyga is a seamstress and she can repair or alter clothes of all kinds. I can clean and cook, and I was preparing to be a doctor before the war."

"Well, you're all in luck. The blacksmith's son is fighting the Red Army and the blacksmith could use an assistant. He's also the closest thing to a trained mechanic that this town has. You, Antanas, could be of great help. Jadwyga, we have a tailor in town who could use your services. Maria, we have a doctor and a nurse in town already, but we have several older women who could use help with cleaning and cooking. Their sons were either killed in the war or are still fighting. They left too young to marry, so these women have no one to assist them."

"You're a good shepherd. You know the needs of your flock," Maria said.

"The people have made me their leader, so I try to take that responsibility seriously," Herr Muller said.

"We'll take all of those jobs," said Antanas.

"These families can't pay you much, but the blacksmith family, Dieter and Gisela Schultze, could provide food and lodging for you and your wife. Frau Karin Richter has lost her husband and two sons on the Russian front. She has a serious heart condition and needs help maintaining her home. She lives on war pensions so she is not wealthy, but she could provide a bed and food for you, Maria."

Jadwyga smiled. "Thank you, for what you are trying to do for us."

Herr Muller nodded and continued. "I will introduce you to the pastor of St. Agnes parish. His name is Father Klaus Lang. While you're with him, I'll present your offers to Frau Schultze and Frau Richter. This should not take long. Most of the homes in town are within half a kilometre of St. Agnes. I'll be back within an hour."

The burgermeister then pointed to a tall priest entering the altar from the sacristy. "Look; here's Father Lang." He then made the introductions and explained that he was going to match the newcomers' needs with those of the Schultze family and Frau Richter.

"Well, if anyone can make these things happen, it will be you," Father Lang beamed his approval.

"I'll return in an hour."

Father Lang addressed the new members of his flock. "Can I offer you some tea and bread?"

Jadwyga spoke first. "Yes, Father, that would be nice, but could you give us confession and then communion first? We've not been able to see a priest for almost a year."

"Certainly, I'll hear your confessions now."

After he had provided them confession and communion, Father Lang invited the trio to the manse next door, where they were given tea and bread. None of them had eaten since leaving Erfurt the previous afternoon.

Father Lang apologized for the quality of the bread. "It's half rye and half sawdust," he said.

"Father, we're used to that recipe. Thank you. We know that you're sharing with us what little you have," Jadwyga responded.

Before Antanas could say thank you, Ade Muller returned.

"I have good news. I have found you all shelter, food, and work."

Chapter 30

Life and Death in Walting

General Zhukov and the Red Army began the Battle of Berlin on March 7, 1945. The Wehrmacht put up strong opposition. On March 12, Franklin Roosevelt died suddenly. The United States and British forces fought to cross the Rhine at Oppenheim on March 22 and 23, while the Luftwaffe continued to fire V-2 rockets at England.

Walting, Bavaria, February–April 1945

Herr Muller brought Jadwyga and Antanas to the home of Dieter and Gisela Schultze and introduced Maria to Frau Karin Richter. Their respective homes were only five blocks from each other.

Quickly, Antanas became like a favourite son in the town. He was an even better mechanic than his host, the town blacksmith. Besides being able to repair cars, trucks, and motorcycles, Antanas could mend electrical equipment, including clocks, radios, light fixtures, and kitchen appliances. The townspeople brought all these things to the blacksmith's shop and asked for Antanas by name. People in the village came to call him "Our Antanas." Dieter Schultze was not the least bit jealous of Antanas's popularity. Antanas was bringing more business to his store and, besides, he liked having companionship at work.

Karin Richter gave Maria her eldest son's old room and she became quite fond of Maria. She was determined to fatten up this poor slim girl, but she knew that this would be a long-term project because she herself didn't have much food.

Maria, in turn, did most of the cleaning, wood hauling, and cooking for Frau Richter. Maria was also introduced to several of Frau Richter's widowed friends and she performed the same services for some of the older ones. The widows formed a weekly card-playing club and Maria became their favourite player. Maria enjoyed their company as well, and felt that helping them all was good experience if she was to become a nurse.

The Schultze's daughters, Diana and Sophia, shared a large bedroom. To accommodate Jadwyga, the two girls took the double bed and Jadwyga got the single one. Frau Schultze gave Antanas the single bed in her son Manfred's room. Manfred was fighting the Red Army somewhere in northeastern Germany, but Frau Schultze did not know his location because his letters were censored. She became teary-eyed when she spoke of Manfred and quickly changed the subject.

Sophia and Diana soon became friends with Jadwyga. Sophia was twenty-four, tall, and blonde. Diana, twenty-two, was a petite redhead. Sophia was a seamstress and owned her own sewing machine. She and Jadwyga took in work referred to them by the local tailor. They alternated hand sewing and using the sewing machine. They traded skills and shortcuts and generally helped one another. Soon, Jadwyga felt that she, Sophia, and Diana had become as close as sisters. The fact that Jadwyga, Antanas, and Maria were all fluent in German gave them a distinct advantage in terms of fitting in with their hosts.

April 15, 1945, 6:15 a.m.

Frau Schultze heard pounding at the front door.

"Wake up, Dieter, someone is trying to wake the dead!"

Dieter threw on his robe and sprinted to the door. He recognized the voice calling out.

"Wake up! Open the door!" It was his friend the burgermeister, Ade Muller.

"What's wrong?" Dieter asked as he opened the door.

Ade entered his friend's home. "It's my wife Alise. She has a fever of forty-four degrees and she's losing consciousness. Doctor Hahn is visiting his sister Magda in Weissenburg. I want Antanas to go and fetch him. For now, Nurse Ilsa and I will give Alise a cold bath for her fever."

By this time, Antanas had put on his pants and shirt and was standing beside Dieter. "I overheard what you said, Herr Burgermeister. But how can I get to Weissenburg?"

"You can take my motorcycle. I know that you can ride one."

"I'll need directions to Weissenburg."

"Here's a map. It's just a little over thirty kilometres but the roads are muddy and slippery. Be very careful."

"I'll pack some tools and leave right away."

Frau Schultze walked in front of Antanas and placed her hand on his arm. "No, you won't. You will have coffee and bread and then you can go."

Antanas objected, but Dieter and Ade joined Gisela in her insistence. He stopped arguing and gulped down the coffee and swallowed the bread. He pitched some tools into a satchel that he fastened over his shoulders. It was always Antanas's custom to bring tools wherever he went. It was a habit that served him well.

He mounted the motorcycle, kicked the starter, heard the roar, and felt the vibration. "This motorcycle has power," he said to Herr Muller.

"My father bought it for me when I became burgermeister in 1936 and I have tried to baby it ever since." Herr Muller gently stroked the motorcycle and then handed Antanas a small piece of paper. "Here's the map and the name and address of Dr. Hahn's sister. Please hurry."

Antanas shifted into first, second, and third gear in rapid succession. He drove off down the muddy road and made excellent progress for the first twenty-five minutes. He found himself entranced by the beautiful pine forest that bordered the road. Just a few kilometres outside of Weissenburg, he spotted a deer bounding across the road. He swerved to miss it but then a second deer followed. The back hooves of the animal hit the handlebars as it leaped over the motorcycle. Antanas and the motorcycle crashed.

Antanas was not sure how long he lay unconscious, but when a truck driver helped him to his feet, it was already 10 a.m. Antanas looked at the bike and his heart sank. He said to the truck driver, "The fender is so bent that it's jammed against the wheel. Some of the spokes on the wheel have been loosened, but my spoke ratchet can fix that. The fender will be more difficult."

The driver offered to drive Antanas to Weissenburg and they heaved the bike into the back of the truck. They arrived at the home of the doctor's sister, Frau Magda Kramer, and the driver helped Antanas to place the broken motorcycle on the front lawn. Antanas and the driver approached the front door and pounded on it until they heard footsteps. When Frau Kramer opened the door, Antanas explained that he needed her brother's help. She called out, "Heinz, come here. There's a man who wants to talk to you."

The doctor came to the front door. "Antanas, what brings you to Weissenburg?"

"I've been sent for you. Alise Muller has a fever of forty-four degrees. Ade is terrified that she's dying. Can you return to Walting right now?"

Doctor Hahn stepped outside onto the front lawn. "Yes, Antanas, I can leave right away. I need to pack my medicine bag and a few clothes. But what happened to Ade's motorcycle?"

"A deer leaped in front of me and knocked the bike over with its back hooves. I think the deer survived, and I lived, but the front fender of the bike is rubbing against the wheel. Your sister and I will fix the fender while you get your things."

Magda Kramer found a metal pole in her basement, which Antanas had requested. The truck driver helped Antanas use the metal bar to try to pry the fender away from the wheel, but the metal of the fender was too thick. It would not budge. Magda joined the two men and, as they pulled, the fender began to bend. When it had bent enough to stop rubbing against the wheel, Antanas used his ratchet to tighten the spokes.

"Okay, Herr Doctor, I'm ready," Antanas declared.

Just before mounting the motorcycle, the doctor noticed that blood had oozed through Antanas's left pant leg, near his calf muscle.

"What's that? Show me your leg." Antanas complied and when he did, Magda flinched. Antanas's leg was cut and burned. It had stopped bleeding, but there was a lot of caked blood. A large area of his calf was bright red from where the hot muffler had singed his leg when he crashed. It was a bad burn and a deep cut.

"We need to disinfect and bandage your leg before infection sets in," the doctor said.

"Not now, Herr Doctor. Frau Muller is dying. I'll clean the wound myself when we return."

"Okay, Antanas but I take you at your word that you will attend to your wound as soon as we get to Walting."

The engine roared to life and they raced back to Walting. In thirty minutes, they were at the home of the burgermeister. Doctor Hahn got off the bike and ran into the house to see his patient. Antanas leaned the motorcycle against the house and limped the five blocks home. In the last block, Antanas felt great pain in his leg, and then he felt dizzy and nauseous. When he arrived at the Schultze's home, Jadwyga rushed out the door to greet him. Antanas fainted on the lawn.

"Help! Antanas is unconscious!" Jadwyga screamed.

Maria was out the door first, followed by Dieter and Gisela. Maria spotted the blood on Antanas's pants and she and Dieter lifted Antanas's upper body while Gisela and Jadwyga gently lifted his legs. They carried him to the kitchen floor, where Maria said, "We have to wash his leg before we carry him to the bed."

They cleaned his calf and leg with soap and water, but when Nurse Ilsa arrived later that day, she bathed his wounds in iodine and wrapped his burns and cuts with a fish compress. Antanas did not move or cry out in pain. He was still unconscious. Nurse Ilsa took his temperature. It was forty-four degrees.

"Jadwyga, Maria, Gisela, you must take turns watching him," Nurse Ilsa instructed. "His fever is very high and we must bring it down. Wipe his face, neck, chest, and arms with a cool facecloth every half hour, and sponge-bathe his entire body every two hours. If his temperature hits forty-five degrees, you and Dieter must carry him into the bath and pour cold water and ice on him."

"We will," Jadwyga sobbed. "We will."

"How is Alise?" Maria asked.

"She's dying. The doctor, her husband, her children, Antanas, and I have done all we can, but it's not been enough. She'll be dead before sundown."

Jadwyga and Gisela gasped.

"With our help, Antanas will live. He's a fighter and so are we," said Maria.

"I believe you, Maria, and I'll be back tomorrow morning. May God be with Antanas and all of you."

It was a terrible two days. The women took turns nursing Antanas. Doctor Hahn visited Antanas once a day and Nurse Ilsa came twice a day to wash the wound and to apply more fish compresses. On the third day, Antanas's fever dropped and he regained consciousness.

"Water," was the first word he spoke.

Jadwyga was thrilled to satisfy his request. After he had swallowed half the water in the glass, Jadwyga hugged him. "Antanas, thank God you're alive!"

Maria teased her brother. "I wasn't worried, because only the good die young."

"It's good to know that I wasn't missed," Antanas replied.

Jadwyga knew better. She had seen Maria go with little sleep for forty-eight hours and she watched her throw herself into her nursing role. She had also seen Maria weep when she thought that no one could see her.

Later that evening, Maria and Jadwyga heard heavy steps mounting the stairs. They were not Dieter's. Jadwyga went silent. *Is it the Wehrmacht? Have they come to punish us for stealing the truck?*

Suddenly, a face appeared at the doorway of Antanas's bedroom. It was Burgermeister Ade Muller. He had his hat in his hand and tears in his eyes.

"My darling Alise is dead. She died two days ago. Antanas, I would have come sooner, but Doctor Hahn told me to stay away until you recovered. He let me come to see you today. I just wanted to thank you. Alise died, but you did everything a human being could do to save her, and so did Doctor Hahn and Nurse Ilsa. I'm here to tell you how grateful I am. Thank you."

Neither Antanas nor Maria nor Jadwyga could form words due to the lumps in their throats, but Ade understood their response nonetheless. He nodded at them, walked down the stairs, opened the door, and entered the morning.

Chapter 31

Black Angels

On April 4, 1945, General Omar Bradley and the United States First and Ninth Armies encircled Field Marshall Walter Model and the Wehrmacht Army Group B in the Ruhr Pocket. Three hundred thousand German troops surrendered. The U.S. armies kept moving eastward. They encountered German resistance, but the Americans sensed victory close at hand.

Walting, Bavaria, April 28 and 29, 1945

The evening and then the night were filled with sounds of war. The roar of airplanes and the shrieking of bombs were reminiscent of British and American raids on Elbing. The rattling of artillery, tanks, trucks, machine guns, and rifle fire was constant. No one could sleep in the Schultze household and Maria was wide awake in the Richter home.

The sounds came from a distance and no shells or bombs hit Walting, but everyone in the town knew that this was the end for the Wehrmacht in Bavaria. At about 6:30 a.m. the bangs and crashes of battle suddenly stopped. Jadwyga and Sophia decided to walk together to St. Agnes church. They both wished to pray. Jadwyga prayed in silence while en route to the church. *May the war be over and may the British or Americans be the army that liberates us. May my mother and father be safe. May my sisters be spared from the Red Army.*

Sophia was also praying as they walked to church. She prayed to Jesus that the army that defeated the Wehrmacht would be a merciful one. *Please God, may this conquering army not kill my parents and rape me or my sister Diana.*

As Sophia and Jadwyga hurried down the cobblestone street, the air was cool and the sun was rising. Jadwyga knew that by late morning, it would be a warm spring day. When the din of battle stopped, the birds began to sing, but now they were silent again. Jadwyga heard vehicles approaching and saw a dozen soldiers. Most were carrying machine guns, but two were hauling bazookas and the leader held a drawn pistol. Jadwyga stood paralyzed. Sophia trembled.

As the soldiers approached them, Jadwyga observed something she had never seen before. She saw a soldier carrying a pistol. His face was black. It was more than the black smudges that she had seen Polish, Soviet, and German soldiers smear under their eyes. This soldier's face was entirely black. Jadwyga suddenly realized that he must be an American. *We're saved! We're saved!*

All the blood drained from Sophia's face when she saw the soldiers. All she could say was, "*Schwartz. Schwartz.*" ("Black. Black.") For a twenty-four-year-old who had been exposed to Goebbels's and Hitler's propaganda for the past decade, it was the most terrifying sight she could imagine: a black conquering soldier. Sophia stumbled and fell unconscious to the ground. The black American sergeant and two of his black comrades came to her aid.

Jadwyga realized that these soldiers might be French colonial troops, but that they were more likely American. This meant that the Wehrmacht was being pushed east by the Allies while the Red Army was forcing the Germans westward. The days of the Third Reich were over.

The captain pulled out his canteen, pointed to it, and said, "Water." Jadwyga spoke Polish, Lithuanian, Russian, Ukrainian, and German, but she could not speak any English.

The captain pointed at Sophia and said, "I'm Captain Hayden. I'll give her my water." Jadwyga smiled vacantly. Jadwyga could see the small U.S. Army insignia on the captain's shoulder. He appeared to be a man in his early thirties and she guessed his two subordinates were in their late twenties. She watched him gently lift Sophia's head and slowly pour water on her brow. Sophia opened her eyes but was too terrified to scream. The captain offered her his canteen. Sophia shook her head and slowly rose to her feet.

Jadwyga said, "*Danka. Danka.*"

The captain and the two privates nodded and moved on towards the town hall.

By 11 a.m., the black American regiment had secured Walting and had moved eastward. A white American regiment relieved them and was issuing orders to the citizens. This second American group did not arrive in stealth. They comprised a mechanized unit accompanied by many tanks and trucks. Antanas counted more than one hundred M3 and M4 medium-sized tanks and ten Sherman T3 Mine Exploders. Maria and Jadwyga lost count of the number of troop-carrying trucks and mechanized vehicles pulling field guns and howitzers. Some of the troops stayed in Walting, but most moved eastward.

The homes that had been emptied were used to house the American troops. The Americans forced many citizens of Walting to relocate from their homes to the homes of neighbours or relatives. The Schultze family and Frau Richter were spared because they had already taken Jadwyga, Antanas and Maria into their respective homes.

The Americans feared that some Germans might try to poison them, so they would not eat local German food, with the exception of eggs. The Americans had therefore brought their own water and food with them. Over time, the U.S. commanders relaxed these restrictions and allowed the use of local water, but they always treated the water before giving it to their men. As the Americans transported more of their own supplies, they shared their food with the citizens of Walting. Although the German citizens of Walting preferred the Americans to the Soviets, they weren't quite sure what to make of them. They were all afraid, sad, and stunned.

Colonel Jeff Neely served as the commander of the occupying American forces in Walting. He was blue-eyed and square-shouldered, with short-cut blond hair. Antanas thought that the Germans would have loved to have recruited such a man. They would have put his face on their propaganda posters as an example of a fine German soldier. Everyone got to know him as an intelligent, hard-working, and demanding yet fair commander. Within two days, he had the entire town fully disarmed, fed, and housed. On the second day, he had posters hung throughout the town inviting all non-German citizens to meet at the town hall at 7 p.m. During the meeting, he told the crowd, "All foreign workers will be transported to Augsburg at 7 a.m. tomorrow morning."

Jadwyga was upset by this news. "We've grown fond of the Schultze family, Frau Richter, Burgermeister Muller, Father Lang, and half the town. I'm especially close to Sophia. I'll miss her deeply."

"But this is a good thing," Antanas explained. "Augsburg is ninety-nine kilometres to the southwest of Walting and farther away from Austria and Czechoslovakia, where the Red Army may already be stationed."

"I understand, Antanas, and I trust your judgement. All I'm saying is that it's hard to make good friends and then have to leave them."

That night they all thanked their hosts for giving them food, lodging, and friendship. Antanas walked down the five blocks to thank Ade Muller for introducing them to Frau Richter and the Schultzes.

"I can't thank you enough for what you've done for my wife, my sister, and me," Antanas said to him earnestly.

"You're most welcome. Walting is a better place for all of you than being here. Thank you for trying to save my wife. I'll never forget you for what you did."

Chapter 32

The End of the Third Reich

Augsburg was the third largest city in Bavaria. It was a major
strategic point that the Americans needed to overtake. Only Munich
and Nuremberg were larger. More importantly, Augsburg had
provided a major base for the Wehrmacht. A massive assembly of
barracks stood in this location.

Walting to Augsburg, Bavaria, May 2, 1945

The three refugees showed up in front of the small city hall by
6:45 a.m. By 7 a.m. sharp, four Ford troop carriers were lined up in a
row. They loaded their luggage inside the first truck and then hopped
aboard. Ten minutes later, they were rolling towards Augsburg. It was
not a long distance, but the fully loaded trucks could not move
quickly on the muddy roads. They finally reached Augsburg about an
hour before noon. The trucks stopped just outside the city hall. They
unloaded their luggage and waited. They could smell sausages, bread,
and coffee, and then they spotted American soldiers cooking on the
other side of the square.

The American commander of Augsburg was Colonel David
Wilmot. He was a man in his fifties with broad shoulders, light-brown
hair, and a warm smile. He welcomed the weary travellers personally
and invited them to partake of the food, coffee, and water. After they
had eaten their fill, he asked everyone to line up according to their
nationality. The Americans wanted to divide up the living quarters
according to ethnic groups. Jadwyga, Antanas, and Maria were
assigned to the Baltic section with the other Lithuanians and refugees
from Latvia and Estonia. The Poles were assigned their own section,
as were the French, Yugoslavians, Dutch, and Greeks. The Russians,
Ukrainians, and Belarusians were located together.

Jadwyga sensed that it would be safe to inform the American soldiers that she was Polish. She feared, however, that she might be separated from Antanas and Maria. It just seemed simpler to continue identifying herself as Lithuanian. *My husband is a Lithuanian and his sister is my best friend, so why confuse the Americans and tell them I'm Polish?* she thought.

The three exhausted travellers were billeted in a large house along with other Lithuanians. They ate at the barracks, which was a huge, austere set of buildings made of wood. The previous occupants had been Wehrmacht soldiers and they had painted the barracks a muddy brown to create better camouflage against Allied bombers.

Their mess hall reminded Jadwyga of the one at their camp in Elbing. It had rows and rows of picnic tables and everything inside was green while everything outside was brown. Still, the Americans prepared food for them and there was almost enough to go around. Every morning, soldiers would drop off containers of porridge and real coffee to the house where they slept. Lunch and supper were served in the mess hall. Meals consisted of canned vegetables, real bread, rations of canned meat or fish, and even some canned fruit. The portions were small, but they tasted considerably better compared to the food served at the work camp.

After lunch, they were driven by truck back to their residence. Maria, Antanas, and Jadwyga had to share one large room, but at least there was a double bed and a single bed to accommodate them.

After they had unpacked, Maria suggested that they explore their new town. "We could use some exercise," she said. Antanas and Jadwyga agreed and they left the house to wander about.

Their new home was perched at the top of a large hill, so they had a good vantage point from which to view the city.

"The citizens of Augsburg weren't as fortunate as the people of Walting," observed Maria soberly. "Look how many buildings have been destroyed by American shelling and bombing."

***

The next morning, an army truck dropped off some large containers of porridge and real coffee at their new home. They also left some powdered milk. Antanas and two of the men carried the food boxes into the house. Everyone made their own breakfast in the kitchen, a large room that could seat a dozen diners. The room had many windows, most of which faced east and south so that the kitchen was flooded with sunlight in the morning and it received rays of light from the south until early evening. It was a cheerful room that inspired social interaction. Conversations with their housemates ranged from the exchange of personal histories, to speculation about the near future, to rumours about the collapse of the Third Reich and the rise of the Soviet and American empires.

May 3, 10 a.m.

An American private and a Lithuanian interpreter arrived at the house where Antanas, Jadwyga, and Maria were staying. They told everyone to assemble in the plaza next to city hall for some important announcements and for lunch at noon. The three walked to city hall together and were standing in the courtyard a little past 11:30 a.m. to hear the announcements.

At 1 p.m., Colonel Wilmot stepped behind the podium at the top of some steps. He cleared his throat a couple of times and then spoke directly into the large microphone. Antanas noticed that five privates had been scurrying around the plaza setting up temporary wires and speakers. He estimated the crowd in this large square to be about 2,000. A few hundred were U.S. soldiers, but the majority were former forced labourers. Judging from their clothes, it also seemed that there were some German shopkeepers, city politicians, and workers on the sidelines.

The colonel spoke only English, but an American corporal who took his place beside him spoke German fluently.

These poor people have heard enough military speeches, Jadwyga thought. *They want to eat lunch.*

The colonel spoke, and the translator repeated his words in German. The crowd went silent, and then a huge roar rose into the sky. A few of the Germans began to cry. The American soldiers slapped each other on their hands, on their heads, and on their backs. Some soldiers broke into a dance. The Germans just looked at their feet. The forced labourers and the American GIs talked joyouslyly among themselves and laughter rang out throughout the square.

The colonel had simply said: "We have it on good authority that Adolf Hitler committed suicide three days ago, on April 30."

After permitting the audience to let this news sink in for a few moments, the colonel resumed speaking. "The Soviet Army captured Berlin yesterday, May 2."

The Americans soldiers jumped up and threw their helmets into the air. The refugees stood and cheered and began to chatter among themselves. The Germans remained silent.

What will happen to Lithuania? Maria wondered.

Jadwyga looked towards the northeast. "What will happen to Poland? What will happen to our families?"

Colonel Wilmot asked the crowd to settle down and everyone complied. "The U.S. Army will continue to house and feed each one of you. We know that boredom, disease, and violence will soon become the new enemy, unless the U.S. Army and all of you work together. We have lots of jobs to be done in the barracks of the refugees as well as in the barracks of the U.S. soldiers. We have posted these jobs on the walls inside city hall. Some of your leaders have spoken to us and have asked for our support to set up various clubs and schools. We will provide space in each of the main barracks and we will provide whatever materials we can afford to share." The crowd roared and applauded. Then everyone but the Germans gave the colonel and his interpreter a loud standing ovation.

Maria told Antanas that she wished to speak to some of the Lithuanian leaders about what the colonel had shared with them and she encouraged her brother and Jadwyga to walk back to their cottage without her. She told them she would follow in about an hour. On the walk home, Antanas expressed his joy that Hitler was presumed to be dead.

Jadwyga agreed but showed little emotion. Antanas asked her what she was thinking.

"The Germans may soon be conquered, but what will it be like to live under the Americans? When can we go home? Can we go home?"

May 9, 3:30 p.m.

A second assembly was held in front of Augsburg City Hall. Colonel Wilmot spoke again. "I'm overjoyed to announce that earlier today, the High Commander of all German Armed Forces, Admiral Karl Donitz, signed a surrender agreement with the Allies and with the Soviet Union. This is the final and unconditional surrender. This is the end of the war in Europe."

The non-Germans went wild. Jadwyga and Antanas jumped to their feet and kissed for a long, long time. The U.S. soldiers blared "Boogie Woogie Bugle Boy of Company C" on the loudspeakers and refugee men and women and American soldiers danced.

The German populace stood still. There were tears in everyone's eyes, but they were all crying for different reasons. The Germans' tears betrayed sadness, bitterness, and fear. The refugees' tears revealed happiness mixed with anxiety. The American tears reflected joy, relief, and triumph.

When the decibel level decreased, Colonel Wilmot leaned into the microphone.

"For those of you who were brought to Germany against your will, I have more good news. A new organization has been formed called the United Nations Relief and Rehabilitation Association, or UNRRA for short. You will be happy to know that over the next few months, this group will be working with the U.S. Army to feed and house all refugees." His translator spoke in German to make the message clear. A tremendous cheer went up from the crowd.

Colonel Wilmot waited for the noise level to subside.

"This same group will also help all of you return to your homelands."

The translator put this message out to the audience. The French, Dutch, Italian, Danish, Belgian, Norwegian, and Greek men and women cheered wildly.

The Polish, Lithuanian, Estonian, Latvian, Ukrainian, Belarusian, Czechoslovakian, Russian, and Yugoslavian men and women stood in stony silence. None of them wished to return to a country occupied by Stalin's armies. A few began to boo. More people joined in the dissent. In a few moments, more than 1,000 Eastern European refugees were booing the colonel. He paused, stared at his translator, and stepped down from the podium.

As the trio walked back to their temporary home, Maria spoke first. "Those Americans are brave and generous, but they are stupid. They refer to Stalin as 'Uncle Joe.' Are they crazy?"

Antanas walked in step beside his sister. "With uncles like Joe Stalin, children would never want to visit their parents' relatives," he said grimly.

Jadwyga gripped Antanas by the hand. "Let's pray that the Americans grow up—and soon. In the meantime, we'll refuse to leave. The Americans are too kindhearted to force us to return to Lithuania and Poland while the Red Army is still there."

A week later, a Soviet colonel, two Soviet majors, five captains, fifteen sergeants, and 200 Red Army corporals and privates arrived in Augsburg. They slept in tents at night and by day they met with every Lithuanian, Estonian, Latvian, Polish, Yugoslavian, Ukrainian, Russian, and Czechoslovakian man, woman, and child. Out of 1,300 people, only ten families, or forty people, left with them. The rest refused to go.

Colonel Wilmot was amazed by this, but his translator, Corporal Giovanni Carlino, was not surprised. "Sir, it's not just the Germans who fear the Soviets. In the past few weeks, I've spoken to refugees from all the ethnic groups here in the camp. Those who have lived under the heel of Stalin hate him and fear him. They all describe him as being more ruthless than Hitler."

The colonel admired Corporal Carlino. He was aware that he was more than a good translator. Colonel Wilmot respected him because he showed initiative. Corporal Carlino had an infectious smile and he put his good looks, his linguistic skills, and his ability to listen to good use. The colonel found him to be invaluable in assessing the needs of the refugees in the camp.

Colonel Wilmot paced for a few seconds and then stopped to face Corporal Carlino. "I'll speak to General Clay. I'll plead the case of the Eastern European refugees. I will not force them to return home against their will. They've suffered enough."

Chapter 33

Dachau

Although the Polish Home Army and Stalin had warned the British and Americans about Hitler's "Final Solution" as early as 1943, it was not until the British liberated the Bergen and Belsen death camps and the Americans liberated the Dachau concentration camp in April 1945 that the Allies began to comprehend the sheer magnitude of Nazi depravity.

Although this horror extended almost everywhere throughout Nazi-conquered territories, it was the worst in Poland and the Baltics. In Poland, six million men, women, and children were killed in concentration camps. Of these six million souls, three million were Jews. In May of 1941, there were 200,000 Jews living in Lithuania. By July of 1945, only 20,000 of them survived—90 percent had been killed.

Augsburg, Bavaria, late May and June 1945

Maria got to know Corporal Carlino well after she first heard him translate for Colonel Wilmot. He tried his best to use his connections to find Private Peter Baur for her. He had limited success. There was one unsubstantiated report that Peter had been wounded in Eastern Germany in late March. Corporal Carlino told Maria that Peter had suffered leg wounds and had been transported to a hospital in Berlin. That's where the trail went cold.

"Is he alive? Is he dead? Where is he now?" Maria asked desperately.

Corporal Carlino was ashamed that he could neither get Maria the answers she needed nor provide comfort to her. He admitted to himself that he was attracted to Maria, but he knew that she was in love with Private Baur. Carlino was a mere corporal, but as a German and Italian translator he had worked with several U.S. colonels who considered him a friend. They pulled strings for him. Still, he was frustrated by the difficulties he encountered in tracking down individuals amidst the confusion following the war.

On June 5, Corporal Carlino, or "Giovanni" as Maria had begun to call him, pulled up to their residence on his army motorcycle. Maria heard his bike and opened the door. She welcomed him into the home that she shared with the other Lithuanians. He ascended the wooden stairs and entered the kitchen. He had shocking news to deliver.

"Tomorrow, Colonel Wilmot is going to announce something that defies belief."

Maria frowned. "What is it?"

Antanas and Jadwyga entered the kitchen where Giovanni and Maria were conversing. "What's going on?" asked Antanas.

"There is news about Dachau and the other German concentration camps as well as the death camps. Whatever you've heard about them, you'll not be prepared for this."

"What's happened exactly?" asked Jadwyga nervously.

"American troops liberated the Dachau concentration camp on April 27, and now General Clay wants the world to know what happened there. People liberated from the work camps are being encouraged to go see it for themselves, but the German citizens surrounding the Dachau camp have been given no choice. They will be forced to witness what happened to Jews, Poles, Gypsies, clergy, and other enemies of the Third Reich."

"Should we go?" asked Maria.

"I went to Dachau today and listened to Major Ray Lalonde's speech. Besides English, he speaks fluent German, Italian, and French. What he told us, what the survivors told us, the photographs he showed, the tour of the camp—it shocked, nauseated, and terrified me. But I don't regret going. A person needs to visit there to understand the horrors that Jews and other victims endured." Giovanni's voice thickened and he stopped.

Maria moved beside him and stroked his arm. When Giovanni could speak again, he asked his three friends, "Do you want to go?"

Antanas rose from the kitchen chair, walked to the sink, and poured himself a glass of water. Then he replied, "Yes, we owe it to those who suffered and died in these camps."

Augsburg, Bavaria, June 15, 1945

Jadwyga and Maria agreed to attend the tour of Dachau as well. Giovanni arranged for them to travel with their Baltic comrades on June 15. They left in convoys of U.S. Army trucks and arrived about an hour before noon. They disembarked from the truck just outside the Dachau camp.

It was hot and bright as they walked slowly towards the camp, fully exposed to the sun. Nothing and no one could have prepared them for what they saw and heard. The first disturbing feature they encountered was the main entrance to the camp itself. It was a huge stone-block archway wide enough for nine men to stand abreast and tall enough to allow a Tiger tank to pass through it. The area of the camp was nine hundred metres by seven hundred metres. About 25 percent of this area had been designated for prisoner barracks and the rest had been used as an SS training school, barracks for the SS guards and SS students, munitions factories, and medical experimentation labs. On top of the entrance archway was a sculpture of the German eagle. It was four metres high and over five metres wide. Below the eagle was a swastika within a circle, one metre in diameter.

This gateway has been built to intimidate all those prisoners who passed through it, and it had just such an effect on Jadwyga. She trembled as she walked beneath the archway.

Just inside the gate, a U.S. corporal awaited them. He asked for their attention. "You can all take a self-guided tour this morning, but at noon you must assemble by the crematorium."

They walked across a grassy field until they reached a large iron gate that Antanas had spotted earlier. Jadwyga read these words in German, sculpted in metal that formed part of the gate itself: *Arbeit, macht frei.* (Work will make you free.)

After they passed through the gate, they saw about twenty similar buildings that had served as the prisoners' barracks. Each building was one story high, standing at six metres, with a gently sloping roof and about five chimneys spread out evenly over a distance of twenty metres. Each barrack was about a hundred metres wide by ten metres deep. These barracks were lined up in rows for well over three hundred metres.

"There must be at least twenty barracks," observed Antanas.

Maria spotted a large brown-brick building in the distance. It had a reddish-brown tile roof with a huge chimney. "Let's go towards that building. It's just on the other side of the field."

When they got closer, a U.S. Army corporal met them by the entrance of the bungalow-style building.

"This was the crematorium. This is where prisoners who had been executed or who had died of disease or sheer exhaustion were burned to ashes. Bodies were being disposed of here right up until we liberated the camp on April 27. That is just a little over six weeks ago."

The smell of stale smoke was still pungent, and it made Maria and Jadwyga nauseous.

Twenty U.S. Army privates appeared and guided everyone behind an imaginary line in front of a wooden platform.

Major Lalonde was introduced, and then he was joined by two Dachau survivors, Gilda Klein and Lou Rose. Jadwyga gasped when she saw this man and woman. She whispered into Antanas's ear, "They both look starved half to death."

The blond, blue-eyed major stood at attention and spoke in a strong, clear voice. At thirty-one, he was young to be a senior officer. He was not tall but barrel-chested. He had distinguished himself as a ski warrior in the Italian Alps in 1944. He was also an accomplished linguist, and this was his most difficult assignment.

The major cleared his throat. "Welcome to Dachau. Welcome to Hades. Dachau started out as a prison for Germans who resisted Adolf Hitler and the Nazi party. In time, it mushroomed in size and, at its peak, it included one hundred off-campus subcamps. We have documented 32,000 deaths that occurred at this camp over the past dozen years, but we know there were many, many more. Since its inception in 1933, Dachau and its subcamps housed over 260,000 prisoners. The types of prisoners it held changed during those years. First, it housed Germans who resisted the Third Reich, but then it housed thousands of Jews, Poles, Soviet POWs, Gypsies, homosexuals, Jehovah witnesses, Catholic priests, other clergy, and anyone else who resisted Hitler and his thugs."

At this point, Major Lalonde beckoned for Lou Rose and Gilda Klein to step up to the microphone. Lou was wearing the striped pants and shirt characteristic of what male prisoners wore. Gilda wore a skirt made of cheap, rough fabric and a top of the same material. Major Lalonde told his audience, "Lou and Rose are both Jewish and they were prisoners here at Dachau. They volunteered to be part of these presentations. They want the world to know the horror of the camps."

Lou appeared to be about thirty years of age while Gilda could not have been more than nineteen. Lou was from Poland and Gilda from Ukraine. Under normal circumstances, they would both have seemed very attractive, but they were extremely underweight.

Gilda spoke first, in flawless German. "We may appear skinny to you today, but please look at the photographs of Lou and me and our fellow prisoners taken on April 27 by the U.S. Army. These photos were taken shortly after our liberation."

Five privates simultaneously distributed photos to the visitors. The men and women were jolted as they viewed the photographs of the liberated prisoners. Lou was more than two metres in height, but at the time the photograph was taken, he weighed less than thirty-eight kilos. Gilda weighed only thirty kilos. Most of their comrades appeared equally emaciated in the photos.

Gilda approached the microphone again. "More than 20,000 inmates were here in the camp, seriously ill, when the Americans rescued us."

Gilda began to cry. Tears streamed down the faces of others as well.

Lou joined the major at the podium and described what had happened on April 27 at Landsberg, one of the many subcamps of Dachau. "In advance of Allied troops, the SS ordered 4,000 men, women, and children into a wooden building. The doors and windows were boarded over and nailed shut. The walls were doused with gasoline and flamethrowers were used to ignite the structure. Most of these prisoners died in the inferno, but a few managed to break out only to die from their burns in the surrounding fields."

"Bastards!" was all that Antanas could utter. His hands were pressed against his forehead and the veins in his neck were pulsing. Jadwyga stroked his shoulders.

Major Lalonde resumed. "Not all the SS camp commanders behaved in this manner, however, and many prisoners, such as Lou and Gilda were spared."

Gilda raised her eyes to heaven and said, "Thank God for the U.S. army who freed so many, but I mourn the deaths of the Jews and non-Jews who died in the concentration camps. However, the horrible truth is that most Jews did not die in concentration camps—they were exterminated in death camps. Dachau was the first concentration camp and all the SS concentration camps were modelled after it. However, the Third Reich designed even worse places than the concentration camps."

Gilda continued. "You are from Lithuania, Latvia, and Estonia and you were forced to leave your homeland and toil in German work camps. You were treated badly and worked hard, but things could have been much worse. At least in a work camp, the purpose of the camp was clear. Concentration camps were more complicated. Yes, people worked in these camps. Here in Dachau and in its subcamps, most of the work involved manufacturing munitions for the Wehrmacht and the Luftwaffe, but it was more than work—it was punishment for the inmates. It was torture. In a concentration camp, you had a chance to live or die. If you worked hard, obeyed the guards, didn't cause trouble with the other prisoners, and somehow managed to stay healthy, then you lived. If you missed out on any of these things, you died, but at least you had had a chance. In the death camps, such as Treblinka or Belzec, a train deposited you there in the morning and you were dead before nightfall. If you were in Ukraine, Belarus, or the western part of the Soviet Union, you were probably shot or poisoned with carbon monoxide in a field. Or killed by inhaling truck or van exhaust. If you were in Poland, Lithuania, Latvia, or Estonia, you were sent to a gas chamber and poisoned with either hydracyanide or carbon monoxide."

At this point, most of those listening were weeping openly, including Antanas, Maria, and Jadwyga.

"Although many Jews were sent to concentration camps and the lucky ones even made it to work camps, like the terrible places where all of you had to work, most Jews were sent to death camps. Others were simply gassed or shot in fields. No one knows how many people died, but the U.S., Britain, France, and the Soviet Union have shared information with one another. They have established some early estimates. There were..." At this point, Gilda's voice faltered and she could not speak at all.

Lou came to her aid. "It's now believed that between 5.5 and 6 million Jews were killed by the Third Reich between 1933 and six weeks ago." A collective gasp went up from the crowd. Many of the men swore.

"Millions of non-Jews were also killed in the death camps. Next to the Jews, those who suffered the most in the SS camps were Soviet soldiers, Gypsies, and Poles, especially Polish priests."

Gilda drew near the microphone. "Lou and I are telling you these things for a reason. As horrible as this war has been, as cruel as some humans have been, we believe that there is hope. The SS has been defeated. The Third Reich is dust. The world has been given another chance. But the world must know the evil that was done; everyone must know what took place so that it never happens again. You can be part of that new world. Tell others what you have seen and heard today. Tell your children what happened in the camps. And be good to your children; be good to one another."

Jadwyga leaned towards Maria and Antanas. "Since the beginning of the war, our life has been a terrible struggle. But compared to what we've heard today, our lives have been blessed." Maria and Antanas both nodded slowly.

The truck ride home was notable for its near-silence. Very few words were spoken among the passengers, some of whom were quietly sobbing. Jadwyga rested her head against Antanas's chest.

Maria held her head in her hands and stared out the back of the truck at the dust swirling up behind them on the old country road.

Augsburg, Bavaria, June 16, 1945, 8 a.m.

Corporal Carlino was riding his Harley Davidson as fast as he could up the dusty road to the camp reserved for the Baltic displaced persons or DPs as they soon were called. The official word would come later that day, but he wanted to inform his friends in person.

The corporal halted just outside the building. He dismounted his motorcycle and ran to the front door. He was breathless when he entered the building and saw Maria.

"Giovanni, you look sad. What's happened?"

He held up his left hand and gently placed it on Maria's lips as he beckoned her with his right to follow him into the centre of the room.

The corporal sat down at the only table in the room. "You and the others are to be shipped out to Nurtingen tomorrow."

"Why?" demanded Maria.

"Because there are too many DPs in Augsburg and the UNRRA has asked Colonel Wilmot to spread people out to live in different German cities. You three are being sent to Nurtingen."

Antanas overheard Corporal Carlino as he entered the room. "How far is Nurtingen and in what direction?"

"Antanas, you'll be delighted to know it's about 140 kilometres to the northwest of Augsburg. You will be even farther from the Red Army."

"Antanas may be happy, but I'm not," Maria sad with a heavy sigh.

"We've been living like nomads since March. The Americans have liberated us from the SS and they are very kind, but they move us around like cattle. We have no home," complained Jadwyga.

"I'm sorry, but Colonel Wilmot has received orders from General Clay and General Clay is being pushed by the UNRRA."

Antanas stepped forward and shook Giovanni's hand. "Thank you for sharing this news with us. You drove all the way out here to tell us. When will official word come down?"

"Colonel Wilmot will come to this Baltic section by noon today and you'll leave tomorrow at 7 a.m."

"Will all the Balts be going to Nurtingen?" asked Antanas.

Giovanni nodded.

"Then, Jadwyga, Maria, let's start packing."

Maria accompanied Giovanni down the corridor and outside to his motorcycle. When they reached the bike, Maria embraced Giovanni and kissed him on the cheek.

"Will you visit us in Nurtingen?"

"I'll try, but Colonel Wilmot told me they'll be transferring me to Sicily. The army is having trouble with pockets of local mafia and they need more soldiers who can speak Italian. They need to gain the trust of the local people."

"Well, then, this is *ciao*," said Maria.

Giovanni put his arms around her and kissed her gently. He let her go, mounted his Harley, kick-started the engine, and drove away.

Maria waved until Giovanni and his motorcycle disappeared over the horizon.

Chapter 34

Life in Nurtingen

There were millions of refugees in West Germany. "Displaced persons," or "DPs," was a new term coined by the Allies to describe people such as Antanas, Jadwyga, and Maria. Many DPs had been forced labourers, some had been Soviet prisoners of war, and some were foreign nationals who had been pressed into military service in the German armed forces. Some were simply people from Eastern Europe fleeing the Red Army. Added to this group were the millions of East Germans fleeing to West Germany to avoid the avenging Red Army.

Nurtingen, July 1946

Jadwyga, Antanas, and Maria had been in Nurtingen for over a year now. Located on the river Neckar, Nurtingen had once been a university town with a population of 10,000. Then, in 1939, the population swelled when the town was chosen as the location for barracks built for the Wehrmacht. With the Allies in hot pursuit in April 1945, the Wehrmacht soldiers escaped through a nearby valley. Thus, the town was spared serious bombing and shelling.

Now that the war was over, the town's population was increasing again due to the influx of refugees from East Germany as well as displaced persons. The U.S. army had used the Wehrmacht barracks to house the DPs, but this was still not enough. They forced some of the townspeople to share their homes with the refugees and the DPs. If citizens refused, their homes were expropriated. Those expropriated were told to build shacks to live in, while the DPs moved into their homes. In 1946, six million DPs had been repatriated from Germany to countries such as France, Italy, Holland, Luxemburg, Belgium, Belarus, Russia, and Greece. But there were one million DPs from Poland, Lithuania, Estonia, Latvia, Ukraine, and Yugoslavia still living in Germany. These people refused to return to sure death or slavery at the hands of Joseph Stalin. Forty-five million West Germans were compelled to accommodate them, along with ten million refugees from East Germany who had fled from the Soviets. It was a great deal to ask from a country that had been bombed and shelled into ashes.

The Paskevicius family were fortunate that they could share a small home together in Nurtingen: a compact, one-story pine building with a thatched roof. Maria had her own room and Jadwyga and her husband shared the larger bedroom. They loved it. This was the first time that they were occupying their own bedroom since they had fled from their flat in Elbing. As a young married couple, they were pleased to have some privacy at last.

Jadwyga was less content when she learned that the German woman who had owned the home had been expelled when she refused to share it with "those swine from Lithuania." Even though this woman was rude and hostile to everyone but Germans, Jadwyga felt sorry for her. Now homeless, the woman was forced to move in with her younger sister who lived in the centre of town. She showed up in front of her house three or four times a week. She simply stood outside and cried. Maria and Jadwyga gave her harvest vegetables from the backyard garden. This seemed to make the woman less miserable, but did not change her attitude towards the DPs who were living in her home.

Antanas, Jadwyga, and Maria were skilled, assertive and lucky enough to each land a paying job. Antanas started work as a full-time mechanic for the U.S. army, fixing and maintaining trucks and jeeps. Jadwyga got part-time work mending soldiers' and officers' uniforms, and Maria was assigned the part-time job of cleaning some of the barracks. Colonel Luke Sulatycki, the United States Commander of Nurtingen, went out of his way to stress how important Maria's work was. "We have a lot of people living close together who are using an assortment of established and temporary latrine facilities. The possibility of an influenza outbreak or even a cholera epidemic is very real. Keeping things clean is the best defence."

Maria acknowledged the importance of good hygiene, but she knew that cleanliness alone was insufficient. Having enough fresh food to eat is also a necessary defence against disease, but food was scarce.

Maria visited the Nurtingen library and began to research basic nutrition. She learned from League of Nations documents that an adult required 1,800 calories per day to be healthy if they were not working, and more if they were. Maria knew that the average DP in their camp was getting much less than 1,800 calories per day. She wasn't worried about Jadwyga, Antanas, and herself because they all had jobs and could buy extra food on the black market. They could pay for food with the cigarettes they were given for their work. Cigarettes were still the currency of the black market. The German deutschmark had no value. Maria was worried about the DPs who did not have jobs and the children of those DPs. *Worrying and praying isn't enough*, she thought. *I have to do something.*

Maria went to the U.S. Army headquarters in Nurtingen. When she arrived, she met a host of army bureaucrats. She pushed for a meeting with Colonel Sulatycki. She didn't get one that day, but she returned to pester the bureaucrats twice a week. It took months, but on July 15 she finally met with the colonel. His office was on the second floor of the building where she had found the notice for her job. She was escorted into the colonel's large but modest office. Colonel Sulatycki got up from his desk, strode up to Maria, kissed her hand, and welcomed her to sit in the chair by his desk. A tall, slim man, he reminded Maria of the American actor Jimmy Stewart.

In fluent German, he declared, "I understand that you're an excellent worker and keep the Lithuanian barracks clean. It appears that you also volunteer as a teacher and as a scout leader for the Lithuanian children."

Maria's eyes widened. "I'm surprised that you know anything about me."

"In many ways, I'm like the burgermeister of Nurtingen. It's important to know the forces of good and evil within the town."

"Which am I?"

"I wouldn't be meeting with you if I thought you to be a villain. What can I do for you?"

"I'm concerned about the lack of food for the DPs and especially for the children. As you know, the League of Nations has clearly outlined that an adult needs 1,800 calories per day to be healthy, and more if they're working. The people in this camp are getting much less."

Colonel Sulatycki took off his reading glasses and peered directly at Maria. "I know. The adults are receiving about 1,100 calories per day. It's not enough, but food is still very scarce. Things are getting better, but Stalin won't let the East Germans trade with us and they represented the agricultural centre of old Germany. France can feed only itself. The English are still rationing food. We're bringing large supplies of canned and dried food from America, but the generosity of the American people can only be pushed so far."

Maria's face flushed as she leaned towards the colonel's desk. "Are the American people starving? Are they aware that 26 percent of the Lithuanians in this camp are children? Do they know that half of these children have rickets because there isn't enough fat in the milk they're given? Do these Americans know that half of these kids have mild to moderate forms of TB? Do they want an epidemic to break out? Do they care at all about us DPs?"

Colonel Sulatycki stood up from his chair, stepped back, and took a deep breath. "Then the reports are true."

"What reports?"

"My spies have told me that you're a natural leader. You've organized many Lithuanian volunteers to help you keep the barracks and the latrines spotless, and this has reduced the chances of an epidemic. They also told me that you are smart, pushy, but fair. Are they correct?"

Maria stood up from her chair and put both hands together and held them close to her chest. "I've suffered under the Nazis and the Soviets and I will be eternally grateful to the U.S. army and the American people for saving us from both. Yet, I must tell you the truth so that you can do all in your power to help these children and their parents."

"I'll do everything I can, but remember—there are millions of hungry people throughout Europe, not just you and your Lithuanian brothers and sisters."

"Thank you. And thank you to the American people."

Maria left Colonel Sulatycki, returned to the barracks, and completed her cleaning shift. Then she went to the section of the barracks reserved for the Lithuanian schools. She got a bucket, some water, and two rags and began to scrub a classroom floor. She couldn't stop thinking about the plight of her fellow Lithuanians. *Lithuanians are a highly educated people and we place great value on the education of our children*, she thought as she squeezed the dirty water from the rag and into the pail. *We have lost our homeland and contact with our parents has been severed. Our careers are on hold.* She scrubbed harder. *All we can do is put our hope in the future—and the education of our children is the future.*

Maria was grateful that during the previous summer, the U.S. army had given each ethnic group a space in the south section of the barracks to establish their respective schools. That was the beginning of the Lithuanian schools. Maria found that it was easy to find teachers. There were many unemployed and underemployed Lithuanian professionals in the camp. Many of these people became part-time volunteer teachers. That was the easy part. What was in short supply were textbooks written in Lithuanian and adequate salaries for the full-time teachers and the principal. Maria stood up from washing the floor and wiped her brow as she thought back to the establishment of the schools.

The Lithuanian DPs were highly resourceful individuals. Beginning in the summer of 1945, Lithuanian tradespeople used whatever scrap materials they could find to make the classrooms bright, cheery, and functional. Many of the teachers were business people who worked late into the night typing copies of books donated by fellow Lithuanian DPs. A child had to share one book or a typed facsimile with three classmates. Care and maintenance of these books was a primary lesson that Maria taught all of her students. Maria took on the role of a seventh- and eighth-grade science teacher. The children found her to be tough, but fair—and always thought-provoking and challenging.

Maria remembered the sweltering night in late July 1945, when superintendent Thomas Benediktas outlined his plan to establish elementary, pre-high, and high schools for the Lithuanian children in their Red Cross camps. The parents questioned him extensively. Not only did they support his ideas, however; they also gave him a standing ovation. With a core of paid staff, free space donated by the U.S. army, and dozens of volunteers such as Maria, the schools became a reality.

On the walk home from that historic meeting, Jadwyga had asked Maria, "Would you like to be a professional teacher?"

"No, I don't think so. I'd like to be a doctor or a nurse, if there's still time."

"I'd like to have my own garage," Antanas declared.

Jadwyga took a long breath. "And I'd like to find a permanent home so that Antanas and I can start a family."

Chapter 35

Family Addition

The United States, Britain, Canada, Australia, and New Zealand had all accepted European immigrants during the past two years, but not at the pace that everyone had anticipated. Life could not be stopped by politics, however, and there was a mini-baby boom happening within the DP camps.

Nurtingen to Plochingen, May 8, 1947, 7 a.m.

Antanas could never remember being this nervous driving a truck. *This is it. This is the day our baby will be born.*

Antanas had borrowed a small army truck from Captain Mario Calla. He packed Maria, Jadwyga, and all the baby items and now they were driving the seventeen kilometres from Nurtingen to Plochingen. The U.S. army had moved them to Nurtingen two years ago and Plochingen was where the U.S. Army hospital was situated. Antanas had been taking Jadwyga there for medical check-ups for the past seven months. *I should be accustomed to this drive, but I'm worried I'll take a wrong turn.* Antanas couldn't stop himself from fretting.

Maria sat in the cab of the truck. She was there to support Jadwyga with the birth. "How are you feeling, Jadwyga?" she asked.

"The contractions are about seven minutes apart now. We're getting closer."

Just then, the Plochingen Hospital came into view. Antanas relaxed somewhat.

The hospital was a beautiful four-story, red-bricked building with a sloping tiled roof. On this fresh spring day, all the white shutters and the many windows were wide open. There was a cluster of lilac bushes growing along the front wall of the hospital. The fragrance of the lilacs wafted in all directions.

This had been the hospital for Plochingen and the surrounding towns and villages for many years. But since April 1945, it had become the main hospital for U.S. army troops stationed in the region, and then it began to take care of displaced persons.

Antanas pulled the truck up to the front door. Maria hopped out first and gave her hand to Jadwyga.

They entered the hospital foyer and crossed over to the large admissions desk. The secretary looked up and frowned. "Jadwyga, your obstetrician, Dr. Kessler, will not be available to assist you with your delivery today. He's already with three other women who are giving birth."

"Is there no other doctor available for my sister?" Maria asked.

"No, but Jadwyga will be ably assisted by two nurses whom she already knows, Anika and Katerina."

Jadwyga smiled. "Oh yes, I'm quite fond of them. I met with them many times when I came for my check-ups with Dr. Kessler."

Maria took Jadwyga's arm and they ambled down the long semi-lit corridor. When they came to the birthing room, it was familiar to Jadwyga but not to Maria. Jadwyga sat in the chair beside the bed closest to the door while Maria scanned the room. She saw that there were windows facing the south, four beds divided by curtains, and a sink and cabinets along the north wall. There was a large bathtub in the middle of the room with curtains encircling it.

As she was surveying the room, she saw that three of the beds were already occupied by German women, about to give birth. At this point, the two obstetric nurses, Anika and Katerina, bustled into the room sharing a laugh. "What's so funny?" asked Jadwyga.

Anika put her arm around Jadwyga and kissed her on both cheeks.

"Hi, Jadwyga! It's your husband. He's clearly nervous about the birth but he won't admit it. He won't even come inside the hospital. He showed us that he parked your truck under the shade of the big poplar tree. He explained to us that he'll be giving the truck a tune-up while we're delivering your baby."

"He's hilarious!" exclaimed Katerina.

"Yes, my brother's quite a joker," said Maria.

Jadwyga stood up and introduced everyone. "Maria, Anika is my midwife and senior nurse, and Katerina is my student nurse. They're both wonderful."

Anika was about forty years old, of medium height with curly brown hair. She was about ten kilos overweight but she had a healthy glow and was always in a good mood. Katerina was taller and slimmer, and her blonde hair was pulled into a ponytail. She was about twenty-one years old, and, while on the quiet side, she displayed more confidence compared to most student nurses.

Anika turned to Jadwyga. "Please remove your clothes and put on this hospital gown."

Jadwyga did as she was told, and Maria placed her clothes in the bag that she had brought with her.

"Please lie down while Katerina takes your pulse, temperature, and blood pressure."

Katerina finished her tasks quickly. "Everything's normal, at least normal for a woman who's close to giving birth."

Anika inquired, "How close are the contractions?"

Jadwyga grimaced. "I'm having one now and the last one was five minutes ago. They hurt more and last longer."

"Jadwyga, now I must examine you to see how dilated you are." Anika raised Jadwyga's gown and completed her examination. "You're only five centimetres dilated. When did your water break?"

"More than an hour ago."

Anika frowned and asked Katerina to boil some water so she could mix it with cold water from the bathtub tap. "I need warm water for your bath."

Katerina did as she was asked. "The bath water's ready."

As Jadwyga began to waddle towards the bathtub, she was stricken with a contraction and Maria supported her. "Thank you, Maria, you're an angel."

"I'm no angel, but I'm your sister and your friend."

Katerina and Maria helped Jadwyga into the bath. Anika asked Jadwyga to do some deep breathing. She did this for about forty minutes. The contractions were now coming every four minutes and they were much more painful. Yet when Anika examined Jadwyga again, she frowned. "You're only dilated to six centimetres."

Anika held Jadwyga's hand. "Okay, Jadwyga, now I'm going to do something to speed up your labour; it will seem strange but trust me."

"I trust you."

"I'll be careful."

Anika gently massaged Jadwyga's stomach; then she began to push down on it. After fifteen minutes, Anika instructed Katerina. "Relieve me and carry on the massage." After another fifteen minutes, Anika checked Jadwyga's dilation and smiled broadly. "You're now at eight centimetres."

The contractions were occurring faster and each one was more painful than the last. Jadwyga was sweating as Maria held her hand. This went on for another two hours. Jadwyga was placed in and out of the bath several times. When Jadwyga was in the bath, Katerina bailed water every fifteen minutes and carefully replaced it with hot water to maintain a warm temperature. Maria was mindful to move Jadwyga far away from the large pot when Katerina poured hot water into the tub.

Suddenly, Jadwyga let out a loud groan and two minutes later she moaned again. "Katerina, please fetch some towels," Anika ordered.

"Jadwyga, I want you to stand slowly while Maria and I help you to get out of the bath." As soon as Jadwyga was standing upright beside the bath, Katerina returned with the towels and began to dry her. "Let's walk back to the bed, slowly," Anika directed.

Once Jadwyga lay in the bed, the contractions increased, as did the pain. Anika told Jadwyga to push and Jadwyga did her very best. Maria remained at Jadwyga's side, gripping her hand. Jadwyga did not scream, but the tightness of her grip almost squashed Maria's hand. Maria said nothing. Anika checked again for dilation and this time she said delightedly, "I can see the top of the baby's head. Whether it's a boy or a girl, the baby has lovely black hair." Jadwyga smiled and then she felt a stabbing pain.

"Push," commanded Anika, and that is what Jadwyga did. "Push," repeated Katerina and Maria, and once again Jadwyga pushed with all her might. While Jadwyga kept pushing, Anika sterilized her hands with soap and water and told Katerina to do the same. The pain was becoming increasingly more intense, but Jadwyga continued to push with each contraction.

Anika walked back to Jadwyga's bed and stationed herself at the foot. She reached forward. "I'm touching the baby's head. Now the head is out and in my hands. One more push and we'll have the shoulders."

Katerina moved beside Anika to see if she needed any help, but everything was going well. One more push and the shoulders cleared. Then the baby arrived in Anika's hands. "It's a boy!" She held him upside down with both hands and he began to cry. Anika handed the baby to Katerina, who carried him to Jadwyga. She and Maria stared at him with wide eyes. Jadwyga placed the baby at her breast and he began to suckle. Jadwyga beheld her son. *The birth of a child is something that happens by the millions, but still each time it's a miracle. Thank you, God, for giving me this healthy baby boy. Please help me to show him one day to my mother and our families in Vilnius and Kaunas.*

Anika approached Maria. "Please fetch your brother while Katerina and I take care of the afterbirth." By the time Maria and Antanas re-entered the room, the little baby boy had finished his meal, was swaddled in a blanket, and was being cuddled by Jadwyga. Antanas strode into the room, broke out into a tremendous smile, bent over, and hugged his wife. He kissed Jadwyga and then Jadwyga held his son up to her husband. Antanas gently picked up his infant boy.

Maria asked, "What are you two going to call him?"

Antanas replied, "Piotr." Their first child would be named after Jadwyga's father.

Jadwyga rolled onto her side to see Antanas and their baby more easily. "Yes, but we'll call him Peter, the English version of Piotr. We really hope that he'll be raised in Canada. They speak English there."

Chapter 36

The New World Scout

When the war ended and the troops returned home, many Canadians feared that another Depression would occur because there would not be enough jobs for everyone. Immigration was restricted for years. Finally, Prime Minister McKenzie King and his Finance Minister CD Howe came up with a plan that allowed Canadian companies and hospitals to recruit refugees to do the jobs that most Canadians did not want to do. Lumberjacks, orderlies, hospital dishwashers, farm hands, nannies for the wealthy, and miners were the most numerous roles offered in this experiment. Single DPs rather than married couples with children were preferred by the Canadian government and Canadian employers.

Nurtingen, July 1, 1948, 6:30 p.m.

Antanas strolled into the kitchen. Jadwyga was holding their son Peter in her arms as she stood by the sink.

Antanas removed his cap and scratched his left ear. "We have to move again. Captain Calla explained to me that the American garage is relocating from here in Nurtingen to Ludwigsburg. He wants me to keep working for him in this new garage, which is forty-eight kilometres to the northwest. But it's too far to travel there and back each day since I don't own a car or a motorcycle."

"You'll be happy because you'll still be working in the American garage and you'll be even farther from the Russians. But what about Peter, Maria, and me?"

"Well, Captain Calla has arranged for Maria to get another job in Ludwigsburg and we'll all live in the same residence together. We'll be housed in the barracks for the DPs from the Baltic area."

Maria entered the kitchen. "Will I have my own bedroom?"

"Yes, but our home won't be as nice compared to what we have now. I'm sorry, Jadwyga and Maria, but we have no real choice in this. I have a paying job now as a mechanic for the U.S. army, and if I want to keep it, we must relocate. The American soldiers will move us in their trucks on July 5, the day after American Independence Day."

Ludwigsburg, July 20, 1948, 4 p.m.

Maria could hardly wait for her brother to come back from work. She had important news, and there he was sauntering up the dusty road. It was a very hot day, and Captain Calla had let Antanas and his men leave work early. Maria waited until Antanas entered their one common room that was separate from the rest of the barracks. Maria called to Jadwyga. "Come out of your bedroom. I have some news."

"We're coming; I'm just looking for Peter's blanket."

"So, little sister, what's the big news?" Antanas asked.

"Wait till Jadwyga and Peter get here."

Peter came running into the room, threw up his arms, and his Aunt Maria picked him up and twirled him around. Peter laughed. Jadwyga walked into the room and grinned at Peter. "You're so happy to be in the arms of your aunt."

Maria could not contain her news any longer. "I've been accepted to work at St. Joseph's Hospital in Toronto, Canada. The Canadian government has agreed to let me immigrate. I start work there on August 25. Remember, I applied over a year ago, and now our prayers have been answered."

"The Canadian Immigration officer Michael Fullan made all the arrangements on my behalf. He has a cousin who lives near the hospital who will let me stay with her at first. She'll help me find a place of my own."

"Do you have your train and boat tickets already?" asked an astonished Antanas.

"Yes, I do. I gave Michael Fullan the money and he purchased them for me."

"Where did you get the money to pay him?"

"I gathered up all the cigarettes and art pieces that I had saved up since we came to Bavaria and I traded them on the black market. I got a loan for the rest from Vytas Balsys, the wealthiest Lithuanian DP in Ludwigsburg."

Jadwyga took a wiggling Peter from his Aunt Maria's arms. "Why didn't you come to us?"

"You need whatever you have to buy food and clothes for the three of you, and soon you'll have to start saving for your own trip across the Atlantic."

Antanas vanished, but then quickly rejoined them holding a small bag of cigarettes. "Take these. They'll help you buy the things you'll need on the train and the boat, instead of using your small bit of cash."

"Big brother, you keep these cigarettes for Peter and Jadwyga and yourself."

"No, we have enough. You're our scout in the New World. You're making a big sacrifice to go first and then sponsor us to come to Canada. We can't afford for you to starve on the journey." They all laughed.

Three weeks later, Maria left them for the first time in six years.

Toronto, January 1949

Maria had been writing them weekly since she arrived in Toronto on August 22. She described Toronto as a medium-sized city.

Dear Jadwya, Antanas and Peter,

... It's not liked the Wild West movies that we used to watch in the DP camps, but it's nowhere near as developed and cultured as the Lithuanian, Polish, or German cities were before the war.

The neighbourhood that I live in is called Parkdale. I think they call it that because on the west side of this neighbourhood is a huge park. Some of the homes in Parkdale used to be mansions for one family and their servants. Now the same homes have been carved up into several flats for German, Polish, Ukrainian, and Lithuanian immigrants.

Love,
Maria

Jadwyga would write back weekly and tell Maria about how smart and handsome Peter was and how all the women stopped her when they went for walks in the parks.

Dear Maria,

They tell me what beautiful hair Peter has. In fact, most people think that Peter's a girl because he's so beautiful and has long black wavy hair. Antanas keeps threatening to cut it off but he hasn't done so. He's a wonderful father and he made a fantastic stroller for Peter when he gets tired of walking. He made the stroller from scraps in the garage.

Peter is my joy, and Antanas and I love him so much, but we miss you, Maria. Even little Peter keeps asking when he'll see Aunt Maria again. He looks at the pictures of you, from when we enjoyed our vacation together in the Bavarian Alps. He looks at them every night before bed....

Love,
Jadwyga

***

In her January 18 letter, Maria was less optimistic than usual, but she opened her heart.

Dear Jadwyga and Antanas,

... I've joined a Catholic church in Parkdale. Holy Family is the name. The 9 a.m. Sunday mass is in Lithuanian. I'm meeting some other Lithuanians there.

I'm slowly learning English. It's a dreadful language with so many exceptions. I have made a few non-Lithuanian friends at work, mostly DPs from Germany, Ukraine, Yugoslavia, and Poland.

Work is drudgery. I can only scrape and clean so many plates. I had hopes that I would be accepted into the nurses training program here at St. Joseph's Hospital. I was turned down by the head administrator, Sister Amelia Comper. She's mean, mean, mean. She claims that I don't have enough science education to start the course and that my English is not good enough to begin the training. She's wrong; my science courses in Lithuania are all I need to start and Sister

Cecelia Dougherty (my immediate boss) says my English is coming along well. Sister Cecelia is a great person and is kind to all of us DPs.

Not all Canadians are as kind as Sister Cecelia. Life isn't easy for a Lithuanian immigrant in Toronto. Most of the business and professional people are either born here in Canada or are from England, Scotland, Ireland, or the United States. English is the only language as far as these people are concerned. Parkdale, Chinatown, parts of College Street, and parts of the Danforth have lots of immigrants, but the rest of Toronto is not so immigrant-friendly. Some Canadians like us DPs, but some fear us.

Anyway, I'm feeling sorry for myself, but it's mostly because I miss you three and I can't wait until you can come here, and we can be together again.

Love,
Maria

May 8, 1949

Dear Maria,

We just received the most wonderful birthday present for Peter. It's from the Canadian government. Michael Fullan just arrived today to tell Antanas and me the good news. We've all been accepted as immigrants to Canada. Thank you so much for sponsoring us. Michael Fullan explained to us that we would never have been accepted to Canada without your support.

We must arrange for passage, but the U.S. Army has set up a system so that you can exchange cigarettes, wine, whiskey, jewellery, and other items at a fixed, predictable rate instead of on the black market. Antanas is going to work these things out with his boss Captain Calla and with Michael Fullan at the Canadian consulate. We will arrive in Toronto at Union Station on July 5 at 4 p.m.

Love,
Jadwyga

Chapter 37

The Final Leg

Louis St-Laurent replaced Mackenzie King as the Prime Minister of Canada in November 1948. Despite the concerns of many Canadian citizens, the new prine minister continued to support pro-immigration policies. On April 4, 1949, Canada joined the United States and ten Western European countries to form the North Atlantic Treaty Organization (NATO). The purpose of this organization was to provide a military counterbalance to the threat of the Soviet Union.

June 22, 1949, 4 p.m.

Antanas, Jadwyga, Peter, and all their earthly possessions were on a train heading for Naples. It was a slow train that stopped everywhere, but the tickets were cheap. They would have to sleep two nights sitting upright, but they would arrive in Naples by 7 a.m. on June 24.

Antanas beamed with happiness. "We got train tickets to Naples. We have enough money for our boat passage to Halifax, our train tickets to Montreal, our hotel stay in Montreal, and our train tickets to Toronto. I exchanged the cigarettes, whiskey, rum, wine, and tools that I've saved for years to pay for these things. I was astounded by what my boss Captain Calla did for us."

Jadwyga held two-year-old Peter on her lap. "What did he do?"

"For my years of dedicated service to him and the army garage, he arranged for the U.S. Army to give me a twenty-five dollar American bonus. We can use this money for our hotel and meals while we stay in Naples, and for tips on the boat passage. He also convinced his superiors to issue us thirty dollars Canadian, for meals in Montreal and whatever we need in Toronto, until I get a job. What makes me happiest is that we didn't have to borrow a cent from Vytas Balsys or any of the money lenders in camp."

"That's great, Antanas. You are such a good provider for Peter and me."

Their slumber sitting upright was fretful that first night, but Peter slept soundly in Jadwyga's lap. Between shallow naps, Jadwyga reflected on their years in Bavaria after the war. She was so grateful for the help they had received from the U.S. army, the American Red Cross, and many German civilians. She was especially thankful for Anika, the midwife at the Plochingen hospital and Katerina, the young nurse in training. Because of their care and expertise and because Maria stayed with her throughout the entire birth process, it had all gone well. Jadwyga knew that Peter's birth had changed her life. His arrival made Antanas a devoted father and Maria a proud aunt.

Antanas had hours to think on the train. He considered how happy he had been working with his men, the mechanics of the Army base. He liked and admired his boss, Captain Mario Calla, and was sad to say goodbye to him. Still, he felt that Canada promised a future for Jadwyga, Peter, Maria, and himself. He was impressed with how brave Jadwyga had been during childbirth and what a wonderful mother she was. He was indebted to Maria for acting as their scout in the new world. He knew how lonely she had been in Toronto without them, but it was the only way they could all have been allowed entry to Canada.

In the early morning of the second day, they descended from the Italian Alps. It reminded Jadwyga and Antanas of their unexpected but fantastic holiday in the German Alps in August 1946. Captain Calla had arranged for Antanas to take his wife and sister with him when he delivered an old Ford truck to a U.S. Ranger outfit. Captain Jack McElroy was part of an American ski battalion during the last eighteen months of the war. Now, he was training the U.S. Rangers how to perform rescue operations using skis. Because of Captain McElroy's graciousness, Jadwyga, Antanas, and Maria had their first holiday in seven years. For three days, they skied, threw snowballs, and, because it was summer, they played in the snow wearing bathing suits. Captain McElroy had lent Antanas a camera, so he had pictures to show his parents one day—if he ever saw them again.

On that afternoon, they dozed off and woke up during one of the many stops the train made. They were about halfway between the Italian Alps and Naples, but on this woefully slow train they still had an entire night of travel ahead of them. They were not sure where they were, but they spotted some women with children Peter's age and younger. The women were begging beside the train and they were shouting in Italian. Neither Antanas nor Jadwyga could understand them. Then the women switched to German. Their German was not good, but Jadwyga knew what they were saying. "We have no bread for our children; please have mercy on us."

They did not have much bread left for themselves, but Jadwyga beckoned two of the women to approach their train window. She stood up and Antanas rolled down the window as far as it would go. Jadwyga passed the women their last loaf of bread.

The women smiled and shouted, "*Gratia. Gratia. Danka. Danka.*" Then one of the women passed an orange through the window to Antanas. Antanas said "*Gratia.*" He peeled the orange and shared it with Peter and Jadwyga. It was a gratifying exchange.

June 27, 1949, 9 a.m.

The passenger ship seemed enormous to Jadwyga and Antanas. Peter took no notice of the ship because he was asleep in his mother's arms as they walked up the gangplank. Antanas and Jadwyga had dozed poorly for three nights on a lumpy mattress. To save money, they had lodged in a cheap hotel in Naples, surviving on bread, water, coffee, oranges, and a little spaghetti. Now they were looking forward to the food provided on their voyage.

They arrived in Naples on June 24 because the ship administrator had written to them to inform them that the boat might have to leave dock anytime between June 25 and June 27. Their liner was a Greek vessel registered in Athens; it had been given the half-Greek, half-English name *The New Heldes*.

Most of the ship's crew were Greek, but its captain was an Italian man named Vittorio Pacione. He was handsome, with brown eyes and light-brown hair. He was thirty-five and he spoke Italian, Greek, and German fluently. He spoke English and French passably. He liked everyone. He was liked and respected by his crew, but he ran a tight ship. He had a wife and three children living in Naples and he missed them on each trans-Atlantic run. To lessen his loneliness, he adopted other people's children on the voyages, and he took a special liking to Peter. He invited the whole Paskevicius family to his table on their first night at sea and he spoiled Peter with gelato and dried fruit. The captain was impressed that Peter knew how to use his knife, fork, and spoon as a two-year-old. This was a trick his mother had recently taught him.

After dinner, Captain Pacione took them to a railing on the upper deck at the stern of the ship. "This is where the kitchen staff dump the uneaten food into the ocean. Over time, many dolphins and even a few whales have learned that *The New Heldes* is a good source of food."

Antanas, Jadwyga, and especially Peter were thrilled to see dolphins leaping out of the water and the occasional whale breaching. Antanas put his arm around Jadwyga and nuzzled his nose into her ear. "This is going to be a great voyage."

Jadwyga kissed Antanas on the cheek and leaned over towards Captain Pacione. "Thank you for inviting us to your table and for such an excellent dinner. I give you special thanks for showing us where the dolphins and the whales come to eat and play."

They brought Peter to see the whales and the dolphins the next two nights, but on the fourth night dark clouds formed, waves swelled, and rain came down hard. The ship began to rock.

The ship handled the storm well, but Jadwyga turned green and started vomiting. She could not eat a thing. She lay on the bed and tilted her head towards Antanas. "You'll have to look after Peter now."

"I'll be happy to look after him until you're well again."

For the next three days, Antanas took Peter to breakfast, lunch, and dinner, brushed his teeth, took him to the toilet, bathed him, and put him to bed. They walked the deck together, met with the other passengers, and visited with the various crew members from the laundry room and the engine room, the cabin cleaners, and the kitchen staff. All the crew and passengers loved Peter. He loved to run on the deck under the watchful eye of his father. He had very long black hair that was wavy near the tips, soft brown eyes, and an angelic face. Antanas did have one concern. *Many of the crew and passengers mistake him for a girl. I'll make sure that they only make that mistake once. When we get to Toronto, I'm taking Peter to the barber.*

On their walks, Antanas loved the engine room best. It was filled with two massive diesel engines and the noise level was high. There he met and befriended Alex Rubis, the chief engineer. Alex was a very tall man of about fifty years of age. He had broad shoulders and a massive chest. He was balding but his most prominent feature was the gaze of his piercing blue eyes. He looked scary to Peter, but Antanas found him to be quite approachable. Antanas was excited to learn from Alex details about the ship's specifications and to observe her powerful twin diesel engines.

"How fast can she go?"

"With both propellers going at top speed, she can reach seventeen knots or thirty-one kilometres per hour, but cruising speed is usually twenty-six kilometres per hour. The crossing from Naples to Halifax usually takes eight days. We should arrive on July 4, American Independence Day."

Antanas may have been fascinated by the engines, but Peter was frightened by the popping sounds they made and he started to wriggle in Antanas's arms. Antanas bid farewell to Alex and started to climb the stairs. When they reached the level of the kitchen and the dining room, they heard the chef, Jennifer Baros, call out to them.

"Antanas, Peter. Wait a minute."

Jennifer was a tall, slim, beautiful young Greek woman with long black hair that she pinned and tucked neatly under her chef's hat. It was unusual, in 1949, for a woman to be employed as the master chef of a Greek passenger ship, but her father was the financial officer of the company and he was the owner's best friend. Besides, Jennifer was a great chef.

In flawless German, she asked, "Would Peter like some pieces of apple and orange?"

Peter raised both hands and said, "*Ja.*"

Antanas corrected, "*Ja, bitte.*"

Peter repeated, "*Ja, bitte.*"

Jennifer smiled and placed two pieces of apple and three pieces of orange segments into Peter's small hands.

Peter ate all of them in a flash and Antanas prompted him. "What do you say to this nice woman?"

Peter looked down at his feet and whispered, "*Danka.*"

"You're welcome, Peter." Then Jennifer walked quickly through the swinging doors and back into the chaos of the kitchen.

July 4, 1949, 7 a.m.

Jadwyga had been up and eating meals for twenty-four hours when she, Antanas, and Peter decided to take a short walk on the deck. Jadwyga spotted two gulls flying above them.

"Don't gulls live close to shore?"

"Yes, that's correct," replied Captain Pacione. "Sorry to sneak up behind you, but I just came to urge you three to hurry in for breakfast. We'll be docking in Halifax in less than an hour."

As they entered the harbour of Halifax, Antanas could see why the British and the French had fought over this magnificent port. The harbour was shaped in a manner that forced ships entering it to pass close to the embankments on the shore. The water was deep enough for big ships, but they were compelled to sail within range of artillery lined up on the cliffs.

Jadwyga formed a different impression. She could see that the port was small and littered with lobster cages. There were the government harbour building, some warehouses, and streetcar tracks, but nothing much else close to the shore. Jadwyga could see downtown Halifax in the distance. It was mostly one- or two-story buildings with some notable exceptions such as the university, the clock tower, and Simpson's department store. She had expected a large city like London or New York, or even a medium-sized port city such as Naples. But Halifax was a small city. Still, it was Canada, and soon they would see Maria again.

When they finally docked, Antanas and Jadwyga knew that they had chosen the right country. Along Pier 21, there were about ten women and two men holding large signs that said, "Welcome to Canada." They didn't read English yet, but one of the crew kindly translated for them.

***

They did not stay long at Pier 21. They boarded a bus and a short ride later, they were at the railroad station. It was 10 a.m.

"What time does our train for Montreal leave?" asked Jadwyga.

"It will be here in an hour," Antanas replied. "It will leave Halifax at 11 a.m."

Antanas took Peter for a walk and then Jadwyga read to him. Finally, they boarded the train. It was a strenuous train ride for both Jadwyga and Antanas. Even though he slept part of the way, Peter was getting bored walking up and down the aisles of their passenger car and looking out the window. It was 11 p.m. when they rolled into the station in Montreal. Jadwyga carried Peter while Antanas carried their luggage. It was eight blocks up St. Catherine Street to reach the inn where they were staying. By the time they checked in and put Peter to bed, it was after midnight.

Everything went smoothly the next morning, and the three of them were on a train heading for Toronto by 8 a.m. They had seen nothing of Canada's largest city, but they promised themselves that they would return to Montreal one day. Many of the Greek sailors had visited Canada. They encouraged the Paskevicius family to settle in Montreal rather than Toronto. "Montreal's bigger than Toronto." "Montreal's more European." "Toronto's boring and other Canadians call it Hogtown." "Montreal's exciting." "Montreal is French."

Antanas explained to them, "My sister is sponsoring our move to Canada, and she lives and works in Toronto. We have to give Toronto a chance."

***

When the train pulled into Union Station, they were asleep and the conductor kindly nudged them awake. Antanas was embarrassed that he'd drifted off to sleep, but he quickly regained his poise. He gave the conductor a twenty-five-cent tip, gathered all their things, and disembarked. Jadwyga had picked up a slumbering Peter and was already a few steps ahead.

When they entered Union Station, they were impressed by its sheer size and by its Beaux-Arts style of architecture.

"This place is huge," exclaimed Jadwyga. "Look at all the people. How are we ever going to spot Maria?"

Then they heard Maria calling their names: "Jadwyga, Peter, Antanas!"

They searched for the source of the sound and spotted Maria wearing a navy-blue dress and a huge smile. They stepped towards her as quickly as their tired bodies would allow. Jadwyga put Peter down and hugged Maria for what seemed like an eternity. Then she picked Peter up while Antanas and Maria embraced. Peter said, "Aunt Maria!" and Maria plucked him from his mother's arms and swung him around. Peter laughed and Maria carried him across the station towards Front Street.

"Where are we going to live?" asked Jadwyga.

"On Fuller Avenue, just north of Queen Street. It's about a five-minute walk east of Roncesvalles, which is the most Eastern European street in Toronto. Our flat is about a ten-minute walk from St. Joseph's Hospital, where I work. It's a great place but it'll be better if I tell you about it once we arrive. I'll give you the short tour."

"How do we get there?" Antanas asked. "Can we walk?"

"No, it'll be too far to walk there with luggage. We'll walk up to King Street and catch a streetcar."

As they descended the stairs from Union Station, Antanas spotted a lush green lawn between the station and the sidewalk. He walked onto the lawn, dropped to his knees, and kissed the grass.

"Thank God, we're alive. Thank God, we're free. Thank God, we're together."

While still holding Peter, Maria took Antanas by the arm, helped him to his feet, and said, "Welcome to Canada, big brother."

Jadwyga slid between Maria and Antanas and pulled Peter back into her arms. "Our journey is finally over. This is Peter's home. This is our home. Canada."

Epilogue

People have asked me why I wanted to write about Jadwyga, Antanas, and Maria Paskevicius and their experiences as forced labourers during the Second World War. The inspiration for this book is easy to recall. In 1972, I met Jadwyga and Antanas's daughter, Chris Paskevicius, and two years later we were married. In the early years of our marriage, Jadwyga and Antanas invited Chris and me to a great many family meals.

I enjoyed these meals tremendously because they were filled with good food and good company, and because sometimes Jadwyga shared stories about their experiences in Europe before, during, and after the war. Most of the family members at the table had heard these stories many times and they tended to be more focused on current events. I, on the other hand, was fascinated. Here was a trio who had been compelled to work for the Nazis for ten months in a camp in northeastern Germany and who had managed to escape. They had lived for four years in American Red Cross camps in Germany while they awaited approval to emigrate to Canada. This was far from normal to me, and I knew that I wanted to capture their experiences for posterity.

Pursuing careers and raising our children, Laura and Paul, consumed most of our time and energy for a few decades. When I retired in 2013, I was determined to record the experiences I had heard about at the family dinner table. By this time, Antanas and his sister Maria were both deceased, but Jadwyga was still alive and her mind was sharp.

Jadwyga turned ninety-three two months after I began to record her story. She was blind, partially deaf, and unable to walk, but her mind was alert and her memory was remarkable. Because Antanas, Maria, and all of her friends had died, and because of her physical disabilities, Jadwyga's life was now quite confined. She often told me that she spent her days remembering the past. She remarked that it was of great value to her that I was interested in her memories and that I wished to preserve them. Usually, she enjoyed our talks together, but describing some of the sadder or more horrific events would make her melancholy. Still, she assured me that she derived much more joy and meaning from sharing her life journey than she suffered pain from it.

Jadwyga made it clear to me that their decision to emigrate to Canada was an auspicious one for Antanas, Maria, and herself. They not only made Canada their home—they made it a haven of happiness. For several years, Jadwyga, Antanas, and Peter shared the same home with Maria in Parkdale. Then, Maria met and married Antanas Vasiliauskas and they lived on the second floor of the house while Jadwyga, Antanas Paskevicius, and Peter occupied the main floor.

In 1952, Jadwyga gave birth to Chris, a sister for Peter. A year later, Maria and Antanas Vasiliauskas welcomed their own baby girl, Giedre. They all continued to live in the house on Fuller Avenue. They worked and saved and, in 1958, the two families purchased their own separate homes in south Etobicoke. Their houses were less than half a kilometre from each other and they visited one another often. Although they were cousins, Chris and Giedre grew to be as close as sisters.

In the early years following their arrival in Canada, Antanas P. worked as a mechanic for a garage near Roncesvalles Avenue, but he later formed a partnership with another Lithuanian mechanic, Joe Tamosiunas. Together, they opened P and T Garage in Mississauga. It was a tremendous success.

Maria worked as an assistant to a renowned photographer until she retired in her sixties. Antanas Vasiliauskas was employed by Massey-Harris in Toronto until his retirement.

Jadwyga remained a stay-at-home mother until Chris started high school and Peter entered the University of Toronto's Engineering Faculty, at which time she went to work as a salesperson in the dress department of Eaton's in downtown Toronto.

Visiting Lithuania or Poland in the late 1940s and early 1950s remained highly dangerous for anyone who had been born there and who had emigrated to other countries. During this time, Jadwyga's mother, Marija, died of cancer. Being unable to bid farewell to her mother in person was a wound that never healed for Jadwyga. Eventually, however, the Soviets became less restrictive, and Jadwyga, Antanas, and Maria visited their homelands in the 1960s and 1970s. Stephania and Antanas (Senior) Paskevicius continued to live a modest but comfortable life well into their nineties. Jadwyga's father Piotr moved to Canada in the early 1970s and resided with Jadwyga and Antanas until he died at the age of 100.

In time, all the children grew up and started their own families; the families remained close and took advantage of every opportunity to visit one another.

Tragically, Antanas Vasiliauskas died from a massive heart attack in his home during the early phase of his retirement. He died in Maria's arms. She was devastated. After a few years, she moved forward on her own and became a world traveller. On a trip to Israel, she met with Peter Baur's daughter, Erica, who confirmed that her father had been wounded in a battle fought late in the war. He lost both legs but recovered and became a watchmaker. In 1950, while visiting Israel, he met Erica's mother. They fell in love and were married, and he moved to Tel Aviv. Erica told Maria that her mother had died three years earlier and that her father had died only one year before Maria's trip to Israel. Erica knew of the history between her father and Maria. Although they never spoke of it, Erica and Maria both understood why her father had never searched for Maria after the war.

When Maria was diagnosed with lung cancer in 2008, Giedre and her husband, Jonas, brought her into their home and nursed her for the last four months of her life. She died on December 8, 2008 at the age of eighty-six.

Two and a half months later, on February 22, 2009, her brother Antanas died at his home at the age of ninety-four. Due to her blindness and overall poor health, Jadwyga moved to a long-term care facility in central Etobicoke. Peter, Chris, and I visited her several times a week, but she deeply missed her husband and her best friend, Maria.

As we entered the spring of 2014, Jadwyga's mental health began to deteriorate along with her physical well-being. It was sad to watch her struggle to maintain her spirit, but nonetheless she remained an extraordinarily loving person until the end of her life. She died on August 5, 2014 at the age of ninety-four.

She left this world before I could ask her all the questions I wanted to ask, but she gave me all I needed.

Thank you, Jadwyga.

Acknowledgements

Thanks go to Alexandra Leggat, Antanas Sileika, Janice Zawerbny, and Jane McNulty, who edited this book with objective eyes and sage advice. I extend my gratitude to Ana Hill, Jennifer Myrie, Mario and Marjie Calla, my nephew Michael Paskevicius, Hazel Reynolds, Monsignor Sam Bianco, Jim Corkery, Glenn Carley, Patti Trudeau, Terry Leeder, Susan Harris, Susan Wright, and a neighbour and long-time friend who all read drafts of the novel and reflected back to me a sample of the average reader's reaction to my telling of the story.

Michael Fullan is recognized for his diligent and faithful work in sharing this story with the public.

Finally, I acknowledge Giedre Abromaitis (daughter of Maria), Peter Paskevicius (son of Antanas and Jadwyga), and my wife Chris Creedon (daughter of Antanas and Jadwyga), who shared their parents' story with me and now with you.

CPSIA information can be obtained
at www.ICGtesting.com
Printed in the USA
LVHW110019041219
639366LV00002B/251/P

9 781771 803601